THE NEW ERA

Also by Hamdy El-Rayes

MENTAL WELLNESS: A Spiritual Journey

Finding Your Own Way to Healing from Depression, Anxiety, and Addictions

Greenview Publishing (http://goo.gl/MDbkr)

THE NEW ERA

Returning the U.S. to Democracy and Prosperity

Hamdy El-Rayes, MBA, Ph.D.

GREENVIEW PUBLISHING

The New Era
Returning the U.S. to Democracy and Prosperity
By Hamdy El-Rayes, MBA, Ph.D.

Published in Canada by Greenview Publishing,
307-1190 W 10th Avenue
Vancouver, BC, Canada V6H 1J1

ISBN 978-0-9865706-2-9

Library and Archives Canada Cataloguing in Publication
El-Rayes, Hamdy
The New Era, Returning the U.S. to Democracy and Prosperity
Includes bibliographical references
1. Political process – elections
2. Political ideologies – Democracy
3. Globalization

To the unknown activists who give selflessly of themselves to a humanitarian cause to make a difference in this world. You are my heroes.

Never doubt that a small group of thoughtful committed citizens can change the world. Indeed, it is the only thing that ever has.

~ Margaret Mead ~

Acknowledgments

I would like to thank everyone who helped me to complete this book and make it available to the reader.

Special thanks go to my editor, Greg Felton, and to Fatima Travassos for designing the book-cover, to Tory Ross for proofreading the book, and to George Xu for designing the websites of Greenview Publishing, the New Era Clubs, and El-Rayes Foundation.

I would also like to express my deep appreciation and gratitude to activists who opened my eyes and led the way to increase public awareness of the role the U.S. government took to serve the interests of the Power Triad—multinational corporations, The Military Industrial Complex, and the Israel Lobby. Most of these activists have been alienated and ostracized for honoring their values and sacrificing their lives and livelihood to make a difference in the world. They spend their little money and their valuable time to enlighten the public selflessly and go the extra mile to deliver their message despite their limited resources. They are the Davids facing the Goliath to save democracy and the economy from the Power Triad. It is a sacred mission and I pray for them that their efforts are fruitful.

I salute those brave American activists who stood up to the cruelty of their government and exposed the crimes committed in their name against the innocent, poor, helpless people in the developing countries.

The work in this book is not in any way complete. It is a starting point for dialogue and offers fundamental important issues that need to be addressed. I appreciate those who will comment on the book and volunteer to offer research that addresses other important issues the book did not cover, or need to be addressed.

I appreciate those who will volunteer to lead New Era Community Clubs (NECCs) and go door-to-door, campaigning to invite their neighbors to join and become active participants in the political affairs of their community.

Special thanks to the authors I quoted in this book. Their writings were educational, inspiring, and rewarding. They helped me to deepen my knowledge, understand the current issues, and offer solutions that serve the common good.

Hamdy El-Rayes

Vancouver, B.C.

July 2013

Table of Contents

Chapter 1

The American crisis

*The most difficult subjects can be explained to the most
slow-witted man if he has not formed any idea of them
already; but the simplest thing cannot be made clear to the
most intelligent man if he is firmly persuaded that he knows
already, without a shadow of doubt, what is laid before him.*
~ Leo Tolstoy ~

In the past two decades, the U.S. has gone through one of the most
critical periods in its history. While it was once the world's only
superpower and the leader of the global economy, the country has
been deteriorating because of policies that favor the wealthy,
corporations, the defense contractors, and certain special interest
groups, rather than the interests of the American people. As a result,
wealth has been sucked up to the top of the food chain and inequality
has increased to the point where it puts the nation at risk of social and
political instability.

After the 9/11 attacks, the Bush Administration indulged in futile
wars that significantly contributed to our unprecedented federal debt
and a lagging economy. In addition, deregulation of the banking
system and corporate greed led to the 2008 economic crisis, but the
government did not hold anyone responsible for it. The economic
crisis severely hurt low income and middle-class Americans, while
some of the wealthiest have even benefited.

The Obama Administration inherited a collapsing economy, but it did
not hesitate to bail out those who caused the crisis and is even
considering austerity measures in the 2013 fiscal budget, further
punishing Americans who are struggling to make ends meet. Indeed,
the political powers in the U.S. seem to be working against the
common good of the American people.

From this crisis, the Occupy Wall Street movement was born. It was an expression of both despair and hope for change. The movement has been successful in exposing the corruption within the political system and making the wealthy elite understand that the people have reached the end of their rope. Although the issues presented by the Occupy movement were important, the movement would have been more successful had it had a defined leadership and focused on the root cause of the current economic crises, which stems from a dysfunctional political system designed by the elite for the elite. What is lacking in the American democracy is "government of the people, by the people, for the people." [1]

Achieving this goal will resolve the issues the Occupy movement is concerned about, whether related to Wall Street corruption, unemployment, health care, education, inequality, or climate change.

This book is designed to help people individually and collectively, respond to these problems. To do this, it looks at the big picture of the U.S.'s economic crisis to highlight its causes and the strategic mistakes that successive administrations have made during the past century. For example, it compares the economies of the U.S. and China to explain why the U.S. economy has stumbled for decades while China's economy has grown rapidly and is one of the world's largest creditor nations. The Organization for Economic Cooperation and Development (OECD), a leading international think tank, says that China will become the globe's economic leader by the end of 2016. [2a]

For its part, the U.S. is today the world's largest debtor nation. The sole superpower that remained after the fall of the Berlin Wall and the end of the Cold War has not been able to maintain its political influence or economic superiority because of its military attempts to control the globe, the beneficiaries of which this book will show. As a result, the U.S. is fast losing its status as a superpower.

The book also offers new ideas for good governance, and solutions to make the world a better place. These are not labeled "socialist" or "capitalist" because labeling them inhibits discussion. Some of them are those the Founding Fathers discussed, while some are outside-the-box solutions designed to explore new venues and free ourselves from ingrained prejudices and opinions. The current crisis cannot be solved using the same ways of thinking that caused it.

The solutions discussed in this book can be applied to any democratic country, but its focus is on the U.S. because solving its political and economic issues will resolve a major part of the world's issues.

Once the people restore democracy and have a government elected by the people, for the people, many things will change.

Restoring democracy

To restore democracy, first, we need to redefine what we mean by "democracy" because the word is understood differently by many people. Once we rediscover its original meaning, we will be able to look at economic and political issues with a fresh mind because what we have been taught about them is designed to brainwash us into serving the Power Triad of the multinational corporations, the Israel Lobby, and the Military Industrial Complex. Armed with this clarity, we can start behaving like shepherds, not sheep, and help communities to become politically engaged.

Knowledge alone will not change the world. It also requires passion. As Khalil Gibran wrote in his book *The Prophet*, [2]

"I say that life is indeed darkness save when there is urge [passion],
And all urge is blind save when there is knowledge,
And all knowledge is vain save when there is work,
And all work is empty save when there is love,
And when you work with love, you bind yourself to yourself, and to one another [the will of the people]."

We are blessed with thousands of activist groups and millions of people, who care about the common good, but they are scattered over a huge number of causes, and consequently they are unable to reach critical mass to bring about change.

As we have seen during the "Arab Spring" of 2011, Egyptians demonstrated against the dictator, Hosni Mubarak, at Tahrir Square in Cairo and in other cities all over the country. Mubarak's ruthless security forces attacked them. The security forces killed more than 1,000 people, but the demonstrations remained peaceful and those involved held on to their sole demand, deposing the dictator. They did not answer police violence with violence. If they had, they would have been massacred and Mubarak and his cronies would have won. The success of the people in defining one goal and staying the course was what made the Egyptian Revolution succeed in deposing Mubarak.

For our activists to succeed, they have to work collectively on one issue at a time. The first challenge is to stop the Power Triad's election funding, the source of most of our problems from health and education to the environment. Once we have successfully addressed the issues that affect the majority of us, we can focus on advocating for our own causes.

My experience under dictatorship

I have lived both in a dictatorship in Egypt and in the North American "democracies." These experiences have enabled me to understand the differences and the similarities between the two systems and realize the difference between the theory and the practice of democracy. I owe a great deal to these countries because they helped me polish my political knowledge.

I wrote this book partly to express my gratitude to these countries and partly to initiate a dialogue that will address important issues. As a freethinking intellectual, I am interested only in the common good, and have no political affiliation.

On warm summer evenings when I was a teenager in a small town at the shore of the Manzala Lake in Egypt, I would listen to the elders discuss the turbulent political affairs of Egypt after the 1952 revolution. At that time, Egypt was under the rule of President Gamal Abdul Nasser, who overthrew Muhammad Naguib, the leader of the military coup that toppled King Farouk I and ended the rule of the Muhammad Ali Dynasty in Egypt and Sudan.

Nasser persecuted anyone who opposed his rule and jailed without trial thousands of members of the Muslim Brotherhood. It saddened me at the time because one of them was my prep school favorite teacher who discovered my gifts as a student and volunteered to help me move three years ahead of my class. The police took him from his home in the middle of the night for no apparent reason. My exposure to such a traumatic event at this young age taught me to look more deeply into the political issues. I began to realize that the way events appear in the mainstream media could be misleading. Later on, I moved to Cairo at the age of 15 and pursued my undergraduate studies in engineering and my graduate studies in management and economics.

History in both the East and the West shows that people can be oppressed for decades, but they revolt when their basic needs are not being met, and when inequality reaches an intolerable level. In the early 19th century, Muhammad Ali modernized Egypt. Then, the British invaded and occupied the country from 1882 to 1952. During that time, Britain created a class system wherein a few Egyptians owned most of the wealth. Although the Egyptian government was oppressive, the Egyptians did not rebel. Nevertheless, inequality triggered the 1952 military coup, which called for redistribution of wealth and abolition of social classes. Nasser nationalized foreign corporations and confiscated agricultural land from the upper class beyond a specific size (100 acres per family). His government redistributed the confiscated land to the farm workers, used profits from state-owned corporations to subsidize food prices, provided affordable housing, paid for building the infrastructure, and maintained other government services. However, despite their good intentions, Nasser and his government gradually turned into a dictatorship. Power and wealth again became concentrated in the hands of a ruling class—a new upper class that continued to grow stronger over the next 50 years, first under Anwar Sadat, and then Hosni Mubarak.

Then, in 1979, a new influence on Egypt's political system emerged that would change Egypt fundamentally, but not necessarily for the better. To support the peace treaty between Egypt and Israel, signed on March 26, 1979, the U.S. required Egypt to adopt its model of capitalism and "democracy." Both the Republican and Democratic parties in the U.S. spent millions of dollars on non-governmental organizations to set up this system. The International Monetary Fund and World Bank also required Egypt to adopt "free market" and globalization policies. To be part of the global market, the Egyptian government had to sell the state-owned corporations for a few cents on the dollar to the ruling class and their cronies, and privatized the utility services.

By selling these corporations, the government could not continue to pay for its services or to subsidize necessities for the poor: about 40 percent of Egyptians live on less than $2 a day. These actions widened inequality and increased inflation to an unaffordable level because food prices were no longer subsidized and the government lost its ability to control commodity prices.

At the same time, the upper class accumulated huge fortunes, while low-income Egyptians could not make ends meet. Then, once again, inequality triggered the February 2011 revolution (known as the Arab Spring) and Mubarak, the dictator who had ruled Egypt for more than 30 years, was overthrown. This time, the people led the revolution. Ironically, the military stood in the way of the revolutionaries and tried to continue to subjugate the people to foreign powers. Had the U.S. not imposed its "democratic system" and its "capitalism model" on Egypt, this revolution might not have happened.

History shows us that "trickle-down" economics has never worked anywhere. It worked neither in a dictatorship like Egypt nor in a democracy like the U.S. It gives false hope to the poor, who end up with the crumbs. It widens the gap of inequality and leads to social unrest. In both economics and politics, the only thing that trickles down is corruption. In Egypt, Nasser and his colleagues corrupted the political system and handed power from one dictator to two others.

My experience under democracy

Like many who live under dictatorships, I aspired to live in a place that espoused values of freedom and democracy. When I moved to the U.S. to obtain my doctorate degree, I was curious about the political process and eager to participate in politics without fear of reprisal. In the U.S., I became an advocate for several causes: protecting the environment, human rights, mental health, world peace, justice, and good governance. When I moved to Canada, I explored the platforms of the existing political parties and discovered the reality of the political process when I ran as a Green Party candidate in the 2005 provincial elections. I was very disappointed to discover that the political systems of both the dictatorship where I grew up and the "democracy" in North America appeared to be essentially similar. It reminded me of what the U.S. author and poet, Charles Bukowski, wrote, "The difference between a democracy and a dictatorship is that in a democracy, you vote first and take orders later; in a dictatorship you don't have to waste your time voting." Since I discovered the flaws in our rigged "democracy," I have stopped wasting my time voting.

My experience as a candidate at the provincial level and a volunteer for candidates at the federal level made me realize that the wealthy elite and a group of self-interested parties have hijacked our democracy.

In the U.S., these self-interested parties invest their money in lobbying and campaign funding to buy control of the Congress. Their investment is paid back to them hundreds of times in the form of subsidies from the taxpayers either as cash from the government (as in the case for the multinational energy companies), or in new laws that helps these organizations take advantage of the taxpayers, as is the case for the Wall Street banks. They succeeded in creating a dysfunctional democracy for the second time in the past century.

Our democracy became so similar to that of the Egypt's dictatorship despite superficial differences. For example, in the U.S., it is legal for the wealthy to contribute to election campaigns and lobby for privileges; in Egypt, such financial manipulation is illegal, although both approaches lead to the same results.

I have always believed that a global awakening is only a matter of time because injustice has reached its limit. I also knew that the brutal wars the U.S. has launched since the shocking event of Sept. 11, 2001, would spur its awakening because these wars widened the gap between the rich and the poor and deepened the U.S.' economic woes.

The Power Triad

Decision making in the U.S. government has been taken away from the American people by the wealthy elite who own or lead three groups of self-interested parties, which I refer to in this book as the Power Triad. These three groups include the Military Industrial

Complex, the multinational corporations, and special interest groups. The Triad controls the White House, Congress, and mainstream media, and plays a major role in shaping U.S. foreign policy and the economy, even if such influence is detrimental to the U.S. national interest.

The power of the Triad increased even further in 2010 after the Supreme Court decided that a corporation is a person, money is speech, and organizations can spend unlimited amount of money on funding the elections. [3] These decisions created gross inequalities and turned corporations into unelected rulers, capable of imposing their will on the nation to the detriment of the American people.

The Triad members are loosely connected. They may seem to work together because they may use the same strategies to achieve their goals, especially when it comes to foreign policy and the business of war. Depending on the geopolitical area and the interests of the Triad members, the level of effort to influence the U.S. foreign policy varies. In addition, some key individuals may belong to more than one group of the Triad. For example, an individual may be part of a special interest group while occupying a key position in the Military Industrial Complex, a Wall Street bank, a mainstream media corporation, or a multinational corporation.

If elected officials do not support the legislative demands of the Triad in Congress, they can expect to be defeated in the next election. This culture of fear prevents representatives from looking after the interests of the American people.

The Military Industrial Complex (MIC)

President Dwight D. Eisenhower coined the term "Military Industrial Complex" in his farewell address on January 17, 1961: "In the councils of government, we must guard against the acquisition of unwarranted influence, whether sought or unsought, by the military industrial complex. The potential for the disastrous rise of misplaced power exists and will persist. We must never let the weight of this combination endanger our liberties or democratic processes." Eisenhower's warning, though, was in vain.

The MIC refers to the policy and monetary relationship between legislators, the Pentagon, the executive branch, the defense industry, and some individuals. "It includes business organizations or individuals that provide products or services to the Pentagon or the CIA. Products typically include military or civilian aircraft, ships, vehicles, weaponry, and electronic systems. Services can include logistics, technical support and training, and communications support." [4] This relationship includes political contributions, election campaign funding, defense spending approval, lobbying, and industry oversight. It is driven in large part by a revolving-door support system between the defense industry and the Pentagon. The defense industry offers retiring high-rank officers generous financial rewards as managers or consultants who then market new projects to their former colleagues at the Pentagon, or as media experts to influence public opinion to support the business of war. In return, the defense industry secures generous contracts and subsidies in the form of open contracts of billions of dollars at cost plus profits. These guarantee the defense industry huge profits, regardless of a project's success or failure.

In its lobbying efforts, the MIC stifles healthy debate on the military and its involvement in perpetual war. It hires public relation firms to inundate the public with advertisements on public TV, radio, and newspapers and hires consultants to be talking heads on TV and other media outlets. In 2011, the defense industry alone spent $60 million on lobbying. [5]

The influence of the MIC is also evident in the federal budget. The Department of Defense and other defense related activities today account for more than 56 percent of all tax revenue. The military employs 1.4 million uniformed personnel on active duty, and more than 700,000 full-time civilians. The defense industry employs another three million people. In the past two decades, the U.S. government has had to support the defense industry from money borrowed from China. The military diverts a major portion of the funds needed to build schools, maintain the aging bridges and highways, improve education, and create new jobs. [5]

Multinational corporations

A multinational corporation, as the name indicates, is an enterprise that establishes its production or service beyond its country of origin. Typically, they are involved in energy, manufacturing, technology, and banking. The relationship of these corporations to the U.S. as its country of origin is parasitic. They ship their operations overseas, and funnel most of their profits to subsidiaries abroad and to tax havens.

U.S. oil multinationals, for example, are interested in controlling the energy and other resources of the Muslim world, as well as the pipelines that flow through their territories. To secure their uninterrupted supply of oil, they help ensure that Muslim populations are oppressed to prevent any popular movement that may threaten the political stability of these countries or access to cheap energy resources. This was evident when the U.S. government supported Saddam Hussein to oppress the Iraqi people as long as he stayed friendly to the U.S. multinationals. They also helped stabilize Libya, during Colonel Gaddafi's rule, and lift the economic sanctions in return for generous contracts with the American oil companies.

Special Interest groups

Political special interest groups are called advocacy groups, lobbying groups, or pressure groups, and may be loosely or tightly organized. More than 1600 organizations participate in the U.S. national politics,[6] and can be divided into two categories. The first speaks on behalf of public groups. These have a broad social base, address a wide range of issues, and balance members' interests with a strong commitment to the common good.

The second, such as the American Legislative Exchange Council (ALEC), a lobbying organization for corporations, has a narrow social base that concentrates on limited issues to benefit their members solely. Some of these groups have a disproportionate influence on policymaking, depending on their ability to spend on lobbying, and election campaigns, recruit campaign volunteers, access the White House directly, mobilize grassroots campaigns, and use the media effectively.

The Israel Lobby is of particular interest here because of its unprecedented influence on foreign policy and its role in driving the war in Iraq and the covert wars in Iran, Libya, Syria, Sudan, and Egypt.

In their book, *The Israel Lobby*, John Mearsheimer and Stephen Walt write: "The Israeli government and pro-Israel groups in the U.S. have worked together to shape the administration's policy towards Iraq, Syria and Iran, as well as its grand scheme for reordering the Middle East. Pressure from Israel and the Lobby was not the only factor behind the decision to attack Iraq in March 2003, but it was critical. The war was motivated in good part by a desire to make Israel more secure." [7]

The "War on Terror," served the interests of the Israel Lobby, but deprived Americans of their constitutionally guaranteed rights and freedoms. The invasion of Iraq cost the U.S. more than $3 trillion [8] and tens of thousands of lives, as well as hundreds of thousands of crippled soldiers whose lives will never be the same. A pretext for this war had been in the making since the early 1990s, and the 9/11 attack on the World Trade Center was the New Pearl Harbor dreamt of by the neo-conservatives at the Project for the New American Century to launch the war against the Muslim world. [9] As you will see in Chapter 6, the main objective of the invasion of Iraq was to serve the strategic interests of the Israel Lobby, which has been the dominant member of the Triad over the past four decades.

The Israel Lobby is led by AIPAC and its influential members at political think tanks, the Pentagon, the executive branch, media, and Christian-Zionist groups. [7] The Lobby coerces the U.S. government to serve Israel's strategic interests, and this coercion is responsible for global terrorist attacks against the U.S. and the resentment of the world's 1.3 billion Muslims whose friendship is needed to secure U.S. economic and geopolitical interests.

Iraq was a perfect target for the Triad as it primarily benefited the Israel Lobby, the most powerful member of the Triad, in addition to the rest of the Triad members—Iraq was a strong Arab nationalist state, which resisted the expansionist policies of Israel in the occupied West Bank and the Golan Heights. It also holds the world's largest proven oil reserves with more than 350 billion barrels. [10]

The invasion of Iraq destroyed a major source of resistance to Israel's expansionist policies, and enabled "American" multination energy companies, defense contractors, and Wall Street banks to improve their bottom line. They succeeded in controlling Iraq's finances, oil exploration rights and national bank, and increased the contracts to manufacture weapons from both the U.S. and the Iraqi governments.[11] They left behind a destroyed country devastated by sectarian violence, poverty, and insecurity. In addition, some areas became contaminated with radioactive material from depleted uranium, making them unsafe for at least another two centuries.

The need for a paradigm shift

> *The liberty of a democracy is not safe if the people tolerate the growth of private power to a point where it becomes stronger than their democratic State itself. That, in its essence, is Fascism—ownership of government by an individual, by a group, or any controlling private power.*
> *~ President Franklin D. Roosevelt ~*

To get engaged in the political process, we need to step back, reflect on what has been happening over the past four decades, figure out why things are not working well, and prepare ourselves to make changes in order to bring our economy and political system back on track.

This book will show that our damaged democracy is the underlying cause of most of the global problems. The financial crisis was a wake-up call to take serious action to abolish inequality. Unfortunately, most of us were not aware of the problem until the crisis reached our own backyards.

Neoliberalism is the belief that states ought to abstain from intervening in the economy, leaving it up to individuals participating in free and self-regulating markets. Globalization and neoliberalism may have led to redistribution of wealth between the developed and the developing nations, but they have also created extremely wealthy individuals who are more powerful than their own countries' governments. Furthermore, majority ownership of multinationals has fallen into foreign hands, especially in Canada and the U.S. Not only do these new owners have no loyalty to our country, but also free market policies allow the multinationals to exploit our financial and taxation systems, without any reciprocal regard for the societies that provide them. Moreover, our political leaders cater to these corporations because of their financial contribution to the election campaigns.

The increasing ownership of American multinational corporations by foreign shareholders has increased these corporations' separation from the U.S. Today, corporations do not care what happens to the U.S. as long as their actions financially benefit their shareholders (see Chapter 5).

In the past, these elites worked behind the scenes. Today, they work openly—emboldened by a sense of entitlement and invulnerability, the elites no longer hesitate to say or do things that used to be considered unacceptable and insulting to the public's intelligence. As Tacitus commented when the Roman Empire started to decline around AD 100: "The worst crimes were dared by a few, willed by more, and tolerated by all."

The economic crisis, which has been painful for millions of people, could become an opportunity to build a better life for our families and ourselves. In fact, the crisis has united working people all over the globe. As it hit the Arab shores, it triggered the Arab Spring, which started in Tunisia, then extended to Egypt and the rest of North Africa. The ripple effects of the Arab Spring have been resonating in Europe, the U.S., and Canada. Like a tsunami, the Arab revolution took us all by surprise, as did the Occupy movement in North America.

To seek shelter from this storm, we need to make drastic changes at the individual as well as the community level. It is evident that what worked well yesterday is not working today, and if we continue to do the same thing, the whole system will collapse.

Since the 2008 financial crisis, the leaders of the developed world have met to address the problems, but their solutions did not help those who have been suffering the most. They have been working on behalf of the wealthy elite. They offered solutions not to get ordinary people out of the hole but to continue to enrich the corporations at our expense. Since we fell into the hole of financial crisis, those leaders simply got us deeper into it.

How you can change the world

Based on previous experiences of Egyptian, American, and Canadian activists in the past two years, we can make a difference if we take these two steps:

Focus activists' efforts

As the Occupy Wall Street movement showed, millions of people were frustrated enough to act, but the message was significantly diluted because too many issues were raised. The movement should have focused on a single issue. Imagine if those millions had focused solely on election campaign funding and achieved that goal, it would have changed not only our country but also the whole world.

Form "The New Era" community clubs

Communities have to be awakened to the importance of participating in politics. It starts with campaigning, and door knocking to invite people to discuss current economic and political issues as described in Chapter 11. When a community becomes well informed and united, it becomes a power to be reckoned with.

Chapter 2

What is wrong with our democracy?

No one is more hopelessly enslaved than those who falsely believe they are free.
~ Johann Wolfgang von Goethe ~

country's economy goes through normal cycles from expansion (growth) to contraction (recession), but the 2008 Great Recession was not a cyclical event. It was the sudden manifestation of a systemic problem that started decades earlier, but we chose to ignore. By the time the crisis made headlines, it had reached a level where minor adjustments would not work. The underlying cause of this crisis is our dysfunctional democracy.

The line between elected officials and special interest groups becomes so badly blurred that one can hardly tell where one ends and the other begins. Those who leave a legislature are rewarded with jobs as lobbyists, consultants, or executives in the corporations. Similarly, corporate executives are rewarded with positions in the U.S. Administration. For Example, Richard "Dick" Gephardt who was a U.S. Representative and served as House Majority Leader (1989 to 1995), turned into a lobbyist. Robert Rubin spent 26 years at Goldman Sachs and served as a member of the board and co-chairman from 1990 to 1992. He was appointed as the U.S. Secretary of the Treasury during the first and second Clinton administration. After his government role, he was appointed as director and senior counselor of Citigroup, then as a chairman of Citigroup until the U.S. Treasury bailed it out. [12]

The Nobel laureate economist Joseph Stiglitz pronounced our age — and the U.S. government to be one "of the one percent, by the one percent, for the one percent." [13] The elite and their representatives provide advice to the U.S. administration on the economy and foreign affairs. Those who are promoted to advise the Administration are connected to powerful corporations and special interest groups who are self-serving and uninterested in the good of the American people. As intelligent and capable as these advisors may be, their conflict of interest prevents them from offering sincere advice to the Administration. For example, "trusted advisors" gave the U.S. government a false image of the Muslim world to drive the U.S. into wars that facilitated its financial collapse. Evidently, our democratic system has to undergo serious changes to save itself. This chapter reviews the theory of democracy, and its mutation into oppressive elitism, leading to the economic crisis and unnecessary wars.

What is democracy?

Democracy comes from a Greek word meaning "rule of the people," and in Western culture reflects the following main principles:

1. All citizens are equal before the law;
2. Every citizen can vote, and each vote carries equal weight;
3. No unreasonable restrictions apply to anyone seeking elected office;
4. Citizens' rights and liberties are protected by a constitution;
5. The majority rules, but minority rights are protected;
6. Elections are free and fair;
7. There is equal participation in the proposal, development, and passage of legislation; and
8. Freedom of political expression, religion, assembly, speech and the press.

Democracy, though, is a double-edged sword—it becomes injurious to a society when it falls into the hands of autocrats, and an uninformed citizenry who are easily misled by lies and half-truths. Here is what has happened to these principles in the U.S.

Principle # 1 – All citizens are equal before the law

In the U.S., the wealthy elite enjoy a level of legal protection and privilege that the average citizen can only dream of. In the court system, for example, the wealthy can afford to hire the best lawyers, whereas the majority cannot afford decent legal representation.

The principle of innocent until proven guilty does not apply to those citizens deemed to be terrorists. It has become legal to deprive these "terror suspects" of their constitutional right to a fair trial and protection under the law. Since 9/11 attacks, the U.S. has tried such citizens based on "secret evidence," whereby the defense lawyer is not permitted to see because prosecutors claim that revealing that evidence could harm national security. How can a citizen have a fair trial if he does not know exactly of what he is accused? To make matters worse, in 2011, Congress passed the *National Defense Authorization Act*, which allows for indefinite detention of citizens (see p. 118).

Principle # 2 – Every vote has equal weight

Election campaigns are very costly and winning an election depends mainly on the amount of money a candidate can spend on an election campaign. Research shows that we usually end up with representatives who can outspend their opponents. [14]

Today, the weight of a vote depends not on an individual's ballot but on how much money is tied to it. A vote will have much more weight if it is tied to a large campaign donation. An election can, therefore, tilt in a candidate's favor because he or she will be able to hire the best campaign managers, who then buy ads on TV, travel widely and hold more campaign events, which lead to more votes. After the election, of course, these corporate donors expect favors from the successful candidate. The corrupting role of money and influence ensures that the most knowledgeable candidates rarely win. In fact, corporations and special interest groups prefer less-intelligent candidates because they are easy to mold and are willing to parrot whatever they are told.

In contrast, independent candidates are often the best informed and driven by a passion to serve their community. However, they cannot compete financially, and often lose when corporations and special interest groups spend lavishly to back an opposing candidate. [15] In addition, campaign donations from ordinary individuals carry little weight relative to those of the Power Triad. Consequently, the Triad decides who will win elections. This subverts the democratic process, rigs elections, and excludes those who truly deserve to win. Since the U.S. Supreme Court determined that, a corporation is a person under the law and money is speech, [3] the idea that every vote has equal weight is officially a fraud.

Principle # 3 – Anyone may seek public office

It may be easy for anyone to run for office, but the chances of being elected are unreasonably restricted if a candidate is not wealthy or cannot secure donations from the Power Triad.

Principle # 4 –Rights and liberties are protected by the Constitution

According to the U.S. Human Rights Network, discrimination permeates all aspects of life. [16] Discrimination by gender, race, religion, against women, African Americans, Latin Americans, and Muslims is widely acknowledged. A survey conducted in September 2009 showed that 52 percent of those surveyed agreed there is "a lot of discrimination" against Hispanics, 49 percent agreed when asked the same question about African Americans, and 58 percent agreed when asked about Muslims.[17] Studies show that 40% of the gap between the wages of men and women is due discrimination. [18]

Since 9/11, constitutional rights and freedoms have been seriously violated by a flood of repressive laws. These laws were decided in brainstorm meetings started on Sept. 19, 2001 by Donald Rumsfeld, then Secretary of Defense, Paul Wolfowitz, Richard Perle, and other neoconservative ideologues who were in control of the government. They decided to launch the "war on terror" against the Muslim world. It would begin with invading Afghanistan, pursuing regime change in Iraq militarily, and re-engineering civil and criminal laws to stamp out Islamic terror. [19]

As part of this war, this group convinced President George W. Bush to violate Americans' constitutional and human rights by claiming the restrictions were necessary to fight terrorism. President Barack Obama has since turned many of Bush's constitutional violations into law.

These laws were not created to protect the American people; they were created to take away their liberties and freedoms. These acts included the *USA Patriot Act, the National Defense Authorization Act (NDAA), Protect IP Act, the Cyber Intelligence Sharing and Protection Act* and the *Stop Online Piracy Act*, and have turned the U.S. into a police state. Meanwhile, under the guise of fighting terrorism, the government has suspended habeas corpus,[i] wiretapped American citizens without warrants, and practiced extraordinary rendition of suspected terrorists.

In the words of Benjamin Franklin: "Any society that would give up a little liberty to gain a little security will deserve neither and lose both."

Principle # 5 – The majority rules, but minority rights are protected

Majority rule is a farce. Elected representatives do exist because they are beholden to those who funded their election campaigns, not their constituents. On the other hand, the majority is either misinformed or uninterested in political and economic issues. As a result, they do not realize the implications when new laws are enacted in their name.

If majority rule is to function properly, citizens must be well informed and politically engaged. For this to happen, the mainstream media must be independent of any influence from its owners and not depend for its survival on corporate advertisers.

Minority rights

In the past, the U.S. has discriminated against many groups— Catholics, Jews, African-Americans—but today the target is

---

[i] Habeas corpus is a judicial requirement that a prisoner be brought before the court to determine whether the government has the right to continue detaining them. This right can only be suspended for the public safety in cases of rebellion or invasion.

American Muslims who are being denied their rights. Discrimination against Muslims and Arabs has been going on in the U.S. since the 1940s, not only in Hollywood movies, but also on TV and in newspaper and magazine cartoons. The discrimination has intensified since 9/11 as Muslims have faced the double discrimination of bigotry and religious prejudice. Their rights have been violated by the police, right-wing, religious evangelical groups, Zionist-Christian groups, the Israel Lobby, right wing Republicans, Democratic hawks and the media. Individuals, places of worship, centers of Islamic culture and Muslim cemeteries have been attacked.

An investigative research project for the Center for American Progress entitled, *Fear Inc, The Roots of Islamophobia Network in America*, reveals that, in the past decade, since 2001, more than $42.5 million has been donated from eight foundations to promote hatred against Islam in the U.S. These foundations include Donors Capital Fund, Richard Scaife Foundation, Lynde and Harry Bradley Foundation, Russell Berrie Foundation, Anchorage Charitable Fund, William Rosenwald Family Fund, Fairbook Foundation, and Newton and Rochelle Becker Foundation. [20] In their research project, Wajahat Ali, Eli Clifton, Matthew Duss, Lee Fang, Scott Keyes, and Faiz Shakir report: "The campaign was led by five key 'scholars and experts' who 'comprise the nervous system of anti-Muslim propaganda including: Frank Gaffney, David Yeushalmi, Daniel Pipes, Robert Spencer, and Steven Everson. They were assisted by Brigitte Gabriel (founder of ACT For America), Pamela Geller (Co-founder of Stop Islamization of America), and David Horowitz (Supporter of Robert Spencer's Jihad Watch). The information is then disseminated through conservative organizations such as the Eagle Forum, the religious right, Fox News, and politicians such as Allen West and Newt Gingrich. These individuals used the mainstream media and their grassroots organizations to promote to the Americans that, mosques are incubators of radicalization and that 'radical Islam' has infiltrated all aspects of American society." [20]

In 2001, acts of violence against Muslims increased by 1600 percent. Then, violence decreased but was soon replaced by discrimination in education, employment, and religious land use. The Federal Bureau of Investigation reported that during 2009 and 2010, "anti-Islamic" incidents motivated by religious bias increased by 20 percent to 800 cases of discrimination annually. [21]

The government takes little action to protect American-Muslims' rights and nothing to stop the media from promoting hatred against them. Sometimes government gives lip service to the issue to appease the Muslim world, but implicitly contributes to these violations to justify its "war on terror."

Preceding the invasion of Afghanistan and Iraq, the media blitz against the Muslim minority and Arabs in the U.S. was so successful that it made some Americans angry enough to kill other Americans they thought were Muslim. [19]

Principle # 6 – Elections are free and fair

Election funding is a decisive factor in any election, and candidates with more funds than their competitors have a much better chance of winning. This practice is unfair to less-wealthy candidates who are well qualified, knowledgeable, and passionate about serving the community.

Jon Corzine, former senator and governor of New Jersey, worked for Goldman Sachs before running for the New Jersey senate. After Henry Paulson forced him out of the company, he was $400 million richer, thanks to Goldman Sachs' 1999 initial public offering. Corzine spent $60 million of his own money to win a Senate seat and went on to run for governor in 2005. [22] Corzine's competitors did not have $60 million to spend on an election.

Rick Scott, the current governor of Florida, led his own private equity firm from 1997 to 2010, when he ran for governor. According to Tom Slade, former co-chairman of Scott's campaign, Scott did not have any political skills, but he won after spending $73 million of his own money on his election campaign. [23]

These examples illustrate that elections are neither free nor fair. The unlimited funds wealthy candidates, corporations, and special interest groups can spend rigs the elections and as a result, the best candidates are rarely elected.

Principle # 7– Equal participation in the proposal, development, and passage of legislation

Although elected representatives are supposed to look after the interest of the electorate, campaign contributors have priority in proposing, developing, and passing legislation. A key factor is the American Legislative Exchange Council (ALEC), a lobbying organization that drafts pro-corporate bills that are then given to representatives to present them as if they were their own proposals. Issues addressed by ALEC include tax treatment of corporations, gun rights, and tightening voter identification rules (See p. 66).

Principle # 8 – Freedom of political expression and speech

Freedom of speech, which includes political expression, must include both content and means of expression. In the U.S., the government and the media have imposed limitations that have opened the floodgates to other repressive measures that harm society, national security and the well-being of individuals. This abuse of a fundamental freedom is more dangerous than terrorism. Acts of terrorism are tangible and physical losses can be quantified, but abusing freedom of speech can pervert the nation's moral values and spread violence. Although media outlets eagerly show or say anything that fits their ideologies, they often do not allow opposing points of view to be heard. Generally, they suppress important news and stifle the diversity of voices.

The U.S. talks loudly in the international arena about democracy and human rights, but many American activists who are well informed and care about the U.S. have no outlets other than the Internet. Ironically, these activists can practice their freedom of speech and expression on Iran's PressTV (http://www.PressTV.com) and Russia's TV station (http://www.rt.com).

Marginalized for daring to dissent

Those who disagree with the government are marginalized and alienated. When Professor Steven E. Jones of Brigham Young University published his research concerning the collapse of Tower 7 at the Trade Center following the 9/11 attack, the university "kindly" reached an agreement with him to retire because he had challenged the absolute veracity of the formal 9/11 commission report. Other professional scientists and journalists who questioned the 9/11 Commission's report lost their jobs because, even though they based their disagreements on scientific evidence, they took issue with the story promoted by the mainstream media and the U.S. government.

Professor Noam Chomsky, the well-known American linguist, philosopher, cognitive scientist, and activist, has been cited as a source more often than any other living scholar according to the Arts and Humanities Citation Index. Between 1980 and 1992, he was the eighth most cited source. Yet, because Chomsky publicly opposes U.S. foreign policy and speaks out against Israel's abuse of Palestinians, the mainstream media shuns him. Despite this marginalization, though, Chomsky's media propaganda exposé *Manufacturing Consent: The Political Economy of the Mass Media*, co-authored with Edward S. Herman, is world famous.

True freedom of expression will not be possible until large media conglomerates are broken up and their ability to influence elected representatives is ended.

Recommendations

Political parties and democracy

Too often, elected representatives are more loyal to their party and its ideology than they are to those who elected them. To address this problem we need to return to the 18th century and the prophetic words of George Washington. In his 1796 farewell address, he warned of the dangers of political parties:

"[Parties] serve to ... put in the place of the delegated will of the Nation the will of a party. ... They are likely in the course of time and things to become potent engines by which cunning, ambitious, and unprincipled men will be enabled to subvert the power of the people and to usurp for themselves the reins of Government destroying afterwards the very engines which have lifted them to unjust dominion."

A non-partisan political system has functioned well in several states – for example, in Nebraska (U.S.), the Northwest Territories (Canada), Nunavut (Canada), and Tokelau (New Zealand). [25]

The Power Triad however, prefers a two-party system such as that of the U.S. because it is easier to fund and control. If we stop the Power Triad from funding the elections, perhaps the influence of political parties will diminish and candidates will be elected based on their merits and be able to vote their conscience.

Term limits for elected politicians

Although people who get involved in politics are supposed to do that out of a desire to serve the public good, history shows that many do so for careerist reasons. Such politicians become part of the machinery of government and seek to perpetuate themselves in power. This renders them not only ineffective as representatives, but also politically corrupt.

If career politicians are faced with having to make an unpopular decision, they have to choose between doing the right thing even though it may cost them re-election or betraying their principles to protect their positions. If all politicians were limited to serving no more than two consecutive terms, the careerist impulse might be eliminated. A candidate who does not plan a career in politics would be more likely to leave a positive legacy. In addition, it would allow other talented people to serve.

Benjamin Franklin and other Founding Fathers understood the importance of limited terms when they drafted the 1776 constitution of Pennsylvania. Thomas Jefferson also urged limited tenure "to prevent every danger which might arise to American freedom by continuing too long in office." Jefferson's proposal was included in the *Articles of Confederation* (1781-1789). Article 5 stated, "… no person shall be capable of being a delegate for more than three years in any term of six years. both Jefferson and George Mason, the father of the Bill of Rights, advised putting limits on re-election to the senate and the presidency. According to Mason, '… nothing is as essential to the preservation of a Republican government as a periodic rotation.'" [26]

Today, term limits apply only to the president of the U.S. as a result of passing the 22nd Amendment in 1947. A two-term limit for all elected office holders would hinder opportunists who run for personal gain and take advantage of the political system and would allow more talented people to contribute as elected representatives.

Representative recall

Recall allows voters to remove elected officials from office through a direct vote before the end of a term if he or she has not delivered on promises or has otherwise betrayed the voters' trust. This remedy differs from impeachment in that it is a political rather than a legal process. Impeachment requires the house to bring specific charges and the Senate to act as a jury.

Currently, recall is not enacted at the federal level, but is enacted in 19 states: Alaska, Arizona, California, Colorado, Georgia, Idaho, Illinois, Kansas, Louisiana, Michigan, Minnesota, Montana, Nevada, New Jersey, North Dakota, Oregon, Rhode Island, Washington, and Wisconsin.

Voters should also have a chance to recall their representatives at the federal level. However, the recall process can be abused if the Power Triad can continue to interfere in the political process. [27]

Referenda

There are two types of referendum, the legislative and the popular. The legislative referendum is a measure a government submits to the voters for their approval. It appears on the ballot in all 50 states, but the practice needs to be extended to the federal level. For example, while the war in Iraq was going on, many Americans could not locate Iraq on a map or answer simple questions about the country. Had a referendum been held on the matter, the U.S. would doubtless be in a better situation today.

The popular referendum is initiated by a petition. It allows voters to approve or repeal an act of the legislature. It empowers the voters to gather signatures and demand a popular vote on the law. Upon gathering required number of signatures, the new law appears on the ballot for a popular vote. If the voters reject the law, it is voided. Currently 24 states have the popular referendum. [27]

Chapter 3

Freedom of the press

*Our liberty cannot be guarded but by the freedom of the
press, nor that be limited without danger of losing it.*
~ Thomas Jefferson, 1786 ~

Today, the U.S. boasts more than 1,400 newspapers, 17,000 magazines, 1,200 TV stations, 12,000 radio stations, hundreds of cable TV channels, and thousands of Internet news sites. Yet, the average American remains remarkably uninformed because the news is filtered. In his book *Empire of Illusions*, Chris Hedges questions how there can be so many media sources and so much conformity. For example, during the buildup to the invasion of Iraq in 2003, two-thirds of Americans believed that Saddam Hussein was involved in the 9/11 terrorist attacks. [28] In a CNN poll taken in February 2010, seven in 10 Americans believed that Iran currently has nuclear weapons. [29]

Juan Gonzalez is cohost of *Democracy Now!* and award-winning columnist at the *New York Daily News*. He is the former president of the National Association of Hispanic Journalists. His previous books include *Harvest of Empire: A History of Latinos in America*. Joseph Torres is the former deputy director at the National Association of Hispanic Journalists. Currently, he is senior adviser for government and external affairs for Free Press, the national media reform organization. In their book, *News for All the People: The Epic Story of Race and the American Media*, Gonzalez and Torres show that the corporate media have no interest in informing us. They have their own practical defined goals: improve the bottom line and maintain a symbiotic relationship with the government at the expense of the public good. [30] They report that government policies have played an important role in concentrating the media in the hands of a few corporations, which then control the flow of information to the public.

Since 1792, government policies have facilitated the flow of news to the public, first by subsidizing the cost of newspaper delivery through the postal system. After the invention of the telegraph in 1840, the governments allowed corporations to own their own telegraph services, and within 20 years, small companies were consolidated. One company bought up almost all the others, and this is how Western Union became the U.S.'s first industrial monopoly and the main source of news.

Later on in 1846, five New York City newspapers funded a "pony express route" [31] to bring the news faster than the U.S. Post Office could deliver it. Since then, Associated Press (AP) became the main source of news. As of 2005, more than 1,700 newspapers and more than 500 television and radio broadcasters publish news collected by the Associated Press. In addition, AP controls about 90 percent of the content of America's small-town newspapers. [30]

In the early 1900s, when radio was invented, it was called "the great liberator of the time," because it enabled thousands of amateurs, churches, and colleges to broadcast from their own radio stations. To reestablish their monopoly, the media industry lobbied the government to centralize radio ownership. By 1927, the *Federal Radio Act* was passed, followed in 1934 by the *Communication Act*, which allowed the government to shut down most non-commercial stations and replace them with just two broadcasters, NBC and CBS. [31]

By the 1970s, cable TV services had been commercialized, but government policies required community access TV through these cable companies, believing that every community would have its own news operation. Unfortunately, media ownership was left to free-market forces, and within 20 years, two major cable companies, Comcast and Time Warner, emerged owning more than 50 percent of the market. The two conglomerates removed all public-access requirements and the media became centralized in their hands. In 1996, the *Telecommunications Act* allowed phone companies to get into cable services.

It is worthwhile remembering that the *First Amendment* to the U.S. Constitution states that, "... Congress shall make no law ... abridging the freedom of speech, or of the press...." Under the current circumstances, freedom of the press is limited to those who own one and serve the interests of corporate advertisers and special interest groups.

Mainstream media in a democracy and a dictatorship

The print and electronic media decide which issues they want us to be concerned about and define them to influence our opinions about any matter of public policy. Consequently, people can easily become victims of political manipulation. [32]

In the U.S. since the end of the 18th century, media corporations have lobbied the government, with the result that eight conglomerates now control news in the country. Their editors, writers, and journalists know, without being told, that their work must reflect the ideologies of their bosses, or they will lose their jobs. In his book, *Rather Outspoken*, Dan Rather, former news anchor for the *CBS Evening News* says, "I was seeking to confront the grave issues raised by bald-faced corporate and governmental intimidation of journalists and by the chilling intrusion of these special interests into newsrooms across the country. If you believe as I do that a free press is the red, beating heart of democracy, then you understand that the corporatization and politicization of the press is an issue that endangers the health and well-being of our country." [33]

The corporate media have to cater to their advertisers, so they offer programs that are superficial and entertaining, rather than provocative and informative. Such programs often center on celebrity gossip, sex, political scandals, and violence, because it is safer to air "news" about scandals than inform the public about what might affect their lives. To maintain access to government sources and establish rapport with the bureaucrats, TV companies prefer not to broadcast negative news about the government unless that news supports their corporate owners.

The media helps the government mold public opinion. Since the 9/11 attack, the media promoted Islamophobia to help the government infringe on the liberties and freedoms of Americans to launch an ideological war on the Muslim world. To promote the business of war, the media featured "military analysts," former military officers, many of whom became consultants to defense contractors, but kept that news from the public.

TV and other media often use certain repetitive and pervasive patterns of images that dominate news, documentaries, and entertainment programs. For example, if people spend several hours a day, year after year, watching television, and they see it mentions stories about terrorism and Muslim "terrorists," then people will come to believe that the world is unsafe.

To control public opinion, mainstream media censors opposing points of view. Indeed, there is little difference between the way the U.S. media are run and the media in a dictatorship. When I was growing up in Egypt, the media told us what the government wanted us to hear, so from a very young age, we were taught not to trust the government or the media. Recently, the Muslim Brotherhood won the hearts and minds of the Egyptian voters because it served Egyptian society for more than 60 years before it was allowed to participate in politics. However, media interference in the presidential election raised suspicions about the intentions of the Muslim Brotherhood, and thus influenced the Egyptian voters' perception. Consequently, the Muslim Brotherhood candidate, Dr. Mohamed Morsi, won only 52 percent of the popular vote.

Those who are interested in knowing what is really happening have to surf the Internet and seek out foreign TV stations or alternative media. It is ironic that in a free, democratic country like the U.S., you have to tune in to Russian TV (rt.com) or Iranian TV (PressTV.com) and other Internet alternative media.

The corporate media's power has given them a sense of infallibility, making them behave like quasi-governments. In the U.K., Rupert Murdoch's company, News International, became so powerful that leaders of political parties were forced to visit the press baron on his yacht in Australia before an election to increase their chances of winning.

Indeed, in the 2012 Leveson Inquiry, which was investigating the U.K. media, former Prime Minister Tony Blair testified: "... certain newspapers are used by their owners or editors as instruments of political power .... in which the boundary between news and comment is deliberately blurred." He said that, as a political leader, certain elements of the media became "… not merely politically partisan in their comment or editorial line but [also] in their news coverage." [34]

Alastair Campbell, Blair's director of communications and strategy, told the inquiry that Rupert Murdoch lobbied the Prime Minister for faster military action against Iraq. A week before the House of Commons voted on joining the U.S. invasion, Campbell said, Murdoch telephoned Blair and urged him to join President George W. Bush and his Republican administration, saying how News International would support him in his war on Iraq. [35]

The media's influence is not limited to the United Kingdom. Rupert Murdoch also owns Fox News, and through it, manipulation of the news has new extremes. During the 2012 presidential primaries, Fox pretty much decided who would be the Republican Party candidate. Newt Gingrich, who ran and lost in the primaries, put it this way: "I assume it's because Murdoch at some point said 'I want Romney,' and so 'fair and balanced' became 'Romney.' And there's no question that Fox had a lot to do with stopping my campaign because such a high percentage of our base [conservatives] watches Fox." [36]

Another candidate, Ron Paul who was the preferred candidate among Republican war veterans because they believed he "felt their pain," was openly marginalized by the mainstream media. As *National Journal* reporter, Sarah Mimms said: "Paul is mentioned on air far less frequently than most of his rivals, including Bachmann and Texas Gov. Rick Perry, both of whom trail him in national and state-level polls. And when pundits talk about him, they frequently do so in a far more negative tone." [37]

Even during the debates, Paul got less time to air his views. University of Minnesota political scientist Eric Ostermeier has calculated that Paul had the least amount of time to speak in three of 10 debates. [37]

Murdoch tried to buy the U.S. presidency in 2012. According to Jonathan Cook of the Global Research, Murdoch tried to persuade Gen. David Petraeus to run against Barack Obama as the Republican candidate. "Murdoch promised to bankroll Petraeus' campaign and commit Fox News to provide the general with wall-to-wall support," Cook says. [38]

American culture in the mainstream media

> *"Our illusions are created for us by publicists, script writers, marketer, advertising professionals, pollsters, news personalities, and celebrities. We live in illusion in politics, religion, news, warfare, and crime."*
> ~ Chris Hedges, The Empire of Illusion ~

Media networks and newspapers appear to be in competition, but they act like an oligopoly with a shared ideology. Individual outlets will rarely interview those who object to war, but they give plenty of time to warmongers who propound distorted, hateful images of Israel's enemies and openly misrepresent the danger to the U.S.

This image is reinforced in the entertainment arm of the media, where movies glorify war and in violent sports programs like Ultimate Fighter Competition. To all intents and purposes, the war in Iraq was presented as an adventure movie—*Shock and Awe*. Beautifully colored explosions and triumphant soldiers were depicted riding in tanks, all driven on the road to victory and glory—No blood, no dead bodies, no maimed soldiers or Iraqis, and certainly no scenes of rape or torture.

America's far-right political culture is, itself, a media creation. As author Ben Bagdikian wrote in *The New Media Monopoly*: "[The media has] produced a coarse and vulgar culture that celebrates the most demeaning characteristics in the human psyche – greed, deceit and cheating as a legitimate way to win." [39]

Consumerism and the mainstream media

In our society, material wealth is over-emphasized as the path to happiness and fulfillment. We are constantly bombarded by messages from advertisers to buy things we do not need. The media, which is sustained by advertising revenue, tries to convince us to work harder to make more money to buy these goods. In the end, manufacturers make higher profits at the expense of the emotional health and wellbeing of society.

Tim Kasser, a professor of psychology at Knox College, reports that seeking satisfaction in material goods is unfulfilling. "When acquiring more things takes center-stage in life and consumption becomes the primary focus, we and our children tend to experience more anxiety and depression, a decreased sense of well-being, and more behavioral and physical problems," Kasser says. [40]

The advent of the Internet

Television used to be the main source of news, and before the age of cable, people got their information from the same few networks. Walter Cronkite, Dan Rather, David Brinkley, and Eric Sevareid were not just newscasters; they were trusted professionals we let into our houses every night. Now, the Internet has democratized news, and our once trustworthy perceptions of news and the media in general have been eroded, perhaps irreparably. This may be for the best because citizens all over the world not only follow the news, but also are more willing to question it as they seek the truth.

When people take the trouble to research news stories on the Internet, they discover how biased the media can be. In the past few years, the number of cable TV subscribers has been decreasing and the low ratings for news stations have reflected the lack of trust in the mainstream media. For example, CNN's ratings hit a 20-year low in May 2012. [41]

How to read mainstream news

If we are to trust what we are told, we need to be politically engaged, analyze stories carefully, consult other sources, and consider whose interests a story serves. For example, regarding information about the Middle East, Western reports should be compared to those from Iran's PressTV (http://www.PressTV.com) or Russia Today (http://www.rt.com). Indian and Chinese reports are also valuable for confirming the accuracy of Western stories. Foreign news sources are especially important for helping readers cut through the propaganda and loaded language of Pro-Israeli/pro-American reporting. Terms like "national interest," "Syrian rebels," "Israeli Defense forces" and "terrorist" are designed to manipulate, not inform.

Manipulation is most conspicuous in the way the media tells how to feel about human casualties. We are supposed to feel sorry for soldiers who are killed or maimed. If a story comes out about

American soldiers raping or killing Afghan civilians in their homes, talking heads can be counted on to mitigate these actions by saying that the soldiers were suffering from post-traumatic stress disorder (PTSD). Meanwhile, the "enemy" is dehumanized and any act of violence committed against "us" is over-reported and blown out of proportion. On some TV stations, right wing Christians cheered the invasion of Muslim countries and the killing of Muslim civilians. They even called for "nuking them." [42,43]

The media's bias is further confirmed by its support for "pre-emptive wars." For example, Iran is accused of developing nuclear weapons, yet no proof exists. However, Israel wants the U.S. to use this as a pretext to attack Iran pre-emptively, and is unhappy that President Obama has so far refused.

Ironically, Israel has more than 400 nuclear weapons, [44] and does not allow the International Agency for Atomic Energy (IAAE) to inspect its nuclear reactor in Dimona. It has been developing its military nuclear capabilities at sea by equipping new German-made submarines with nuclear-tipped cruise missiles. [45] It has also been disposing its nuclear waste in southern Hebron, in the Occupied Territory, causing the level of radioactive contamination among Palestinians in the area to rise to 10 times the allowable limit. [46] These issues have never been discussed because Israel influences almost all-mainstream news.

The media keep telling us that we live in a free country, but in the past decade, our freedoms have been eroded to the point where our democracy is now closer to a police state. The non-mainstream "independent" media is therefore vitally important to defend our freedoms and to help the people determine if what is published or broadcast is factual and trustworthy.

Independent media

Independent or "alternative" media are newspapers, radio, television, magazines, movies, and Internet sites that provide marginalized or otherwise critical points of view. Many of these media are small-scale, non-profit organizations that are community based, and owned or run by volunteers or collectives. The Internet has enabled these media to flourish and effectively compete with mainstream media, as can be seen in the decrease of the number of TV network subscribers.[41]

In January 2000, the U.S. Federal Communications Commission (FCC) authorized a special broadcast class, low-power FM (LPFM) stations, to provide non-commercial, educational broadcasting. These stations cannot operate with power of more than 100 watts, far below the power of commercial, public, or state-run broadcasters. The Prometheus Radio Project, a U.S. grassroots organization that advocates the establishment of LPFM stations, provides assistance to startups. [47]

Noncommercial broadcasters in the U.S. have an exclusive use of the FM band between 88.1 and 91.9 megahertz. This portion of the dial includes some radio stations, which could be classified as alternative media, including community-run and student-run radio stations, although there are many stations affiliated with large national broadcasters, such as National Public Radio or large religious organizations.

Interaction among activists and alternative media outlets, whether local, national, or international is crucial for democratic reform, but just because media are alternative does not necessarily mean they are not directly or indirectly linked to corporate media. [48]

Understanding the pitfalls of alternative media

Thanks to the Internet, the role of alternative media has grown astronomically. In October 2009, YouTube views numbered one billion per day, exceeded two billion in May 2010 [49] and by 2011, YouTube viewers had increased to four billion. [50] Small wonder governments are turning to the Internet to influence public opinion. The leading states in this arena are Israel and the U.S.

In July 2006 during its invasion of Lebanon, the Israeli government manipulated the Internet using software called Megaphone. The Israeli lobby used it to vote down stories questioning Israeli actions and to send pro-Israel communiqués to volunteers, who then used these communiqués to write letters to politicians and media.

The software was developed by Give Israel Your United Support (GIYUS) and distributed by the World Union of Jewish Students, World Jewish Congress, The Jewish Agency for

Israel, World   Zionist   Organization, StandWithUs, Hasbara fellowships, Honest Reporting and other pro-Israel public-relations organizations. It was supported by Israel's foreign ministry, [51] which orchestrates propaganda efforts to flood news websites with pro-Israel arguments and information. It also recruits pro-Israel "media volunteers" and sends them a list of media links that the ministry would like addressed by pro-Israel comments. It uses the Hasbara brigade of "cyberspace soldiers" and "cyber insurgents" like those involved with GIYUS.

By June 2011, GIYUS replaced the tool by an RSS newsfeed that casts vote of a pro-Israel volunteer automatically if the volunteer chooses to go to a particular site with a poll about Israeli policies or actions. [52] On its website, GIYUS says that the organization's special software exists to save its propagandists from having to search the website to vote manually. As the GIYUS website says: "If you have arrived at the poll results, it means that you were directed straight to the voting action and have already successfully voted." [52,53] In later versions, the software directed users to anti-Israel websites, giving users an option to click a button labeled "act now!" that would direct the user to a poll or e-mail address.

After a volunteer signs up, the Department of Information and Internet sends an official communiqué with talking points about current issues for the volunteer to use in their propaganda efforts. Examples of target sites may include *The Times* of London, *The Guardian*, Sky News, the BBC, Yahoo News, *The Huffington Post* and the Dutch *Telegraaf*, in addition to other media sites in other languages considered critical of Israeli policies. For example, Richard Silverstein of *The Guardian* reports that, when peace activists held a rally at a federal building in Seattle attended by 500 protesters, the next day the Foreign Ministry issued a communiqué directing activists to comment on the *Seattle Post Intelligencer*'s article about the demonstration. [54] Silverstein believes that the comment thread was riddled with Hasbara "plants," who distorted the balance and tone of the discussion. [55] Such messages are designed to narrow the gap between the position of a specific country's government and public opinion, which may oppose Israeli actions.

As the Israeli foreign ministry has said, in a communiqué during the attack on the Gaza Strip in December 2008, "It is our goal to shift public opinion, as conveyed on the Internet; avoiding, or at least minimizing, sanctions by world leaders. We need to buy the Israeli Defense Forces enough time to achieve its goals," [55] as well as talking points provided by Israel's foreign ministry to pro-Israel web activists. The Israeli foreign ministry also offers online pro-Israel material to link to their comments, such as Britain Israel Communications and Research Centre (http://www.Bicom.org.uk/) [55] "The Foreign Ministry itself is now…urging supporters of Israel everywhere to become cyberspace soldiers in the new battleground for Israel's image," says Silverstein. [56]

A computing website known as The Register [57] has described the use of this software as "highly organized mass manipulation of technologies that are supposed to be democratizing," and reiterated that Megaphone is "effectively a high-tech exercise in ballot-stuffing." [58]

Control of the Internet

Under the post-9/11 Homeland Security laws, the U.S. government has been targeting, and demanding access to, social media, including popular news sites, and spreading black propaganda in the international media. Black propaganda is false information and material that purports to be from a source on one side of a conflict, but is actually from the opposing side.

A Washington blog has mentioned that polls at Digg, Reddit, YouTube, and other mainstream news sites have suddenly disappeared entirely if insufficiently pro-government sentiment was expressed. [59] In 2002, the Pentagon established the Office of Strategic Influence to manipulate public opinion abroad by planting black propaganda and misleading stories. Since the Internet has no boundaries, there is nothing to stop an American newspaper from picking up such a foreign plant and then having it show up on the computers and television screens of Americans.

In 2003, an official Pentagon report titled *Information Operations Roadmap* was put out as part of the military's psychological operations or "Psyops." The report described a range of military activities that engaged in misinformation operations, such as public affairs officers who brief journalists, psychological operation troops who try to manipulate the thoughts and beliefs of an enemy, and computer hackers who seek to destroy enemy networks. The report explains: "Information intended for foreign audiences, including public diplomacy and Psyops, is increasingly consumed by our domestic audience...Psyops messages will often be replayed by the news media for much larger audiences, including the American public." [59]

The roadmap recommends establishing global websites to support America's strategic objectives. The website would use content from "... third parties with greater credibility to foreign audiences than U.S. officials." [59] It also recommends that Psyops personnel should consider a range of technologies to disseminate propaganda in enemy territory. The "strategy should be based on the premise that the Department [of Defense] will 'fight the 'Net' as it would an enemy weapons system." [59]

In 2005, the Pentagon paid a private company, the Lincoln Group, to plant hundreds of stories in Iraqi newspapers. The stories, which were supportive of U.S. policy, were written by Pentagon personnel and placed in Iraqi publications and websites that appeared to be information sites on the politics of Africa and the Balkans. "The articles, written by U.S. military 'information operations' troops, are translated into Arabic and placed in Baghdad newspapers," wrote Mark Mazzetti and Borzou Daragahi [60,61] of the *Los Angeles Times* on Nov. 30, 2005.

Use of "sock puppets"

A "sock puppet" is an online identity used for the purpose of deception. It is created to praise, defend, or support an organization or a third party. The difference between a pseudonym and a sock puppet is that the sock puppet poses as an independent third party unaffiliated with any organization. [62]

In March 2011, Nick Fielding and Ian Cobain of *The Guardian* [63] reported that the U.S. Central Command (Centcom), which oversees U.S. armed operations in the Middle East and Central Asia, was developing software to manipulate social media sites using fake online personas to create a false consensus in online conversations and crowd out critical opinions. The software was to be used to influence Internet conversations and spread pro-American propaganda. The interventions would be directed at the Muslim world in Arabic, Farsi, Urdu, and Pashto. However, the instant translation part of web browsers would not prevent the message from reaching the American homes.

The software could allow U.S. service personnel, working around the clock in one location, to respond to emerging online conversations with any number of coordinated messages, blog posts, chat room posts and other interventions. However, the military could face legal challenges in the U.S., where a number of people engaged in sock puppetry have faced prosecution. [63]

Jeff Jarvis of *The Guardian* noted that the practice is needlessly risky: "It is appallingly stupid for there is little doubt that the fakes will be unmasked. The net result of that will be the diminution, not the enhancement, of American credibility...[I]t is sad to see the U.S. government taming the power of the Net to stoop to the morals of a clumsy Nigerian spammer." [62]

What the U.S. and its European allies also failed to appreciate is that Muslims have been subjected to black propaganda from their own totalitarian regimes for many years, and so can read between the lines to distinguish between what is fake and what is not.

Recommendations

A lack of public awareness and knowledge makes it easy for the media to decide which issues will be discussed. However, it has little power to set the agenda if people are well informed about propaganda techniques, think for themselves, and can be convinced to take an active interest in politics. For this reason, it is important to set up "the New Era" clubs at community centers and schools to educate and inform the community about the current political issues.

Regarding the media itself, a mechanism needs to be developed to free it from the control of corporate owners, government, self-interest, and special interest groups. Misinformation will continue as long as there is no opportunity for an opposing point of view to be heard. We need TV, radio and print outlets that present the news with integrity and help ordinary people make up their own minds, based on facts. Laws should be enacted requiring the media to give equal time to those who have opposing points of view, and have an independent body to observe this process and ensure its implementation.

Today, the Internet has subverted the existing order and the mainstream media are on the verge of losing control. The media's major players will try to develop new policies that enable them to control and centralize the Internet. They have done it successfully in the past. It is up to us to prevent this from happening; otherwise, the freedom to access unfiltered information through the Internet will end.

Chapter 4

Lobbying and campaign finance to Control the White House, Congress and economy

It is necessary that laws should be passed to prohibit the use of corporate funds directly or indirectly for political purposes, [and] it is still more necessary that such laws should be thoroughly enforced.
~ Theodore Roosevelt ~

The Power Triad spends a huge amount of money on lobbying and election campaign funding in order to control the White House, Congress, and the economy. The money the Triad members spend for this purpose is their best investment. This chapter explores the Triad's strategies to buy political influence and discusses the efforts of the multinational corporations to manipulate the congressional representatives in order to generate huge profits at the expense of the ordinary Americans.

The discussion of special interest groups in this book focuses on the Israel Lobby because it is, without doubt, the greatest threat to the national interests and security of the U.S. and it citizens. Through bribery and coercion, the agents of Israel push the Congress to fight futile wars of aggression against Muslim states. These wars deepened the debt crisis, impoverished millions, and inflamed the Middle East against the U.S. No serious talk of political reform is possible until this internal threat to U.S. democracy is addressed.

The Israel Lobby

> *Real power does not lie with the White House or Congress.*
> *It lies with the Zionist, Christian and Straussian pressure*
> *groups that tell the president and Congress what to do.*
> *These lobbyists, academics, and 'think tanks' constitute the*
> *real governing class... Some of these 'think tanks' display*
> *their bias openly, while others carry deceptively neutral*
> *names and masquerade as tax-deductible educational*
> *foundations, but all of them are part of a fascist network*
> *that fosters Straussian econo-theology, Israeli colonialism,*
> *and anti-Muslim bigotry.*
> *Greg Felton, Author of The Host and the Parasite—*
> *How Israel's Fifth Column Consumed America*

Since the creation of Israel in May 1948, the Israel Lobby has played a major role in influencing U.S. Middle East policy. From the founding of the American Israel Public Affairs Committee (AIPAC) in 1951, the Lobby has developed a wide network of advocates and sympathizers (neo-conservatives) in key posts in the executive branch, the Pentagon, Congress, media, and think tanks. It has the power to steer millions of dollars of political contributions to reward or punish candidates based on their loyalty to Israel. It ensures that no representative would endorse an even-handed policy toward the Middle East or put the interests of the U.S. ahead of those of Israel.

AIPAC is a lobby group uniquely positioned to influence the U.S. foreign policy, yet it is not required to register under the Foreign Agents Registration Act. Despite being a single-issue group, AIPAC acts on behalf of a foreign government and interferes in U.S. election campaigns. Many Americans concerned about the independence of the U.S. from foreign influence have raised this issue. Gus Savage, who served a member of the U.S. House of Representatives from 1981 to 1993:

"[AIPAC is an] organization operating within America composed of Americans, in the interest of a foreign nation, and interfering in the internal affairs and the elections of this Nation. The group's top political operatives are actively involved with pro-Israel political action committees (PACs) to help raise money for several candidates in the Senate races." [15]

"Several prominent Americans filed complaints with the Federal Elections Commission charging that AIPAC works so closely with legally established PACs to target political candidates based on their positions toward Israel. These PACs are in effect affiliates of the lobby group. AIPAC's formidable ability to monopolize congressional support is based not upon an appeal to American national interests, but upon threats by a special interest group that has resorted to conspiracy and conclusion. The complaint demanded that the FEC force AIPAC to register as a political action committee and reveal the sources, amounts, and beneficiaries of its unique and still-secret ways of corrupting the U.S. political system." [15]

The complainants claim that AIPAC has helped establish more than 100 deceptively named political action committees. By pooling their resources, these committees can, and have, grossly violated laws limiting the amount a PAC can contribute to a political candidate during an electoral cycle.

AIPAC's pervasive influence is well known. *The New York Times* has described it as "the most important organization affecting America's relationship with Israel," [64] and one of Washington's most powerful lobbying organizations. [15] In a 2005 National Journal survey of Congress, AIPAC ranked the second most powerful lobby that works for Israel not only in Washington, but also in wherever there is a perceived challenge to its interests in the news media, the religious community, or on college or university campuses. [65]

In his book, *They Dared to talk*, a U.S. representative for more than 22 years, Paul Findlay, reports that, "Since WWII, Israeli lobbyists succeeded to dominate Capitol Hill. They muffled free and open debate in the USA in public and in the legislative chambers on Capitol Hill, whenever the discussion related to the Middle East. As a result, U.S. backed Israel in its aggressions whether financially, militarily, or politically." As a result, the U.S. has backed Israel in its aggressions in the region, and allowed Israel to become a nuclear power." [65]

The price Americans pay for supporting Israel

In their book, *The Israel Lobby and U.S. Foreign Policy*, John Mearsheimer and Stephen Walt argue that, "Israel has continued to be a strategic burden on the U.S. due to the influence of 'the unmatched power' of the Israel Lobby over U.S. foreign policy…[Today] the U.S. has a terrorism problem in good part because it is so closely allied with Israel not the other way around." [7]

The economic cost

The U.S. has spent more than $7.4 trillion pursuing policies dictated by the Israel Lobby, and the U.S. economy continues to bleed because of them. Writing in *The Washington Report on Middle East Affairs*, retired U.S. Foreign Service Officer, Shirl McArthur said direct U.S. aid to Israel between 1949 and 2011 totaled more than $123.2 billion; however, this amount does not take into account the substantial indirect cost to the U.S. economy because of its blind support for Israel. [66]

For example, she reports that money collected by charitable American Jewish groups, to help Israel build illegal settlements [colonies] in the occupied Palestinian territories, is exempt from U.S. taxes. This tax-exempt status amounts to a direct subsidy that costs the U.S. treasury at least 20 percent of the funds sent for illegal construction. [66] Some of the recipients of this money include groups designated by the U.S. as foreign terrorist organizations.

Why the U.S. has to give any aid to Israel is the real question. According to the UN's Human Development Index[ii] Israel ranks 21st out of 194 nations (adjusted for on 2011 estimates), two places ahead of the U.S. [67] Despite this higher standard of living, Israel continues to be the largest recipient of U.S. aid. It receives $3 billion annually in military grants, yet the Israeli government is allowed to apply 26.3 percent of this to investment in its military manufacturing sector and job creation. This unusual practice deprives the Americans of job opportunities while enabling Israel to establish an increasingly

---

[ii] The Human Development Index, which is used by the United Nations Development Program to rank countries, is a composite statistic of life expectancy, education, and income indices.

sophisticated defense industry, making it the seventh-largest arms exporter to the world from 2001 to 2008.

Dr. Thomas R. Stauffer, former Harvard professor of economics and Middle East Studies, conducted an October 2002 study for the U.S. Army College and the University of Maine and reported that the cost of the Israeli-Palestinian conflict to the American taxpayers from WWII to 2002 amounted to more than $3 trillion—$4.4 trillion in 2012 dollars. [68a] This amount includes "the actual indirect consequential cost to the U.S. unbalanced attitude of its foreign policy in the Middle East." In addition, the support for Israel costs the U.S. more than 275,000 American jobs annually. [68]

Despite these immense losses and the $3 trillion spent destroying Iraq, the Israel Lobby is now pushing the U.S. to start a war with Iran, a much bigger and stronger country. Such a war could well pronounce the end of the U.S. supremacy both economically and militarily and plunge the world into a depression.

Political cost

The unconditional backing of AIPAC's foreign policies in the Middle East has led to increasing political isolation. As Chuck Hagel cautioned the Senate Foreign Relations Committee on Jan. 24, 2007, "Today, in the Middle East whether in Iraq, Iran, Syria, Lebanon, it is more dangerous for the U.S. than we have ever seen. We have destroyed our standing, reputation, and influence in the Middle East by what we are doing. And the more we sink down in this bog, the harder it gets to get out of and the more enemies we make." Then he added, "The world needs American leadership. When America loses the trust and confidence of the world, it makes the world more dangerous." [69]

The increasing loss of the U.S.'s global standing was evident in 2012 when the Palestinian Authority sought U.N. recognition in defiance of the U.S. administration. The successful vote in the General Assembly to upgrade Palestine to nonvoting observer status was not only an embarrassment for the U.S., but it showed how much Israel had diminished the influence of the U.S. Of 188 nations, only nine voted against the resolution: Israel, the U.S., Canada, the Czech Republic, Panama, the Marshall Islands, Micronesia, Nauru, and Palau. [70]

Israel and the business of war

U.S. Middle East policy is prepared from Israeli proposals. Before the Clinton presidency, the U.S. acted as an "off-shore balancer in the region," using local powers against each other. That is why the Reagan administration supported Saddam Hussein against Iran during the Iran-Iraq War (1980 – 88), and then illegally funneled arms to Iran (the Iran-Contra scandal) to tilt the balance against Iraq and to continue the destruction of both countries.

The Israel Lobby has been interested in changing the map of the Middle East and having the U.S. station large numbers of troops in Kuwait and Saudi Arabia permanently to contain both Iran and Iraq in what is called "dual containment." In this policy, the U.S. would stop playing off Iraq and Iran against each other and maintain hostile relations with both countries. [7] This strategy led to the invasion of Iraq, which Israel supported because it put the U.S. personnel in harm's way to help Israel achieve its strategic objectives, at no financial or human cost to Israel.

This same thinking is behind the U.S. Middle East policies that date to the beginning of the Clinton administration in 1993 when the Israel Lobby campaigned to have the U.S. attack Iran. At that time, Israeli Prime Minister Yitzhak Rabin and his foreign minister Shimon Peres started to claim that Iran was a growing threat to both Israel and the U.S. They indicated that Americans and their political leaders needed to be convinced of the urgency of the need to restrain Iran. Soon afterwards, Martin Indyk of the pro-Israel Washington Institute introduced the Israeli proposal of "dual containment" for Near East Policy. As director for Near East and South Asian Affairs at the National Security Council, Indyk began implementing dual containment [7] despite the potential human and financial costs to the U.S.

Mearsheimer and Ward [7] affirm that Iraq was not a threat to the U.S. On the contrary, the invasion of Iraq was against the security and national interests of the U.S., but served the interests of Israel because Iraq was an obstacle to Israel's expansion policy in the Middle East. Following 9/11 attacks, AIPAC and its sympathizers launched a misinformation propaganda blitz, through mainstream media, portraying Iraq as a threat to the U.S. They succeeded in making two-thirds of the Americans believe that Saddam Hussein was linked to

Al-Qaeda. [28] Within the U.S., the main driving force behind the war, as Mearsheimer and Walt explains, "Was a small band of neo-conservatives, many with ties to Likud [Israeli political party]," and the Israeli intelligence MOSAD. [71] It participated in fabricating the infamous report about the Iraqi weapons of mass destruction, which was used by the U.S. as reason for the war. According to Israeli Brigadier-General Shlomo Brom in an analysis for Tel Aviv University's Jaffe Centre for Strategic Studies, "Israel was a 'full partner' in American and British intelligence failures that exaggerated former president Saddam Hussein's nuclear, chemical and biological weapons programs before the US-led invasion of Iraq, a report by an Israeli military research Centre has alleged." [72]

The futile wars the U.S. launched over the past two decades on behalf of Israel have understandably increased anti-American sentiment in the Muslim world. If radical Muslims hate the U.S., it is not because of its freedoms as President George W. Bush fatuously proclaimed; rather, it is because the U.S. supports Israel's continued occupation of the Golan Heights, the West Bank and violation of the Palestinian human rights.

Strategies to dictate the U.S. foreign policy in the Middle East

The Israel Lobby has been very successful in using money, coercion, and the media to determine who is elected to Congress so that Israel gets consistent diplomatic backing, even when it undermines U.S. interests and national security. It has also been successful in using coercion and intimidation to stifle open dialogue about the U.S.-Israel relationship. The Lobby's all-purpose weapon is the accusation of "anti-Semitism." The Lobby aggressively attacks politicians who dare to provide details about Israel's brutal treatment of the Palestinians or its systematic defiance of international law.

Control of Congress

Any politician who does not toe the line of the Israel Lobby can expect to be targeted. The Israel Lobby will smear their character, fund their opponent's election campaign, or push for redistricting electoral areas where the incumbent elected representative has well-established connections. In the eyes of AIPAC, politicians commit an "offense" against Israel if they:

- Advocate an even-handed U.S. foreign policy in the Middle East;
- Put the interests of the U.S. ahead of Israel's;
- Interact with the American Arab community;
- Show empathy towards the Palestinians;
- Seek a peaceful settlement for the Israeli-Palestinian conflict;
- Refuse to sign a Pledge to Israel, or
- Not support an AIPAC initiative.

Paul Findley, a 22-year congressman from Ohio (1961 – 1982), was a victim to such a coordinated attack. In his book *They Dare to Speak Out*, he wrote: "AIPAC's ex-executive director Thomas A. Dine credited Jewish money, not votes, to the defeat of Republican senators Charles Percy of Illinois and Roger Jepsen of Iowa, and Democratic senator Walter Huddleston of Kentucky, all of whom voted to sell AWACS planes to Saudi Arabia. Dine said these successes, 'defined Jewish political power for the rest of this century.'" [73]

Americans like Findley who stand up to Israel do not do so lightly. They know that challenging the Israel Lobby was, as President Carter puts it, "almost politically suicidal." [7]

As far back as 1973 on CBS's *Face the Nation*, Sen. William Fulbright pointed out that around 80 percent of the Senate was completely in support of anything Israel wanted and that the U.S. bore a great share of the responsibility for Middle East violence. He indicated that, "It's quite obvious [that] without the all-out support by the U.S. in money and weapons and so on, the Israelis couldn't do what they've been doing...We should be more concerned about the U.S.' interests." [73]

During Ronald Reagan's presidency, AIPAC's influence over the Republican Congress was stronger than that of the president himself. When he needed votes of some Republican representatives to keep the marines in Lebanon in October 1983, he sought the help of

AIPAC to secure those votes. In addition, AIPAC made Congress increase aid to Israel even though it was in violation of international law and contrary to White House policy. [73]

The supremacy of Israeli interests is evident in policymaking forums, where conflicts of interest ensure that Israel, not the U.S., comes out on top. In February 1983, Reagan's secretary of state George Shultz named a panel of prominent citizens to recommend changes to the federal foreign aid program. Shultz selected AIPAC's executive director, Thomas Dine to be a member even though Israel is a beneficiary of this aid. AIPAC representatives were also invited to the White House for private meetings with Reagan's national security adviser to give advice on issues concerning Lebanon and Jordan. Consequently, most congressional actions affecting Middle East policy must be either approved or initiated by AIPAC. [73]

On the matter of Israeli intimidation of U.S. lawmakers, former congressman Paul N. 'Pete' McCloskey put the matter most succinctly: "Congress is terrorized by AIPAC. Other congressional representatives have not been so candid on the public record, but many House and Senate members privately agree. In practice, the lobby groups function as an informal extension of the Israeli government. This was illustrated when AIPAC helped draft the official statement defending Israel's 1981 bombing of the Iraqi nuclear reactor, then issued it the same hour as Israel's embassy." [73]

More recently, the reception Benjamin Netanyahu received during a joint session of the Congress on May 24, 2011, demonstrated the subordination of both Republicans and Democrats to Israeli interests. In his speech, Netanyahu arrogantly rejected President Barack Obama's peace proposal, which had been presented the previous day, and for this, he received more standing ovations from both parties than the president had during his State of the Union address. In a comment on this scene, Mitchell Plitnick of Jewish Voice for Peace said that the U.S. had never been as shameless in its blind support for the Israeli right, "placing support for the Likud [Israel's Right wing party] leader over the interests of justice and human rights and even its own self-interest." Indeed, many Israeli journalists even considered that what Netanyahu suggested in his speech was a threat to the peace and stability of Israel. [74]

To demonstrate their loyalty to AIPAC, high-level policymakers and politicians from both parties attend the annual AIPAC Policy Conference. Candidates visit AIPAC to "explain" their positions on foreign aid, and U.S.-Arab relations in general. Despite AIPAC's claims of non-involvement in political spending, "no fewer than 51 pro-Israel PACs are directed by AIPAC officials or people who hold seats on AIPAC's two major policymaking bodies." [15]

In addition to Jewish organizations, Zionist Christian preachers use their pulpit to pressure their congregations into intimidating elected representatives to support Israel. In a film about AIPAC produced by Dutch TV (VPRO), Pastor John Hagee of Christians United for Israel said, "We want to let our elected officials know that if you reduce your support to Israel, we will do everything in our power to see that this will be their last term in office." [75]

Largely because of Zionist Christians, and pro-Israel PACs to raise funds to influence election campaigns, AIPAC has successfully ended the political careers of patriotic representatives such as Paul Findley, Charles Percy, Gus Savage, Cynthia McKinney, Earl Hilliard, Adlai Stevenson III, and Jesse Jackson.

On the other side, politicians who do toe the line are rewarded with generous campaign funds and volunteers to help with the election campaign, and many other rewards including junkets to Israel. While AIPAC does not itself conduct the tours, it facilitates them through its affiliate organization, the American Israel Education Foundation. During the recess in August 2011, the Foundation sponsored 81 House members on a visit to Israel and the West Bank. [76] Over half of the members of Congress have traveled to Israel, about half going on what is deemed official business at the expense of the U.S. government.

Control of freedom of speech on University Campuses and the media

Intimidation extends not only to members of Congress, but also to university professors, journalists, and the public. Professor John Mearsheimer, co-author of *Israel Lobby and U.S. Foreign Policy,* describes his predicament: "It is not fun to be called an anti-Semite, hounded day after day and see very few people standing in your defense. They [AIPAC] are going after people in a very hard-hitting way to shut us down and to send a message to other people that if you follow the footsteps of Jimmy Carter, Tony Judt, John Mearsheimer, or Stephen Walt, you will pay a serious price for your transgression. That is their deterrence model." [75]

In his paper in February 2009, *"Is it Love or the Lobby? Explaining America's Special Relationship with Israel,"* Mearsheimer and Walt write, "we were routinely smeared as anti-Semites and accused— incorrectly—of making numerous scholarly errors. Critics routinely misrepresented our arguments; indeed, they often accused us of saying the opposite of what we actually wrote." [77]

Mark Shields of PBS explains in a comment on January 4, 2013 on PBS' Newshour, "There are some people who view any criticism of whatever the administration is in Likud as somehow disloyal to the state of Israel. If you say what the Labor Party in Israel says about Benjamin Netanyahu in this country [the U.S.], you would make yourself vulnerable to charges of anti-Semitism." [78]

Corporate lobbying

> *[Legally] you can't take a congressman to lunch for $25*
> *and buy him a hamburger or a steak or something like that,*
> *but you can take him to a fundraising lunch and not only*
> *buy him that steak, but give him $25,000 extra and call it a*
> *fundraiser, and have all the same access and all the same*
> *interaction with that congressman. So, the people who make*
> *the reforms are the people in the system.*
> *~ Jack Abramoff, veteran lobbyist ~*

In both a democracy and a dictatorship, money buys influence, but with a difference. In a dictatorship, politicians and bureaucrats can be bribed directly with cash but the transaction carries some risk. In our democracy, lobbying (bribery) occurs at all levels of governments and is safe and legal.

Lobbyists can give politicians campaign funds as well as gifts to facilitate what their corporate or special interest clients want to achieve. In addition, loyal politicians are implicitly given an assurance that, if they are not re-elected, they will be taken care of. In return for faithful service in the legislature, they may be offered positions as lobbyists, paid consultants, or corporate directors or executives. In a study published in March 2012, The Republic Report indicates that when a Congressman becomes a lobbyist, he gets a 1,452 percent raise in salary. [79a] This may be legal, but it corrupts the political system. If an elected representative remains committed solely to the interests of the electorate, he/she will ruin their potential opportunity to work as a lobbyist after leaving the Congress.

Any relationship with lobbyists jeopardizes our democracy. A lobbyist's job is to convince elected officials to enact laws and create loopholes at the expense of the public good, so that their clients (corporations and special interest groups) shirk their financial or legal responsibilities and improve their bottom line. The Center for Responsive Politics reports that in 2012, the Power Triad spent $3.28 billion on lobbying in addition to their contributions to election campaigns. [79]

Money and gifts may be offered to a party or its candidates to buy their loyalty, and once elected these politicians will be expected to pay back their corporate donors, and financial subsidy is one method. In 2011, for example, British Petroleum, Chevron, ConocoPhillips, Exxon Mobil, and Royal Dutch Shell received $2 billion in subsidies from the U.S. government, while their profits reached more than $137 billion, an increase of 75 percent over 2010 profits. In 2011, these oil-and-gas companies spent $1.6 million on campaign contributions and $65.7 million on lobbying. For every $1 spent on lobbying in Washington, the Big Five received $30 worth of tax breaks. [80] In 2012, these companies spent $49.5 million of $138 million spent by the whole oil and gas industry. [81]

Oil companies are not the only corporations to benefit from this corruption. The Center for Responsive Politics reported that in 2012, the defense sector invested $129 million in lobbying, of which the big military corporations—Lockheed Martin, Boeing, and Northrop Grumman—accounted for $48 million. [82] In addition, the military industry donated some $200 million to presidential candidates to ensure future contracts. As a result, just six months before the election, President Obama signed an agreement to remain in Afghanistan for another 10 years. [83]

The military industry has the best and most profitable arrangements with the government. U.S. taxpayers fund its research, development, and construction of new weapons systems, so it has no limits on spending and incurs no risk. These defense contractors are allowed to have huge cost overruns, and charge the government the cost of the research plus profit margin. Then, they sell the newly developed weapons to the U.S. and other countries at an inflated price that they set. In addition, most of the foreign aid given to countries like Egypt and Israel is used to buy equipment from these same corporations.

Lobbyists promote ideologies, which work against the common good. For example, the health care system is unsustainable—one of the most expensive and least effective in the developed countries. Although a universal health care program funded from the income tax revenues, without any extra cost to citizens, would be very cost effective, the healthcare industry lobbyists have been successful in preventing this from happening.

The American League of Lobbyists claims that its members have a role to play in formulating sound public policy, but in a democracy, that role should be played in the open without any gifts or campaign funds to legislators. If there is a conflict between the public good and private interests, the public good should prevail.

Jack Abramoff

In November 2011, the CBS show *60 Minutes* aired a provocative segment about lobbying in Washington D.C. and lobbyist Jack Abramoff in particular. [84] Abramoff was a very successful Republican lobbyist in the mid-1990s and the center of one of Washington's biggest corruption scandals. In his *60 Minutes* interview, Abramoff revealed that he was able to influence politicians and their staffers through generous gifts and job offers. He showered gifts on congressional representatives and persuaded his clients to make substantial campaign contributions to select members. In return, they would vote on legislation and tax breaks favorable to his clients. As *60 Minutes* reported:

"[Abramoff's gifts included] access to private jets and trips to the world's great golf destinations such as St. Andrews in Scotland, free meals at his own upscale Washington restaurant and access to the best tickets to sporting events—including two Skyboxes at Washington Redskins games. He also offered congressional office staffers jobs that could triple their salaries. In this way, he virtually owned the

Chief of Staff and Office of Congressional Representatives, and got whatever he requested for his clients." [84]

One of Abramoff's strategies was to ask the chair of a congressional committee to insert some language into a reform bill that would help his clients. In order to do this, Abramoff crafted language that "was so obscure, so confusing, so uninformative but so precise" that no one would have known about it but the chair of the committee. Abramoff says he could get away with this because committee members often do not read bills carefully and sometimes have no idea about what a bill contains. In all, Abramoff claimed his office exerted a strong influence on 100 of the 335 congressional offices. [84]

After the scandal, the Congress instituted a package of reforms in order to make it illegal to buy members of Congress expensive meals, but Abramoff said the reforms were ineffective because the members of Congress know how to fool the system. [84] Moreover, lobbyists can find a way around whatever rules Congress comes up with.

Abramoff admitted that lobbying is a sort of bribery, and has come to believe that the system needs to be fixed. For that to happen, he said that members of Congress and their staff must be prohibited from ever becoming lobbyists in Washington: "If you make the choice to serve the public, then serve the public, not yourself. When you're done, go home." [84]

The American Legislative Exchange Council

The American Legislative Exchange Council (ALEC) is an ideologically conservative group consisting of business interests and conservative state legislators who believe in limited government and free markets. It became a powerful lobbying force on behalf of business since the early days of the first Reagan administration. [85] ALEC has more than 2,000 legislative members representing all 50 states, amounting to nearly one-third of all sitting legislators, as well as more than 85 members of Congress, and 14 sitting or former governors. Members include approximately 300 corporate members. [86]

ALEC has drafted model legislation on issues such as tax treatment of corporations, tightening voter identification rules and promoting gun rights. [87,88]

The Granite State Progress Organization (GSPO) is a non-profit organization that engages the citizens of New Hampshire to advance progressive solutions to critical community problems. The GSPO states that, "The American Legislative Exchange Council hands state legislators the changes to the law they desire that directly benefit their bottom line. Corporations sit on all nine ALEC task forces and vote with legislators to approve 'model' bills. Participating legislators, who are overwhelmingly conservative Republicans, introduce these proposed bills in the statehouses without disclosing that corporations drafted and voted on the bills. ALEC has over 1,000 of these bills introduced by legislative members every year, with one in every five of them enacted into law." [86]

Senator Bernie Sanders (Independent, Vermont) explains how some members, owners and executives of the Power Triad have taken advantage of working people: "U.S. statistics show that in 2011, the average tax paid by the rich was 17 percent, down from 60 percent in 2000. Loopholes in the regulations enable large corporations to make billions of dollars and not pay a nickel in federal corporate taxes. Congress will not close these loopholes because many congressional representatives stand for the wealthy and fight for the large corporations. On the other side, the polls say do not cut social security, Medicare, and Medicaid. Day after day, we have to fight against many members of Congress who want to cut social security, Medicare and Medicaid."

However, lobbying to fund election campaigns or influence public opinion must not continue to be confused with free speech.

History of campaign finance

Those who cannot remember the past are condemned to repeat it.
~ George Santayana ~

Since the beginning of the 20th century, the Court has flip-flopped regarding free speech and its relation to campaign funding according to the political inclinations of its members. In 1905, President Theodore Roosevelt called for campaign finance reform that led to the "Acts of Congress," designed to ban corporate contributions for political activities. The acts limited the influence of wealthy individuals and special interest groups, regulated campaign spending and deterred abuses by mandating public disclosure. The 1907 *Tillman Act*[89] banned corporations from contributing to political parties or candidates for any federal election campaigns.

In 1910, the *Federal Corrupt Practices Act* (the *Publicity Act*) established campaign spending limits for political parties in general elections, and required public disclosure of financial spending by political parties, but not the candidates. The parties were required to file post-election reports regarding their contributions to individual candidates, as well as their own individual expenditures. When the *Federal Corrupt Practices Act* was first amended in 1911, financial disclosure by candidates was required and limits were established on the amount of money candidates were allowed to spend on their campaigns. For House of Representative candidates, expenditures were held to $5,000. For those running for the Senate, expenditures were limited to $10,000, which was increased to $25,000 in 1925. This act also required reporting any contribution over $100. However, the law did not regulate total contributions, and that loophole encouraged parties and donors to set up multiple committees and make multiple donations (all under $100) to get around the limits. Further, enforcement was left up to Congress, which rarely acted. [90]

In 1947, the *Taft Hartley Act* restricted the activities and power of labor unions or corporations from spending money to influence federal elections, and prohibited labor unions from contributing to candidate campaigns. However, labor unions allowed individuals to contribute by establishing political action committees (PACs) to work around these limitations. [91]

The 1972 *Federal Election Campaign Act* (*FECA*) increased disclosure of contributions for federal campaigns, put a $1,000 limit on contributions of individuals, including candidates running for election. It also defined a political action committee (PAC) at the federal level as an organization that receives or spends more than $1,000 for influencing an election. A PAC may campaign for or against candidates, ballot initiatives, or legislation. [92]

Since that time, *FECA* has undergone several amendments, as corporation and special interest groups strived to hijack elections by pressuring Congress and the Supreme Court. *FECA* was amended in 1974, 1976, 1977, 1979, 2002, and 2010. In 1974, due to abuses during the 1972 presidential election, the Congress established the Federal Election Commission (FEC), set rules to restrict the contributions of individuals and corporations to election campaigns, and placed legal limits on:

- Expenditures by candidates and associated committees,
- Independent expenditures, and
- Candidate expenditures from personal funds.

The FECA also required the disclosure of political contributions.

The 1974 amendments enabled the wealthy and the Triad members to control the Congress and politicize the Supreme Court. In January 1976, the Supreme Court ruled in *Buckley v. Valeo* that spending money to influence elections was a form of free speech and thus constitutionally protected. [93] The court also ruled that candidates could spend unlimited amounts of money on their own campaigns. These rulings enable the wealthy individuals to drown out the speech of ordinary citizens, and put congressional seats on sale for the rich as we have seen in in many cases. For example, Michael Bloomberg, the Mayor of New York, ex-senator and ex-governor, Jon Corzine, and Governor of Florida, Rick Scott spent out of their own pocket on their election campaigns $7.5 million, $60 million, and $73 million, respectively. [22]

In 1977, the Supreme Court ruled in *First National Bank of Boston v. Bellotti* that corporations had a First Amendment right to use their money to influence elections. It said prohibiting corporations from this right infringed on their "protected speech." The ruling struck down a state law that criminalized corporations for spending money to advertise their views prior to a state referendum. This ruling declared that corporate "persons" have the same free speech rights as natural persons, could spend unlimited sums in the form of advertisements and campaign contributions, and engage in other forms of political speech. Justice Lewis Powell ruled that a Massachusetts criminal statute prohibiting the expenditure of corporate funds for "influencing or affecting" voters' opinions infringed on corporations' "protected speech in a manner unjustified by a compelling state interest." Powell's ruling equated corporate donations with free speech and allowed corporate money to govern politics. [94]

In 1990, in *Austin v. Michigan Chamber of Commerce,* [95] the Supreme Court recognized the importance of combating a different type of political corruption. It upheld the *Michigan Campaign Finance Act,* which prohibited corporations (but not unions) from using their money to support or oppose candidates in elections, because it did not violate the First and 14th Amendments. The Court upheld the restriction on corporate speech based on the idea that "corporate wealth can unfairly influence elections." The case recognized that the concentration of wealth in corporate hands had little or no correlation to the public's support for the corporations' political ideas.

In 2002, the *Bipartisan Campaign Reform Act (BCRA),* also known as the *McCain-Feingold Act,* amended *FECA* once again, this time to prohibit national political party committees from raising or spending any funds not subject to federal limits. The amendment applied to state and local races and even the discussion of issues, as well as federal campaigns. The *BCRA* also prohibited "electioneering communications," defined as advertisements that advocate on issues and name a federal candidate within 30 days of a primary or caucus or 60 days of a general election. In addition, the act prohibited advertisements paid for by a corporation or "unincorporated entity" that used any funds from a corporation's or union's general treasury.

In the 2010 *Citizens United v. Federal Election Commission* ruling (known as the *Citizens United* decision), the Court decided that, indeed, money *is* speech, and that corporations, as "persons," have a First Amendment right to use their money to influence politics. The decision enabled corporations and special interest groups to strengthen their hold on Congress and the White House, giving them the legal rights to decide who would be elected. At that time, Jamie Raskin, a constitutional law expert at American University and Maryland state senator cautioned: "This is a moment of high danger for democracy so we must act quickly to spell out in the *Constitution* what the people have always understood: That corporations do not enjoy the political and free speech rights that belong to the people of the U.S." [96]

President Barack Obama went even further: "With its ruling today, the Supreme Court has given a green light to a new stampede of special interest money in our politics. It is a major victory for big oil, Wall Street banks, health insurance companies and the other powerful interests that marshal their power every day in Washington to drown out the voices of everyday Americans. This ruling gives the special interests and their lobbyists even more power in Washington, while undermining the influence of average Americans who make small contributions to support their preferred candidates. That is why I am instructing my administration to get to work immediately with Congress on this issue. We are going to talk with bipartisan Congressional leaders to develop a forceful response to this decision. The public interest requires nothing less." [97]

Freedom of speech should go hand in hand with *equality* of speech. To do this, money must be taken out of politics and the equation of a corporation as person must be overturned. [98]

Reform of election campaign funding

To be elected under the current system, candidates' experience, qualifications, and skills are irrelevant. What matters is how much money they can raise and spend on their election campaigns. In most cases, the candidate with the most campaign funds wins. Even still, the differences between candidates are largely cosmetic, and those who win do so based on looks, eloquence, and promises.

If we expect the best-qualified and experienced candidates to run for office, we need to prohibit private campaign contributions. Some people may frown upon this idea, claiming that it infringes on individual rights or that the idea is socialist, but it would be more cost-effective and honest.

The idea of funding election campaigns through taxes is not new. ACE Electoral Knowledge Network is a non-profit organization that promotes credible and transparent electoral processes with emphasis on sustainability, professionalism, and trust in the electoral process. According to data from the ACE Network, out of a sample of over 180 nations, only 25 percent do not provide public electoral funding, 58 percent provide direct public funding, and 60 percent provide indirect public funding. Some countries provide both direct and indirect funding to political parties. [100,101,102,103]

In the end, the people pay for election campaigns, either directly or indirectly. Currently in our democracy, they are funded indirectly, and many times higher than the real cost because campaign spending is also a form of private investment. As discussed, the contribution of the Power Triad to the political process is returned to them many times over in the form of tax breaks, subsidies, and loopholes to help them save billions of dollars. For the Israel Lobby, a few million dollars of spending on the elections is returned in the form of $3 billion in aid and other invaluable political support for Israel.

Election campaign funding from tax revenues would be immeasurably cheaper and more transparent. The government would set a limit on candidate spending and fund candidates at minimal cost to taxpayers. Those who use their own money or get funds (directly, indirectly, or in-kind), from individuals, corporations or other organizations would be disqualified. Under such a program, candidates would be more likely to be elected based on merit. If elected, they would dedicate their time to serving the public without worrying about raising funds for the next election. Re-election will only be dependent on how well they served their community.

The role of the media has to be overseen by an independent committee to prevent it from favoring one candidate over another, and must not be allowed to interfere in an election. Equal time must be available to each candidate.

An election committee from the community could identify candidates based on defined criteria. For example, candidates would have to collect a specific number of signatures from their constituents to certify that they meet the necessary ethical and professional criteria. They would also need to present their resume to the electorate during the election campaign in the same way they would if they were applying for a job, and to prepare their platforms in order to show their understanding of the issues and their relevant experience.

The role of the voters is also important. They have to remain actively engaged in politics and meet with their candidates, individually or in groups, during and after the elections to stay up-to-date and monitor their representatives' words, actions, and performance.

President Roosevelt's New Deal of 1933 was a courageous step that improved equality, raised the standard of living for ordinary people, and enhanced economic growth. However, it would have not been successful had it not been backed by the people. Similarly, if the people do not work together to change election funding, both the economy and the quality of life of the American people will continue to deteriorate.

Chapter 5

Corporate domination of the U.S. economy and political system

In 1886, the Supreme Court granted corporations the same rights that living persons have under the Fourteenth Amendment. [104,105] However, with the New Deal (1933-1936), [106] President Franklin Roosevelt reined in corporations, revived democracy and made the political system work for ordinary people. The New Deal lasted for about 50 years, until Ronald Reagan promoted "free markets," globalization and deregulation—the same policies that led to the Crash of 1929.

Putting corporations back in the driver's seat has led to the deterioration of the American middle class's liberties and wealth. Deregulation of the financial industry, for instance, has driven the U.S. to the verge of bankruptcy and forced more than 47.8 million Americans to depend on food stamps. [107]

Understanding the concept of "corporate personhood" will shed the light on how the American people can restore their freedom and liberties, and encourage corporations to work for the common good.

Corporate personhood

Under "corporate personhood," a corporation is treated as "a natural person" and enjoys all the rights under the U.S. Constitution. Corporations are now entitled to "due process" and "equal protection" under the law, rights originally entrenched in the Constitution for human beings. The decision to give corporations the status of persons changed the relationship amongst the people, corporations, and government, and pronounced the end of democracy as we knew it.

Corporate personhood has enabled corporations to do the following:

- Buy politicians through campaign funding and lobbying;
- Lobby legislatures to enact preferential laws to permit the violation of environmental, labor, industrial, and other regulations in the public interest;
- Create media monopolies and oligopolies;
- Stifle free enterprise by driving small local businesses out of the market; and
- Prevent the government from protecting the health and safety of the workers.

Corporate personhood violates the democratic principles mentioned in Chapters 2 and 3 because individuals can be neither equal to a corporation before the law, nor can they have equal access to the legislative process. For example, in a dispute with a corporation, an ordinary person faces prohibitive costs for lawyers, but a corporation, can easily afford these costs, which are tax deductible. [108]

Individuals also cannot compete with corporations who propose, develop, and lobby for passage of legislation into law. In addition, corporations can influence political thought and push for new laws through ALEC (see p. 66) and the corporate media.

If corporate personhood were revoked, corporations would not be protected by the First, Fourth, and 14th amendment and that would stop them from lobbying, rigging elections, or influencing public opinion, especially during referenda. Corporations would be forced to operate according to their charters and within the law, and would no longer be able to buy their way out of admitting guilt for a crime they commit. Corporate executives would be tried according to law and held financially liable and personally responsible for their crimes.

If corporate personhood did not exist, ordinary people could enjoy real democracy. They could discuss a particular issue in the public arena without corporations misleading them. For example, the main roadblock to a single-payer, universal health care system has been lobbying by corporations and the American Medical Association. According to William Meyers, a teacher and writer at III Publishing, "By prohibiting corporate-sponsored election campaign funding and issue advocacy advertisements (electioneering communications) to misinform the public about the universal health care system, the national consensus in favor of universal health care could no longer be foiled." [108]

In addition, the American people would have a more just Supreme Court, since the current one is politicized by corporations. "[The Supreme Court] is a product of the corporate-dominated appointees, who are designated by corporate-dominated presidents and approved by a corporate-dominated Congress," says Meyers. [108]

The corporate search for power and control

Today, U.S. multinationals have weakened the government's ability to protect the American people, their culture, and their livelihood. A corporation is loyal only to its executives and shareholders. It is not loyal to a country, a political system, or a community. Currently, some of the world's largest and most powerful corporations have their headquarters in the U.S. and maintain the privileges of a national company, even though they have moved their manufacturing operations to China and other emerging markets, and stashed their profits in tax havens in order to pay very little in taxes.

Corporations do not prefer one political system to another because of principle or ideology; many regularly do business with totalitarian and authoritarian regimes. During the Second World War, General Motors in Germany built trucks for Hitler's army, and IBM helped run the Nazi concentration camps and slave-labor programs. [109]

Corporations are without morals and do anything to increase profits. This focus on profits alone does not serve the common good, as in the case with the tobacco and alcoholic-beverage industries. Nicole Winfield of *The Washington Post* reported that, on World Youth Day (an event for young people organized by the Catholic Church on August 18, 2011), Pope Benedict XVI's visited Madrid, Spain where unemployment had reached nearly 21 percent. In his speech, he denounced corporate ideology and criticized corporations' goal to increase the value for the shareholders, ignoring ethical and environmental considerations.

"[Profit-at-all-cost] is behind Europe's economic crisis," the Pope said. "Ethics must play a greater role in formulating economic policy.

Man must be at the center of the economy, and the economy cannot be measured only by maximization of profit but rather according to the common good."

The Pope then said that ethics has been left out of economic policy at both local and international levels. He affirmed the importance of government oversight to consider policies and enact laws to rein in corporate power, so that corporate activities serve the common good. "The economy doesn't function with market self-regulation, but needs an ethical reason to work for mankind. The debt crisis shows that a moral dimension is not 'exterior' to economic problems but 'interior and fundamental," the Pope said. [110]

This moral dimension will not be possible until the people restore democracy, "elect a government of the people for the people," and forbid the corporations from using their money to influence elections.

Until 1776, a few powerful corporations controlled Colonial America and effectively governed Virginia, Maryland, and the Carolinas. New York was founded by the Dutch West India Company. By declaring independence, the American people freed themselves from the control of the English corporations, which exploited their resources and controlled trade. [108,111]

During the 18th century, U.S. corporations were chartered by states for a limited period, in order to undertake a specific project and then dismantled upon completion. [109] Corporations were not allowed to participate in politics, fund political campaigns or own stock in other corporations. Their owners were responsible for any criminal acts their corporations committed. Governments kept a close watch on their activities and revoked the charters of corporations that did not serve the public interest. For example, in 1832, President Andrew Jackson refused to extend the charter of the Second Bank of the U.S., and the State of Pennsylvania revoked 10 banks' charters. [113]

The Founding Fathers were wary of the corporations. In 1816, Thomas Jefferson expressed his concerns saying: "I hope we shall crush in its birth the aristocracy of our moneyed corporations which dare already to challenge our government in a trial of strength, and bid defiance to the laws of our country." [112] However, in the early part of the 19th century, states began to enact corporation laws to attract more business. In 1811, New York enacted a law for manufacturing companies. New Jersey, Connecticut, and Delaware followed by enacting a law to allow incorporation of any legal business in 1816, 1837, and 1883, respectively. Later on, Delaware general corporation law dominated in the U.S. [114] Corporations were allowed to exist permanently, merge with and acquire other corporations, and own stocks in other corporations. To maintain their competitiveness, other states followed suit. According to Joel Bakan, author of *The Corporation: The Pathological Pursuit of Profit and Power*, about 1,800 corporations were consolidated into 157 between 1898 and 1904. [109] As the corporations grew, the number of shareholders increased. They became widely spread away from the corporation's head office. Their ability to influence managerial decisions by acting collectively diminished and their power ended up in the hands of corporate management teams.

During the Industrial Revolution in the 19th century, the U.S. enjoyed enormous economic expansion and progressed rapidly in agriculture, international trade and manufacturing. Production moved from home-based businesses to large factories and corporations dominated business life, America's politicians, courts, and culture.

The eruption of the Civil War (1861 – 1865) accelerated the growth of manufacturing and corporate power. Owners accumulated great fortunes, which helped them influence policymaking and change the rules governing their corporations. For example, they enacted the limited liability doctrine, which allowed corporate owners and managers to avoid responsibility for harm and losses and offered protection for the personal assets of owners. The government's role shifted from that of keeping a close watch on corporations to encouraging their growth, mainly because of their ability to offer employment. Accordingly, their influence extended so that corporations began to dominate the economy and the political process.

In 1868, after enacting the 14th Amendment to protect the freed slaves, corporate lawyers requested for corporations the same constitutional rights as a natural person. In *Santa Clara County v. Southern Pacific Railroad Company* (1886), Chief Justice Morrison Waite announced: "The court does not wish to hear argument on the question whether the provision in the 14th Amendment to the Constitution, which forbids a state to deny to any person within its jurisdiction the equal protection of the laws, applies to these corporations. We are all of the opinion that it does." [115]

At the beginning of the 20th century, corporations became big enough to overpower social institutions and governments and managed to increase their powers through deregulation. State laws transformed corporations into powerful "natural persons" with their own identity, separate from their owners. With the growth of conglomerates, corporations became more powerful than the government itself.

During the 1930s, corporations' negative impacts on society became evident. People believed that corporate greed, deregulation, and mismanagement had caused the 1929 Crash and the Great Depression. To improve their public image, business leaders led a publicity campaign to inform the public that they would adopt "corporate social responsibility" as a strategy to restore peoples' faith. Nevertheless, they did not deviate from their own sole purpose—to increase profits and investment value for their owners. Corporate social responsibility was merely used as a tool to enhance corporations' public image.

The New Deal and the conspiracy to overthrow Roosevelt

In 1933, President Franklin Roosevelt created the New Deal, a package of regulatory reforms designed to restore economic health. Although it saved the U.S. economy, a small group of businessmen was so enraged with Roosevelt that they plotted to overthrow his administration. They wanted to turn the U.S. into a fascist dictatorship modeled after Mussolini's Italy and Hitler's Germany. [116]

The conspiracy was backed by some Wall Street firms, including Goodyear Tire, Bethlehem Steel, Andrew Mellon Associates, Rockefeller Associates and General Motors, as well as the Pitcairn family and the V. Pew family. The conspirators asked Gen. Smedley Darlington Butler, a former U.S. Marine, to lead the operation.

Butler was a lifelong Republican and a celebrated military hero who had spent most of his military career in wars in Asia and Central America. He was twice decorated with the Congressional Medal of Honor and was adored by veterans.

The conspirators planned to fund Butler to recruit an army of soldiers and veterans. Backed with his army, Butler would demand that Roosevelt appoint him as assistant president and be called "Secretary of General Affairs." Then, "Butler would announce that Roosevelt's health was failing, assume power over the nation, and make the president a mere figurehead. If Roosevelt refused to cooperate, Butler's army would overthrow the government," Bakan reports. [109]

On November 20, 1934, Butler reported the plot to the House Un-American Activities Committee. The findings of the committee were submitted to the House of Representatives on February 1, 1935, and the conspiracy was spoiled. Roosevelt managed to continue with the New Deal, which saved businesses from themselves. [109]

The spirit of the New Deal prevailed for 50 years, and during these decades, the growing power of corporations was offset by the continued expansion of government regulation, trade unions, and social programs.

The New Deal focused on three elements in what was known as the "Three Rs:"

- Relief for the unemployed and poor
- Recovery of the economy
- Reform of the financial system to prevent another stock market crash

The New Deal decreased inequality and protected the public from the misuse of corporate power, strengthening the government's control of big corporations and banks. It reflected Roosevelt's conviction that the Great Depression would end once the government was able to enact new rights and protections for workers, debt relief for farmers, and fairness and transparency for investors.

Corporation battle to restore personhood

The New Deal reined in corporations, but they did not give up on having the government, through the Supreme Courts, affirm their personhood. In 1967 and 1978, the Supreme Court ruled that a corporation, like a "person," has Fourth Amendment constitutional rights and consequently, it cannot be compelled to have its facilities subjected to random inspection (See *v. City of Seattle,* 1967), [117] and in *Marshall v. Barlow's, Inc.* (1978). [118] The *Occupational Safety and Health Act* (*OSHA*) of 1970 was enacted to ensure a safe working environment, and allow for surprise inspections of workplaces. However, using the Fourth Amendment right for corporations as a person, the Supreme Court struck down the surprise inspections and required that the inspections be done with either corporation's permission or a warrant. This decision helps corporations get away with environmental violations because, without random inspections, it is virtually impossible to enforce meaningful pollution prevention, health, and safety laws. [108]

The New Deal era finally ended in 1976, when the Supreme Court ruled in *Buckley v. Valeo* that spending money to influence elections is a form of constitutionally protected free speech. [119] Two years later, in *First National Bank of Boston v. Bellotti*, the Supreme Court declared that corporate persons have the same free speech rights as natural persons, and could spend unlimited sums of money "speaking" in the form of advertisements and campaign contributions. [120,121]

In 2002, the *Bipartisan Campaign Reform Act* (known as *McCain-Feingold*) amended the 1971 *Federal Election Campaign Act* to end the use of nonfederal, or money raised outside the limits and prohibitions of federal campaign finance law (soft money) in federal election campaigns. The law prohibited national political party committees or federal candidates from raising or spending funds not subject to federal limits, even for state and local races or issue discussion. It also prohibited issue-advocacy advertisements (electioneering communications) that name a federal candidate in a targeted electorate from being broadcast within 30 days of a primary or caucus, or within 60 days of a general election, and prohibited any such advertisements paid for by a corporation or an unincorporated entity using any corporate or union general treasury funds. [122]

Nevertheless, in 2010, with *Citizens United v. The Federal Election Commission*, the Supreme Court ruled again that, "money is speech and a corporation, as a person, has a First Amendment right to use its money to influence the political process." [123,124]

Ending of the New Deal era

The New Deal protected the American people from exploitation and created the most affluent middle class in history, but during the 1970s, the U.S. economy experienced a decade of rising unemployment and inflation (stagflation). By the 1980s, President Ronald Reagan ended the New Deal era by adopting economic ideology, known today as Neoliberalism, which prevailed in the U.S. before the 1929 Great Depression. [125] He argued that economic stagnation was due to misguided government policies, too much tax, too much government spending, and too many regulations. Neoliberalism ultimately sought to maximize the role of the private sector in determining the political and economic priorities of the world and limit the role of government in the economy.

Reagan promoted predatory capitalism, creating a widening gap of inequality and a more unstable economy that lurches from one crisis to the next. Professor Robert Brent Toplin believes that President Reagan's ideas caused the 2008 financial crisis. Deregulation, according to Toplin, "has contributed more to today's unstable business climate than any other policy. Reagan's long-standing campaign against the role of government in American life produced conditions that ultimately proved bad for business. He failed to recognize that government regulation could serve business interests quite effectively." [127]

Reagan's deregulation policies, free markets and globalization, and privatization of government-owned entities got a boost with the collapse of the Soviet Union and led many economists to consider neo-liberalism the answer to our economic problems. However, neoliberalism has failed to improve the American economy or its citizens' quality of life. Its failure culminated in the 2008 financial crisis.

Neoliberalism has been bad for the U.S. political system and the economy in the early 1980s as they were at the beginning of the 20th century because the financial markets need regulations to align the interests of the private sector with those of the public. Deregulation has caused the Savings and Loans crisis of the 1980s and 1990s, and contributed to the Great Recession of 2008. In addition, it caused extreme fluctuations in the U.S. economy since the 1980s. These economic crises will repeat unless the Glass-Steagall Act is restored.

During the 1980s, deregulation enabled Savings and Loan institutions (S&Ls) to invest recklessly, causing the greatest banking crisis since the 1929 crash. By 1989, more than half the S&Ls had failed. Losses amounted to more than $153 billion, costing the taxpayers $124 billion, while the S&L industry paid the rest.

This crisis demonstrated that deregulation was not good for business, but it did not prevent some European governments from pursuing Neoliberalism. By the early 1990s, neoliberalism had become the economic model to follow in both Europe and the emerging markets.

Reagan's free market and globalization policies enabled corporations to outsource the manufacture of their products. With the progress in communications and the low transportation costs, they were able to move their manufacturing operations to emerging markets where cheap skilled labor was available and environmental laws were lax. As a result, profits of U.S. multinational corporations skyrocketed, but Americans lost their high-paying jobs.

Reagan's policies ignored the importance of the government's role in making the economy work for the majority to decrease inequality. He lowered taxes for the rich and cut spending by slashing social programs. Under Reagan, the top marginal individual income tax rate decreased from 70.1 percent to 28.4 percent. In 1986, capital gains were taxed at 28 percent. This tax reduction mostly benefited the wealthy and increased the inequality gap between the rich and the poor. Cutting social services degraded the social net for the poor, the sick, the elderly, and the most vulnerable Americans.

To encourage public acceptance of neoliberal ideology, corporations launched a successful, sophisticated public relations campaign in support of deregulation and limiting government's role in protecting the public and the environment. However, Neo-liberalism ideology has not been successful. The Fraser Institute, a right-wing think tank based in Vancouver, Canada, has reported that neo-liberalism has been declining globally since 2007. In his article on Globalization, Rajesh Makwana writes, "The neoliberal experiment has failed to combat extreme poverty, has exacerbated global inequality, and is hampering international aid and development efforts." [128]

Monopolies

The laws for protection of consumers and the public have not been updated to address the exponential growth in technology and global economy. Since the 1980s, the U.S. has been enjoying the fastest growth in scientific and medical discoveries and technology development, which has led to creating monopolies for technology and pharmaceutical products and services. As a result, technology companies increased their wealth in just a few years to become bigger than many well-established corporations that took a century to get to that stage. This exponential growth made many individuals and corporations richer and more powerful than the state. Over the past four decades, technology companies in particular have underpaid their employees and overcharged their customers because they have a monopoly over new products or services. The corporations also either bought out or otherwise destroyed their smaller competitors. The government's policies did not discourage these predatory practices.

The attitude of technology companies and pharmaceutical companies is similar to that of the 19th-century oil and railroads trusts. The trusts with a monopoly over certain activities could impose prices on their customers for fuel and other products and services. These trusts led to the Sherman Antitrust Act of 1890, followed by the Clayton Act of 1914. The Sherman Act outlawed such restrictions on competition by large companies and those who co-operated with rivals to fix outputs, prices, and market shares. [129]

The Clayton Act of 1914 clarified and strengthened the Sherman Act. It limited the power of corporations by prohibiting price discrimination between different purchasers, as well as exclusive tying agreements and mergers and acquisitions that could substantially lessen competition. The Clayton Act also prevented anyone from being a director of two or more competing corporations.

Today, most technology companies and pharmaceutical manufacturers have monopolies over necessary products and services that are sold at excessively high prices. There has been no oversight by government to ensure fair prices, and as a result, technology and pharmaceutical companies have become more powerful than the government.

Preventing corporations from owning other corporations is another way to curb their power and make them pay their fair share of taxes. This policy allows competition to grow and benefit the society in both lower prices and higher quality products and services. In addition, this practice prevents the corporation from evading taxes and taking high risk by parts of its operations at the society's expense. For example, a multinational pharmaceutical company may have a very high-risk operation that could result in very high profits, but if it fails, it could drive the corporation into bankruptcy. The corporation can limit its liability by incorporating its high-risk operations into a subsidiary. This arrangement can be highly rewarding because the cost of capital will decrease. In case of a catastrophic event, only the subsidiary is affected—the losses of the mother corporation is limited to its assets in the subsidiary. However, this arrangement is unfair to society. For example, a pipeline may assign high-risk portions of its lines to a subsidiary. In case of a major spill, its risk is limited to that smaller part of the operations. As a result, society ends up with the risk and will have to pay for clean-up costs.

Globalization

After the Second World War, several institutions such as the International Monetary Fund and the World Bank were established to promote international economic cooperation. In 1947, the General Agreement on Tariffs and Trade (GATT) was established to regulate international trade of goods and substantially reduce tariffs and other trade barriers. The General Agreement on Tariffs and Trade (GATT), lowered tariffs and extended trade rules into several new areas, including services and intellectual property. [127]

The World Trade Organization

Reagan's globalization policies worked against the interests of the Americans as they lost the high paying jobs to the developing countries, but enriched the American corporations. In 1986, 123 members of GATT met in Uruguay to expand its rules from trading in goods to trading in services and intellectual property, and agreed to create the World Trade Organization (WTO). [130]

On January 1, 1995, the WTO replaced GATT. By August 2012, the WTO had grown from 77 to 157 members. The objectives of the WTO are to supervise and liberalize international trade, develop policies and champion corporate interests. While GATT was just a set of rules agreed upon by its members, the WTO is an institutional body that provides a framework for negotiating and formalizing trade agreements and dispute resolution. Governments of participating countries are required to adhere to WTO agreements, which are signed by representatives of member governments and ratified by their legislatures. [131]

The WTO is a corporate-controlled organization with the power to overrule government mandates to protect citizens and the environment. As the world's dominant institution, the WTO can force a member state to change or repeal laws that protect the environment, consumers or other public interests, or be penalized.

Because of the WTO, corporations are now able to repeal the local laws instead of being controlled by them, and governments must censor their behavior to ensure that they comply with WTO rules.

American corporate control of world resources

During the 18th and 19th centuries, European governments enjoyed enough military power to establish colonies in Asia, Africa, and the Americas, and take raw materials at little or no cost. Manufactured products were then exported back to the resource-rich colonies at relatively high prices. In this way, European nations managed to raise their citizens' standard of living at the expense of those living in the colonies. It was considered acceptable to invade and subjugate people in those countries because it served the imperial interest. This exploitation in raw materials also extended to people. From 1619 to 1807, in one of the greatest human tragedies in history, between 12 and 13 million Africans were uprooted from their homelands and forcibly transported to the Americas in the trans-Atlantic slave trade. This forced migration is known today as the African Diaspora.[132] Professor Edward Curtis IV of Purdue University reports in his book, *Muslims in America: A short History*, that Ayuba Suleiman Diallo from Senegal was the first Muslim to be brought to the U.S. as a slave in 1730. [133]

In the 20th century, the West found it too costly to keep their hold on its colonies. Local resistance increased the fatalities of the European soldiers and looting operations became uneconomical. Europeans changed their strategies towards their colonies. As if they owned them, they granted the colonies their independence. However, before they left, they appointed an indigenous ruler who proved to be a loyal servant to the interests of his masters in Europe. These new "leaders" were given a free hand to abuse, oppress, and violate the human rights of their people, as long as they maintained the flow of resources and served the interests of their masters in the West. In this way, Europe secured resources for their corporations at a lower cost.

The West has never repented or atoned for its crimes, past or present. On the contrary, the U.S. and its European allies in NATO continue to invade countries like Iraq or pursue covert operations to control countries such as Libya and Syria. The only significant difference between the old imperialism and the new imperialism is the use of the United Nations to legitimize this aggression.

Ownership of natural resources and the transfer of wealth

We live in a world with finite natural resources, a growing population and escalating demand from the most populous developing countries—China, India, Brazil, Indonesia, Pakistan, Bangladesh and Nigeria, which collectively represent more than 50 percent of the world's population. Scarcity of non-renewable natural resources will limit economic growth and those who control the natural resources will control the world economy.

China has been actively addressing this issue, using its trade surplus to buy resources around the globe. Every dollar China spends to buy oil fields or mineral resources will multiply in a few years. Cofounder and chief investment strategist of Grantham Mayo van Otterloo (GMO) reports that the days of abundant resources and falling prices are over forever. [134] It is surprising that the Canadian and the U.S. governments do not understand this concept and encourage foreign companies, such as China's state-owned corporations, to buy mining, oil and gas companies.

Of course, we must consume these resources wisely, knowing that what is left belongs to future generations. Governments do not have the moral right to trade these resources away to individuals or corporations in return for meager royalties. They must realize these resources will soon be very scarce and what we sell to the Chinese today will be needed for our own use in the near future. Resources should belong to all citizens, with the government acting as guardian to use for the benefit of all.

Under the current system, the state gives corporations the right to explore and develop the oil and mineral deposits they find. Current technologies enable geologists to predict with high accuracy the potential of finding oil and minerals. Selling mineral and oil rights to corporations creates a few wealthy individuals and widens the gap of inequality. Those who can afford the exploration cost will get wealthier and those who cannot will become relatively poorer.

Outsourcing jobs to China has created a transfer of wealth that needs to be addressed. Modern China has become the global center for manufacturing everything from shoelaces and clothing to computers and other sophisticated equipment. North America's natural resources are the means to secure a better life for future generations. For example, take the hypothetical event of a Chinese state-owned corporation deciding to purchase agricultural land in the U.S. The Chinese will operate the farm, but may hire local farmers to work in it. However, the Chinese owners legally have control over the food the farm produces. International trade laws allow them to sell their products at market rates wherever they want. If we cannot afford to buy their products, the products that Americans produce will be shipped to China or other parts of the world where buyers can pay the highest price.

The same scenario applies to resources. In the past two decades, China has been on a buying spree of mining and oil-and-gas companies. The Chinese know that mineral and petroleum ownership will be the controlling factor in the global economy in the 21st century. While Canadians have been discussing the environmental impact of the Alberta tar sands, the Chinese had bought a significant part. They are partners in the proposed pipeline that is to transport it to ports on Canada's West Coast for shipping to China using Chinese shipping companies.

In a very short period, China could own all the tar sands and Canada's citizens will be reduced to workers for a Chinese state-owned oil company.

In future, when oil becomes scarce, will the oil from the tar sands be used to provide for Canada's needs, or China's? If a spill occurred, Canada's valuable water resources and soil would be contaminated. Such a spill would ruin our pristine water resources and take decades to clean up, but would have little impact on the Chinese or their oil supply.

We can learn from the Chinese. In China, a corporation must have 51 percent Chinese ownership. The government could buy out other investors, and this will probably happen in the near future. Selling resources to foreign corporations under the banner of globalization and free market is very shortsighted, especially when "American companies" cannot do the same in China. It is imprudent for the Canadian government to sell Canada's resources to the Chinese and celebrate it as if it were an achievement. In the future, this move will be seen as one of the most serious mistakes of the Harper government.

State-owned corporations and Western capitalism

The crisis of Western liberal capitalism has coincided with the rise of a powerful new form of state capitalism in emerging markets.
~ Adrian Wooldridge, managing editor, The Economist ~

What is the role of the state in shaping the economy and social policies? What is best for the people—Western capitalism or state capitalism? [135] The questions must be considered without prejudice or preconceived ideas.

Statism, or state capitalism, is the belief that government should control either economic or social policy or both, to some degree, with high concentrations of government-owned commercial enterprises and/or high degrees of strong directive, as opposed to merely regulatory, economic participation by the state. [136] In state capitalism, the state either owns companies or plays a major role in supporting or directing them. The state is able to secure sufficient funds for its operations and hire professional managers to run them.

On the other hand, Western capitalism (neo-liberalism) is an ideology based on the ideas of economic liberalization, free trade, and open markets. [137] It supports privatization of state-owned enterprises, deregulation of markets and promotion of the private sector's role in society.

According to this neo-liberalist ideology, the government does not intervene in the free market in an attempt to regulate supply, demand, and prices. These factors are theoretically regulated by the market itself. This means that a company with an innovative product, such as software or a new pharmaceutical product, can ask for any price, regardless of the impact of its pricing policy on society. Between 1900 and 1970, statism prevailed and many nations, such as the U.K. and Canada, where established social safety nets are major parts of the economy.

Due to neo-liberalism, the economy in the U.S. has been volatile and the inequality gap has widened. Between 1973 and 2008, total household income of 99.5 percent of the US population decreased from 93.7 to 83.1 percent. In other words, the income of the majority of Americans decreased by 10.6 percent, whereas the top 0.5 percent of the population saw its income increase by 186 percent. By 2011, in the richest country in the world, 46.3 million Americans were living on food stamps and one in four children lived in poverty. Aimee Picchi of MSN reported that, in 2012, the number of Americans enrolled in the food stamps program increased to 47.8 million despite the recession's end and a stronger economy. [107]

While Western capitalism in the developed world is stumbling, state capitalism—merging the power of the state with the power of capitalism—in the developing countries has been flourishing. China's brand of state capitalism represents a significant advance over older state capitalism, like that practiced in the Soviet Union. It is developing globally on a much greater scale and has far more sophisticated tools that enable it to lead and innovate more effectively than private corporations. [139]

China has successfully expanded its annual GDP over the past 30 years by an average rate of 9.5 percent, and increased its international trade by 18 percent. Over the past 10 years, it has become the world's second-biggest economy and the world's biggest market for many consumer goods, surpassing that of the U.S.

Joshua Kurlantzick of *The Economist* reports that, "the Chinese government is the biggest shareholder in the country's 150 largest companies and guides thousands more. China shapes its overall market by managing its currency and developing its economy according to a state plan." [138]

State-owned corporations are growing globally at a very high rate relative to private corporations: "From 2004 through 2009, 120 state-owned corporations made their debut on the *Forbes* list of the world's largest corporations, while 250 private companies fell off it," Kurlantzick reports. [138] Successful state-owned corporations can be found in many sectors of the economy, such as the world's biggest natural-gas company, Russia's Gazprom; China Mobile with 600 million customers; Saudi Basic Industries Corporation, one of the world's most profitable chemical companies; Russia's Sberbank, Europe's third-largest bank; and Dubai Ports, the world's third-largest port operator. [139]

"State-owned corporations make up 80 percent of the value of the stock market in China, 62 percent in Russia and 38 percent in Brazil," says *Economist* managing editor Adrian Wooldridge. "They account for one-third of the emerging world's foreign direct investment between 2003 and 2010 and an even higher proportion of its most spectacular acquisitions...Three Chinese state-owned corporations, Sinopec Group, China National Petroleum Corporation, and State Grid, rank among the world's 10 biggest companies by revenue," Wooldridge adds. [139]

The concept of state-capitalism is not foreign to the Western economy. In the developed countries, states have incubated many innovative corporations such as Bell Labs in the U.S. and Airbus in Europe.[138] The rise of innovative state capitalists could even push multinationals out of some markets entirely. State-owned corporations now control about 90 percent of the world's oil, as well as large percentages of other resources. When a state-owned company like Petrobras becomes as innovative as the multinationals, their country will not require foreign companies for exploration, deep-water technology or refining. In addition, these state-owned corporations will be able to dominate, within their own country, sectors such as oil and gas and mobile communications. [138]

With the West's sagging economy and the flourishing emerging markets, China's state-owned firms have proved a sustainable model. These corporations have redesigned capitalism to make it work better, as a growing number of emerging-world leaders agree. The Brazilian government, which embraced privatization in the 1990s, is now using companies like Vale and Petrobras to foster growth and employment, and compelling smaller companies to merge to form national champions. Other countries such as South Africa are also considering this model. [140]

State-owned corporations have access to the state's considerable financial resources, and governments can use the profits of these corporations to improve public services. As the profits of the state-owned corporation increase, government services can be increased correspondingly, without adding to the tax burden on its citizens.

In January 2012, the World Economic Forum (WEF) in Davos, Switzerland, discussed the state of the global economy. "This forum used to be the triumph of the Western model of capitalism," Wooldridge said. "This year the delegates have admitted that the Western model of capitalism is not working and that state capitalism, such as the Chinese model, is succeeding. German Chancellor Angela Merkel told the Forum, 'It was time for a radical rethinking of the Western model among European policy-makers...and debate new methods.'" [141] Because of the success of state-owned corporations in Russia, Prime Minister Vladimir Putin said that the Russian economy must move away from its dependence on natural resources towards high-tech products, but he insisted that the change should be led by state-run firms. [142]

The Economic Times reported from the WEF that David Rubenstein, managing director of Carlyle Investment Funds, cautioned the delegates that the West had three to four years to improve its economic model: "The game will be over for the type of capitalism that many of us have lived through and thought was the best type of capitalism." This admission is ironic since Rubenstein is a billionaire who has done very well under the existing model. In January 2012, the Carlyle Group paid him a $134 million "annual bonus." [141] Western-style capitalism is, of course, the best type if you are at the top of the food chain. Nevertheless, while Rubenstein warned that the West needed to get its deficits under control and return to growth, he did not consider a problem—the huge inequality that predatory capitalism has created.

Of course, many in the West consider state capitalism to be a form of communism, to be shunned at all costs, but when a company is mostly owned by the state, like China Mobile, it is loyal to the state and does everything to protect the state's financial interests. It will not move its manufacturing operations to a foreign country. It will not raise prices in order to earn a 900 percent profit as some American technology companies have done. Even if it did, the profit would return to the Chinese government and, in theory at least, the citizens of China.

This model of state-owned corporations might be used to run our resource companies to ensure national independence. For example, as of June 2010, state-owned China National Petroleum Corporation (CNPC) was the world's second highest valuated company in market capitalization. It has oil fields in Peru, Sudan, Kazakhstan, Venezuela, Canada, Iraq, Iran, Syria, and Uzbekistan. [143]

When oil becomes scarce, the price will skyrocket. Chinese companies will then be able to buy oil, regardless of the price. If CNPC were not owned by the state, the oil would be sold to anyone who would pay the highest price.

Note that, for a Chinese-owned corporation, even a very high price for oil would not hurt the Chinese economy because the profits will benefit the Chinese people.

Recommendations

Reining in the power of corporations

An effective government of the people and for the people is one that is able to regulate businesses to generate a sustainable economy and a healthy environment. A corporation will not become socially responsible voluntarily because such principles contradict its mandate. Only government regulation and active enforcement will curtail corporate exploitation. For that to happen, we must curb the WTO's ability to override governments in passing laws that protect the economy, citizens, and the environment. The existing U.S. government, which is owned by corporations, cannot pursue these goals. The first step is to have overturned the Supreme Court decisions that state that corporations are natural persons and money is a form of free speech and banning its interference in politics.

- Government funding of elections will enable the people to elect representatives who are responsible to them, and not to corporate interests.

- Government key members and advisors should not be permitted dual citizenship. It is almost impossible to receive impartial advice from individuals with divided loyalty.
- The U.S. must actively enforce the *Clayton Act* of 1914 to improve economic efficiency and limit the power of corporations, which has clearly undermined democracy in the U.S. and many other parts of the world.
- Monopolies in pharmaceuticals, software and computer technology, along with computer corporations such as Apple, must be limited. Currently, these monopolies accumulate huge profits and buy other corporations, thus increasing their power and dominating both the economy and the political process.
- Corporations must be prevented from merging, acquiring, or owning stocks in other corporations. This would prevent corporations from becoming so large that they can influence the political process and extend their control over other sectors, as has been happening during the past three decades.
- Subsidiaries should be separated from the mother company and the stocks of the subsidiaries be distributed directly to the individual shareholders.
- Any excess cash within the corporation can be used either to enhance the corporation or distributed to the shareholders. This practice will improve the economy because the corporations' boards of directors will begin to focus on their business and the distribution of dividends will increase citizens' purchasing power and revive the economy.

Non-renewable resources

- Our non-renewable resources do not belong to us. They are ours to use wisely and steward for the use of future generations. All resources should belong to the state and the benefits should be used to provide services to all citizens.

- Corporations should not be allowed exploration licenses, act as facility operators on behalf of the state, and be paid for that function, but the state—in other words, the people—should own the oilfields and mines.

- The revenues that come from these operations could then be used to pay for healthcare and social services, or construction and maintenance of the infrastructure.

State-owned Corporations

The state-owned corporation model could be very effective, especially when resources are finite. Strategic planning will become an important tool to optimize the use of national resources (workforce and other natural resources). Currently, China produces regular five-year strategic plans. The U.S. government needs to consider this model to maintain natural resources for the benefit of their citizens, instead of giving them away to multinationals, foreign state-owned corporations or private owners.

Chapter 6

The Business of war

War is a racket. It is not what it seems to the majority of people. Only a small 'inside' group knows what it is about. It is conducted for the benefit of the very few, at the expense of the very many. Out of war, a few people make huge fortunes.
~ Major-Gen. Smedley D. Butler, U.S. Marine Corps ~

Many people in the Third World perceive Americans to be aggressive, violent, coercive, and disrespectful of human life because of what the U.S. government has done in their countries. The U.S. destroys resource-rich developing countries if they decide to pursue independent policies in the national interest instead of subjugating their country to the demands of multinational corporations and special-interest groups. In the history of man, no nation has ever spent so much on war or destroyed so many countries as has the U.S. Between 1890 and 2011, the U.S. was involved in 147 military interventions, and since World War II has been in a military conflict with 48 countries. [144] Today, the U.S. devotes more than 53 percent of its tax revenue to the business of war.

In their election campaigns, U.S. presidential candidates compete with each other to fabricate excuses to justify aggression. Campaign funding is the carrot that convinces the U.S. president and elected representatives to continue the business of war. Kimberly Dvorak of *The San Francisco Examiner* reports that $200 million in campaign donations from the military contractors convinced President Barack Obama to sign an Executive Agreement in May 2012 (just six months before the presidential elections), to remain in Afghanistan for another 10 years. "The industry gurus have deduced that campaign donations of $200 million can produce a return on investment of billions in lucrative Pentagon contracts," wrote Dvorak. "The defense lobbying effort certainly pays out high returns and the forecast confirms smooth sailing." [83]

Why did the U.S. launch so many wars, kill so many people, and destroy so many countries?

Who benefits from these wars and who pays the price?

This chapter shows that American people would be better off if their country pursued the goals of its Founding Fathers—a more peaceful approach in its relationships with other nations, rather than coercion. This chapter also reviews the motives of the U.S. for invading other countries, as well as how war affects the U.S. economy and Americans' quality of life. In addition, it sheds light on the rampant violence within the American population, evident in the number of people incarcerated in American jails.

Why the U.S. invades other countries

Since the end of World War II, the primary reason for invasion has been to serve the interests of the Power Triad. [109,145] Wars significantly improve their bottom line and enable the military industry to secure more federal research and development contracts to sell arms not only to the U.S. military but also to the invaded countries after their defeat and occupation. The U.S. military allows multinationals, as part of the spoils of war, to take over natural resources such as oil, gas and other minerals in the defeated country for pennies on the dollar. Other contractors get reconstruction contracts.

Major-Gen. Smedley Darlington Butler, one of the nation's most honored and decorated military men, realized that after 33 years in the military he had wasted his life in wars in Asia, Africa and Central America. He admitted that he had mistakenly believed he was protecting the U.S. liberty and freedom.

After awakening to the truth, in one of his speeches, he said: "I spent 33 years .... being a high-class muscle man for big business, for Wall Street and the bankers. In short, I was a racketeer for capitalism...I helped purify Nicaragua for the international banking house of Brown Brothers in 1909-1912. I helped make Mexico, and especially Tampico, safe for American oil interests in 1916. I brought light to the Dominican Republic for American sugar interests in 1916. I

helped make Haiti and Cuba a decent place for the National City
[Bank] boys to collect revenue in. I helped in the rape of half a dozen
Central American republics for the benefit of Wall Street. In China in
1927, I helped see to it that Standard Oil went its way
unmolested...I had a swell racket. I was rewarded with honors,
medals, promotions. I might have given [American gangster] Al
Capone a few hints. The best he could do was to operate a racket in
three cities. The Marines operated on three continents." [109,145]

Is the business of war good for the American economy?

In the past, the business of war improved the economy. The
government increased spending to provide salaries for military
personnel, purchase arms and equipment, and develop weapons, while
arms manufacturers increased production and hired more workers.
The result was increased consumption and demand for American
products as well as increased tax revenues, which made up for the
costs of funding a war.

Today, the structure of the U.S. economy has changed, and
consequently it cannot sustain this strategy. Since 2001, this strategy
has put the U.S. deeper in debt because the business of war has not
improved the economy for several reasons:

- Ownership of American multinational corporations has
  changed. Owners are mostly non-U.S. residents, who
  incorporate major parts of their operations abroad and so
  do not pay much tax or spend their profits in the U.S.

- The American wealthy elite are the main beneficiaries of
  wars, but they stash a major portion of their fortune and
  income in tax havens (See p. 183).

- Multinationals have shipped their manufacturing
  operations to China, which means the U.S. depends on
  imports from China for everything from jeans to
  computers. Any increase in consumer spending from
  armaments production no longer expands manufacturing
  operations in the U.S.

As a result, war increases the trade deficit with China and the U.S. government can no longer recover its war costs. Therefore, war has become a losing strategy for the U.S. treasury and the American people.

Unfortunately, financial losses and the death toll of American personnel do not appear to deter the U.S. government from launching new wars. The nation will continue on this path until it becomes bankrupt or the American people wake up to demand a government that works for their interests.

The Military Budget

> *Every gun that is made, every warship launched, every*
> *rocket fired, represents, in the final analysis, a theft from*
> *those who hunger and are not fed, who are cold and are not*
> *clothed. This world in arms is not spending money alone. It*
> *is spending the sweat of its laborers, the genius of its*
> *scientists, the hopes of its children.*
> *~ President Dwight D. Eisenhower, 1961 ~*

The U.S. military budget is not allocated just for defense purposes. On the contrary, the U.S. military is used to bully, intimidate, coerce, invade, and destroy developing countries that dare to challenge the demands of the government, American multinational corporations, and certain special interest groups, such as the Israel Lobby.

Since the 2008 economic crisis, all government spending has been subjected to budget cuts, from medical care for children of laid off workers, to unemployment benefits, education, social security benefits, post office services, Medicare, and Medicaid. Despite cuts to social programs, the Department of Defense budget has increased by 13 percent annually, [146] although many Americans are losing their homes to foreclosure, some are dying because of lack of health care, and millions are struggling to make ends meet.

Despite the deterioration of the U.S. economy, money for the Pentagon appears infinite and without any accountability. In September 2001, then-Secretary of Defense Donald Rumsfeld announced in a press conference that he was declaring war on the Pentagon bureaucracy. "Money wasted by the military poses a serious threat," Rumsfeld said. "According to some estimates, we cannot track $2.3 trillion dollars in transactions. That is $8,000 for every man, woman and child in America...As a matter of fact, it could be a matter of life and death." [147]

Rumsfeld promised change, but the very next day, the world changed forever when the 9/11 attacks occurred. The money the Department of Defense could not account for was completely forgotten and has not been accounted for since then. President George W. Bush announced that his 2003 budget called for an increase of $48 billion in defense spending, while, according to Vince Gonzales, the Pentagon's own auditors admitted that they could not account for 25 percent of what had been spent. [148]

While the U.S. owes more than $16 trillion, a "weekend trip" made by then-Defense Secretary Leon E. Panetta from Washington to his walnut farm in California cost taxpayers about $860,000 between July 2011 and April 2012, less than nine months. How many families could have used this money to feed themselves, buy medicine for sick children or hire more teachers for public schools?

When asked about his excessive expenses, Panetta said that he would consider other alternatives that might save money and enable him to fulfill his responsibilities. [149]

American investigative reporter, Dave Lindorff described just how much U.S. tax money goes towards the country's war chest when he said: "... 53 cents of every dollar that they [Americans] are paying into taxes is going to the military ... an enormous, enormous amount of money being blown on war and killing and destruction." [148]

In the breakdown of the budget for fiscal 2012, the Department of Defense's budget was $716.3 billion, but the total defense budget, including all defense-related expenditures in other departments totaled $1.4 trillion, that is 37 percent of the total U.S. budget and the highest ever in the history of nations. It is as much as all the rest of the countries of the world combined. [151]

Expenditures included:

- FBI counter-terrorism;
- International affairs;
- Energy Department defense-related spending;

- Veterans Affairs;
- Homeland Security;
- NASA satellites;
- Veterans' pensions;
- Other defense-related mandatory spending; and
- Interest on debt incurred in past wars, amounting to $431.5 billion. [152]

Since 2001, the U.S. has increased its military spending by 81 percent. Today, its military spending accounts for half of total global expenditure, six times more than that of its nearest rival, China that has more than 4.3 times the population of the U.S. It challenges reason and logic that the most indebted country in the world should waste so much money and resources while millions of Americans depend on food stamps, and more than 25 percent of Americans have no or insufficient health insurance.

In 2010, the U.S. defense budget amounted to $698 billion (not including $700 billion in defense-related activities), while China, with the second largest military budget, spent $119 billion. [153] On a per capita basis, the U.S. spent 46 times what China did.

The U.S. Government Accountability Office (GAO), part of the legislative branch responsible for auditing, evaluating, and investigating government branches, was unable to provide an audit opinion on the 2010 and 2011 financial statements of the U.S. government because of "widespread material internal control weaknesses, significant uncertainties, and other limitations." The principal obstacle to its provision of an audit opinion was "serious financial management problems at the Department of Defense that made its financial statements un-auditable." [152,154]

Because of the 2008 financial crisis and diminishing tax revenues, the U.S. will be unable to continue supporting the business of war. If the nation continues to fund wars at the current pace, the U.S. might not be able to pay the interest on its debt, which will hasten the deterioration of its economy. At the same time, interest rates will rise because many nations, including China and other Asian and South American countries, have been gradually using currencies other than the U.S. dollar as their international trade currency (see p. 148).

Strategy of the Military Industrial Complex

Both the Republican and Democratic parties' share of funding from the Power Triad depends on their ability to serve its organizations. The Military Industrial Complex spends around $146 million lobbying Congress to fund wars. In 2011, several big oil companies, including British Petroleum, Chevron, ConocoPhillips, ExxonMobil, and Royal Dutch Shell spent $1.6 million on campaign contributions and $65.7 million on lobbying efforts. [155] That is why politicians in all parties favor spending money on war, rather than spending it at home to improve the American people's quality of life. [156,157]

To justify this irrational military budget, the U.S. administration, its "advisors," and the two main parties create fictitious enemies and spread fear and hatred. During the Cold War, the enemy was the Eastern Block; today, in the "War on Terror," it is the Muslim World. The more animosity candidates display toward Muslims, the better the chances of winning election. The Israel Lobby had a common interest with the defense contractors and played a major role in manipulating the public opinion to support the wars against the Muslim world.

This following section briefly discusses the activities of the Military-Industrial Complex after WWII to promote the business of war, first against Soviet communism until it collapsed in 1991, and then against Islam.

The war against Communism

The Union of Soviet Socialist Republics (U.S.S.R.) emerged from World War II as one of two superpowers. After occupying much of Central and Eastern Europe, the U.S.S.R. sponsored communist revolutions in Hungary, Poland, and several developing countries in South America, Africa, and Asia. These "revolutions" were opposed by the U.S. and several Western countries.

Communism became the enemy of choice during the so-called Cold War because it met all the requirements. It was an intangible, credible enemy. It could be engaged in a continuous war that seemed endless. Had the U.S.S.R. not collapsed, the Cold War would likely have continued. As it was, it lasted from 1945 to 1991.

After WWII, American political leaders led a campaign blitz to instill fear of Communism in the hearts of the American people. The campaigners even spread rumors that high-ranking U.S. government officials were secret Communists.

Republican Senator Joseph McCarthy, for example, claimed that thousands of government officials, journalists, writers, actors, and moderate politicians were Communists or Communist sympathizers working to overthrow the U.S. government. He accused hundreds of people, without regard to evidence, of selling or giving American security secrets to Communist governments.

The accused were subjected to aggressive investigations and questioning before government or private-industry panels, committees, and agencies. The evidence was greatly exaggerated and suspicions were often accepted as evidence, despite being inconclusive or questionable. As a result, many people lost their jobs, their careers were destroyed, and many others were even jailed. Most of these punishments came about through trial verdicts later overturned. [158]

When the U.S. launched proxy wars in Latin America, Southeast Asia and the Middle East to stop the Soviet Union's "expansionist tendencies," Americans could not object for fear of being branded as Communists or Communist sympathizers. This campaign, later known as McCarthyism, lasted from 1950 to 1954. [159,160]

Islamophobia and the war against Islam

During the Cold War, the U.S. and Soviet Union were involved in conflicts and proxy wars in Latin America, Africa, the Middle East, and Southeast Asia. The conflicts were expressed in military coalitions, strategic military deployments, massive propaganda campaigns, and military science research.

The Israel Lobby influences U.S. foreign policy through think tanks—such as the Washington Institute for Near East Policy (WINEP), the Hudson Institute, the American Enterprise Institute, and the Brookings Institution—as well as neo-conservatives in key decision-making posts in the U.S. government. During the Cold War, the Israel Lobby managed to get the U.S. to back Israel's aggression in the Middle East and guarantee Israel's military superiority over its neighboring Arab states.

In 1983, U.S. aid to Israel increased by $510 million, just after its indiscriminate bombing of Beirut and the massacre of Palestinian refugees in the Sabra and Shatila refugee camps. [65] On September 16, 1982, the Israeli military allowed the Phalange, a right wing Lebanese militia and Israeli collaborator, to enter the camps in Beirut. The militia raped, killed, and dismembered thousands of Palestinians, assisted by the Israeli army, which used flares to illuminate the camps' grounds for the militia. In the *New York Times*, Seth Anziska reported that nearly all of the dead were women, children, and elderly men. The U.S. could not stop the crime although it had pledged to protect those refugees just weeks earlier. Nevertheless, U.S. diplomats in Beirut "were bullied into accepting the spurious claim that thousands of 'terrorists' were in the camps." [161] By 1984, AIPAC managed to increase aid to Israel to more than $2 billion a year. [73]

The Israel Lobby succeeded in making Israel a nuclear power that can threaten the globe with nuclear annihilation. In an interview on *Face the Nation* in 1973, Sen. William Fulbright mentioned: "The U.S. bears a very great share of the responsibility' for the continuation of Middle East violence." [73] In the past 20 years, the U.S. vetoed 14 U.N. Security Council resolutions against Israel's violations of international law and human rights. [162] In addition, the U.S. acted as an offshore balancer using local powers against each other. For example, the Reagan administration encouraged Saddam Hussein to attack Iran and backed both Iraq and Iran militarily during the Iran-Iraq War (1980 – 1988) to ensure complete destruction of both countries.

The end of the Cold War in 1991 created a void that threatened the existence of NATO, the bottom line of the Military Industrial Complex, and the interests of other members of the Power Triad. Hence, there was an urgent need for the Triad to replace the Soviet Union as an enemy to justify continuous wars.

The Israel Lobby saw the collapse of the Soviet Union as an opportunity to get the direct military involvement of the U.S. in the Middle East to increase Israel's control of the region. Martin Indyk of WINEP proposed the policy of "dual containment" of Iraq and Iran, and implemented it when he was appointed director for Near East and

South Asian Affairs at the National Security Council. [7] Then, the Israel Lobby led a campaign in 1993 to have the U.S. attack Iran during the Clinton administration. Israel's Prime Minister Yitzhak Rabin and Foreign Minister Shimon Peres reiterated that the Americans and their political leaders "need to be convinced that Iran is a threat to the U.S.," but they were unsuccessful in driving the U.S. to attack Iran. The Israel Lobby realized that it would take a catastrophic event to make the U.S. attack the Muslim world. In its report, the American Enterprise Institute indicated that it would take another Pearl Harbor to get the U.S. in a war with the Muslim World. The 9/11 attack was the Pearl Harbor that Israel Lobby dreamt of.

The Islamophobia network spent millions of dollars to promote hatred against Muslims and created a bogeyman, Osama bin Laden, who was said to live in the mountains of Afghanistan. The day after the 9/11 attack, bin Laden was accused, without any evidence, of being the mastermind behind the attack. Presumably, he managed to outsmart the CIA, the FBI, and the North American Aerospace Defense Command (NORAD), in order to hit the World Trade Center and the Pentagon with such accuracy. If that was the case, leaders of these organizations were negligent and contributed to this tragedy.

The *9/11 Commission Report* has been publicly questioned within the U.S. and globally by thousands of well-established and credible scholars, academics, journalists, military leaders and activists, including:

- Mike Gravel, a U.S. senator and a member of the Alaska House of Representatives. He demands a new 9/11 investigation; [163]
- Cynthia McKinney, Former U.S. Representative (Dem. Georgia;
- Richard Gage, a member of the American Institute of Architects for more than 25 years. He is the founder of Architects & Engineers for 9/11 Truth;
- U.S. attorney James Gourley, Founder of the International Center for 9/11 Studies;
- Professor Lance deHaven-Smith of Florida State University;

- Professor David Ray Griffin who published several books about on 9/11;
- The University of Massachusetts Professor, Lynn Margulis who was awarded the National Medal of Science in 1999;
- Dr. Mahathir Mohamad, Malaysia Prime Minister who held the 9/11 Revisited Conference in Kuala Lumpur;
- Distinguished McKnight University Professor Emeritus, James H. Fetzer, Founder of Scholars for 9/11 Truth; and
- Retired Major General Albert Stubblebine III, who was the commanding general of the U.S. Army Intelligence and Security Command.

In August 2011, an international scientific conference was held at Ryerson University in Toronto to dispute "the myth of 911." The Toronto Hearings was sponsored by the Texas-based International Center for 9/11 Studies. The conference examined various conspiracy theories stemming from the attacks, including suggestions that the wars in Afghanistan and Iraq were planned before September 11, 2001, and that no plane ever hit the Pentagon. [164] In addition, in November 2012, the Perdana Global Peace Foundation held an international conference in Kuala Lumpur to investigate the 9/11 attack. [165]

The CIA placed Osama bin Laden on the world stage, and when he was no longer useful he was killed in a dramatic movie-style assassination. However, many Americans questioned whether the government had real evidence against him or whether the stories about him were fabricated. When he was located, it would have been wise to catch him alive and put him on trial, rather than to kill him assassination-style.

However, the 9/11 attack was used as a pretext to intensify the war against the Muslim World and was affirmed by the propaganda machine that worked relentlessly since 1990 to emphasize the inevitable confrontation with Islam in their most embraced and promoted theory of some of the infamous Zionist "scholars" Bernard Lewis and Samuel P. Huntington—clash of civilization.

To gain the public opinion in support of Israel's objectives, Zionist organizations, some "Christian" churches and "Zionist-Christian" organizations in collusion with mainstream media portrayed Muslims as terrorists in movies, talk shows, public lectures, and "news." They repeated a simplistic story, similar to what was said about Communism—that Muslims intend to take over the country, impose Sharia law, and force everyone to convert to Islam.

The integrated campaign blitz all over the mainstream media, government, military talking heads, and the Congress was very successful in misleading the American public about Islam. However, Americans do not know that democracy was one of the founding principles of Islam and is embedded in the Islamic Law.

In his book, *Islamophobia, The Ideological Campaign against Muslims,* [19] Professor Stephen Sheehi reports that racism against Arabs and Muslims has been common in Hollywood movies since the 1940s. To prepare the American people for a new series of wars, Islamophobia was promoted aggressively in the 1990s and grew exponentially after the 9/11 attack on the World Trade Center. Sheehi suggests that anti-Muslim sentiment pervades contemporary America: "Islamophobia should be looked into as an ideological paradigm used to structure and justify U.S. policies, both domestic and international. A deep-seated psychological fear of Islam and Muslims has been produced and circulated to enable not merely war, but globalized militarism on a historically unprecedented scale that most Americans have come to take for granted as necessary and inevitable in the post-September 11 world." [19]

Just as Sen. McCarthy's tactics forced the American people into submitting to drastic measures that deprived them of their liberties and freedoms, so had the "War on Terror." The U.S. government has explained that curtailing civil liberties was necessary for "homeland security" and has justified funding various wars to protect "national security" and "national interests." A media blitz was launched following the 9/11 attack to exaggerate the level of threat posed by Muslims and instill fear in Americans concerning their personal security and way of life.

The Israel Lobby silenced opponents by raising doubts about their loyalty. In addition, they raised doubts about the loyalty of American Muslims to their own country. On November 15, 2006, Keith Ellison, the first Muslim American Congressman, was interviewed on CNN by Glenn Beck. He started the interview by saying, "I have been nervous about this interview with you, because what I feel like saying is, 'Sir, prove to me that you are not working with our enemies." In fact, Ellison can track his American ancestors back to the 1700s. [166]

In their book, *Islamophobia: Making Muslims the Enemy*, Peter Gottschalk, professor of religion at Wesleyan University, and Gabriel Greenberg say: "Many members of the media characterize Muslims as Muslims to the exclusion of any other aspect of their identity [and] cartoonists frequently conflate terrorist groups or the Taliban with Muslims or Arabs in general, although Muslims differ [culturally and religiously] from one country to another." [167]

Terrorism and Islamophobia

The Israel Lobby had been planning to invade Iraq and Afghanistan since 1990. The 9/11 attack offered pretext to invade and overthrow the Afghan government, even though the Taliban government would have agreed to extradite Osama Bin Laden had the U.S. provided proof that he was behind the 9/11 attack. In addition, Iraq was invaded, although Saddam Hussein led a secular government and was an enemy of Al-Qaeda. Not only were the rumors of weapons of mass destruction, the pretext for invasion, found to be baseless, but also a CIA report confirmed that there was no relationship between Saddam Hussein and Al-Qaeda. [168]

The Iraq invasion was based on false information provided by "experts" and pseudo-scholars who had a stake in launching a futile war that caused the death of a million Iraqis. It may take Iraq a century to recover from the damage inflicted since 2003. More than 38,000 American soldiers were killed or injured and 300,000 soldiers were left with brain injuries. War cost totaled more than $3 trillion. [8] Although they have been proven wrong, those advisors to the Administration have not lost their positions. On the contrary, they were rewarded. For example, the U.S. Deputy Secretary of Defense, Paul Wolfowitz, the main architect of the Iraq War, was appointed as the President of the World Bank Group.

Those who advise the Administration deliberately misrepresent Islam and the Muslim World. For example, Fareed Zakaria, in his article "The Politics of Rage: why do they hate us," [169] reflects the poor advice he gave to the Bush Administration. It was he who gave Bush his famous expression, "they [Muslims] hate us because of our freedoms." Surprisingly, the article was published one month after the 9/11 attack, and described the plan President Bush would follow in his "War on Terror." It was evident that the policies Bush pursued only served the military, multinational corporations, the Israel Lobby, and the personal interests of those advisors.

The Israel Lobby and its members of religious organizations, mainstream media, think tanks, opportunistic individuals, and pseudo-scholars joined an Islamophobia network of military and multinational corporations' consultants, and some politicians and journalists who joined network to enhance their political and professional careers.

The media have played a huge role in keeping Islamophobia at the forefront of U.S. politics and made it a flourishing industry for so-called "terrorism experts," who are welcomed on various TV programs. During this time, anybody promoting Islamophobia likely sold more books, got better ratings, and found themselves in demand as keynote speakers at political and religious conferences. Even some cartoonists became famous because of their Islamophobic work. In *Islamophobia: Making Muslims the Enemy*, Greenberg and Gottschalk indicate that Islamophobia is prevalent among both the political left and right. They offer a comparison of cartoon depictions of Jews prior to World War II and today's Muslim caricatures and analyze Islamophobia and its manifestation through political cartoons:

"Islamophobia—a racist-like bias against Muslims based on stereotypes, manifesting in some cartoons that are obviously biased. Cartoons, symbolic of wider feelings and paranoia about Islam, reflect misunderstandings and prejudice among Westerners and, like a self-fulfilling prophecy, often serve to widen cultural chasms, particularly between Muslims and American Christians."

The fear of terrorism was completely irrational, as Charles Kenny reports, in his article on terrorism in *the Bloomberg Businessweek*, that you are 185 times more likely to be killed by a lightning bolt than by a terrorist attack. [171] However, the government and the media used scare tactics, which proved effective in controlling the masses. Following the 9/11 attacks, Bush created the Department of Homeland Security (DHS) to protect the U.S. from and to respond to terrorist attacks. Secretary Tom Ridge gave the impression that the U.S. has been turned into a war zone. DHS spread fear of terrorism almost daily following the 9/11 attacks, using a color-coded terrorism threat advisory scale. DHS announced that there was an eminent threat of nuclear, biological, and chemical attacks, as well as a possibility of armed aggression by hostile governments or extremist groups.

In 2003, as part of the anti-terrorism scare campaign, Ridge appeared on TV and asked the American people to keep a three-day supply of water, canned food and make sure that they have ample duct tape and plastic sheets to cover windows in the case of a biological or chemical weapons attack. [172] Ridge looked ridiculous, causing John Tierney to write in *The New York Times*: "Tom Ridge has become a one-man economic stimulus package for the comedy industry." [173]

On the Tonight Show, Jay Leno quipped: "More warnings issued by all branches of the government today that another terrorist attack is imminent. We're not sure when, we're not sure where, just that it is coming. Who is attacking us now, the cable company?"

In most of the "terrorist" plots uncovered to date in the U.S., an FBI informer played a leading role. Similarities can be seen in plots uncovered in Canada and the United Kingdom.

People in the Muslim world were not fooled by the speeches of the Secretary of State Hillary Clinton about democracy and freedom and her claim that the U.S. was not in a war against Islam. The demonstrations in Egypt against Mubarak and after he was deposed on February 11, 2011, showed anti-U.S. sentiment because of its interference in the internal affairs of Egypt to derail the democratic process. The elected Egyptian Parliament was eager to stop the $1.7 billion annual aid Egypt receives because they believed it was a price for surrendering their will to the U.S. As a result, the military junta dissolved parliament.

In their memoires, President Bush, Vice President Cheney, and the Secretary of Defense, Ronald Rumsfeld proudly justified the war to "free" the Iraqi people. They neglected to mention the more than one million Iraqis who were killed and the chaos they left behind. More than 18 months after the U.S. withdrew on December 18, 2011, Iraq was still an unstable country, and hundreds of Iraqis were being killed in fighting between various conflicting factions. The outcomes of the war were the destruction of Iraq, its economy, its culture, and its infrastructure for the benefit of Triad with Israel being the major beneficiary.

The Obama Administration has continued to pursue the plan of the Israel Lobby to change the map of the Middle East in covert wars against Libya, Egypt, Tunisia, Iran, and Syria.[170] The U.S. uses the old imperialistic "divide and conquer" strategy. So far, in addition to Iraq, and Afghanistan, the U.S. has succeeded in destroying both Libya and Syria, their people are divided, their resources are stolen, the human rights of its people are violated, and violence became rampant. In Libya, genocide against blacks was committed, and a new government was "democratically" elected. Syria has been on the same path to "freedom and democracy," but Russia and China realized that the U.S. model of "liberation" might extend to their borders if they did not resist it. Although Al-Qaeda is claimed to be our enemy, it has been armed and funded by the U.S. and its allies to destroy Libya and Syria. [174,175]

It is interesting to notice that Gadhafi and Assad were leaders of the friendly governments that did the dirty work of torturing terrorism suspects during the Condoleezza Rice rendition program.

Cost of the War on Terror

The wars and security measures at home and abroad in the past 11 years cost the U.S. more than $5.4 trillion including $1 trillion—the cost of interest on borrowing the money to fight these wars. [176]

The War on Terror has cost the U.S. within its borders significant economic losses and the loss of lives domestically due to the increase of driving fatalities. In his *Bloomberg Newsweek* article, Charles Kenny reports that the direct total toll, physical damage, and economic loss due to the 9/11 attacks amounts to $178 billion." However the total cost related to increased homeland security and counter terrorism spending, as well as the wars in Iraq and Afghanistan, totaled $5.4 trillion of which, $580 billion spent on homeland security over the period between 2002 and 2011. [176]

A study by Noble laureate, Professor Joseph E. Stiglitz and Linda Bilmes indicate that the invasion of Iraq was the most costly war since World War II, the true cost was much more than $3 trillion.[8] In a study by Cornell Univesity researchers show that the homland security alone has become a burden on the U.S. economy. It made travel very inconvenient, pushing travellers to use car instead of using airlines, resulting an increase of driving fataliteis by 242 per month. Kenny does not blame the Homeland Security officials for this loss. He blames politicians, the media, and the traveling public who are ignorant of the fact that it takes more than four plane disater on the scale of 9/11 to occur every month to match the fatalities related to traveling by car. [177]

Victims of the Military Industrial Complex

America's leadership and prestige depend, not merely upon
our unmatched material progress, riches, and military
strength, but on how we use our power in the interests of
world peace and human betterment.
~ President Dwight D. Eisenhower, 1961 ~

The U.S. did not use its power for spreading peace as the Founding Fathers desired. [178] Since World War II, the American governments have wasted a huge amount of resources that could have been used to serve Americans. On the other hand, those Americans are used to fuel the war and their taxes are spent on covering its costs, but the spoils of wars are given to the Power Triad. The wars undermined the life quality of millions of Americans. Thousands of Soldiers lost their lives, and those who came back home injured and maimed or afflicted with mental illnesses were ignored. The Middle class and low income Americans are those who lose the most. If you examine the list of Americans who have been killed or maimed in the wars with the Muslim world, you will find that none of them relates to the wealthy elite or the politicians who sent them to war.

In 2009, the Program on International Policy Attitudes at the University of Maryland conducted World Public Opinion poll in 20 countries representing more than 60 percent of the world's population. Andrew Tully reports that the majority of these countries believe that the U.S. does not obey international law and uses its powerful military to bully other countries. [178] Steven Kull, the director of the polling center says, "People still perceive the U.S. as having this kind of coercive quality and not following the rules... There is certainly a widespread perception that interest groups and the military as an institution play a big role in driving U.S. foreign policy." [178]

After Obama's speech in Turkey in early April 2009, a survey was conducted in the Muslim countries and Russia. The majority of the Iraqis, Egyptians, Pakistanis, and Palestinians indicated that they have "not too much confidence," or "no confidence at all," in Obama. In Russia, the poll shows that 55 percent of Russians did not trust the Obama Administration as it interferes in the sphere of influence of their country. [178]

In June 2012, Pew Research Center undertook another study on global opinion of the U.S. international policies. [179] The U.S. received very low ratings in the Muslim world Including Egypt, Turkey, Pakistan, and Jordan. In each of these countries, fewer than one-in-five have a positive opinion about the American foreign policy. More than two thirds of the population sees the American people in an unfavorable light. This study confirmed that people not only in the Muslim world, but also across much of the globe believe that the U.S. acts unilaterally in world affairs. Moreover, the vast majority of nations polled oppose the U.S. drone campaign against the Muslim world. Most of the people in the countries polled disapprove of the U.S. drone missile strikes that target "extremists" in places such as Pakistan, Yemen, and Somalia. About nine-in-ten people in the predominantly Muslim countries oppose these strikes. [179]

President Bush summed up the foreign policy of the U.S. in his statement, "You have to be either with us or with the terrorists." To become a friend of the U.S., rulers of the Muslim countries have to subjugate the will of their people to the dictates of the multinational corporations and special interest groups. If a country does not support U.S. aggression, the U.S. will impose economic sanctions, or invade that country and make it an example to scare other countries. As a result, U.S. puppets, such as Hosni Mubarak of Egypt, and Ali Abdullah Saleh of Yemen ruled the Muslim countries. When Saddam Hussein, a puppet of the U.S., decided to pursue the national interests of Iraq, his country was destroyed first by sanctions, then by the 2003 invasion. The Islamic Republic of Iran has been a victim of the U.S. economic sanctions and a covert war since 1979 because the Iranian people dared to overthrow the Shah whom the U.S. government imposed on the Iranian people.

Crimes committed in the name of the American people

War crimes

U.S. administrations demand the world to do what they say, and put themselves above the international law. In 1945, the United Nations established the International Court of Justice, of which the U.S. was a member until 1986. After the court ruled that the U.S. violated the international law with its covert war against Nicaragua, the U.S. withdrew from the compulsory jurisdiction.

The *United Nations Charter* authorizes the Security Council to enforce World Court rulings. However, the five permanent members can veto any enforcement. Ironically, the U.S. is very active at the International Criminal Court in prosecuting presidents of the developing world who disagree with its policies and ignores war crimes committed by its leaders and its allies.

Michael Haas, a Nobel Peace Prize nominee for his work on human rights and author of *America's War Crimes Quagmire, from Bush to Obama*, reports that the Bush Administration can be prosecuted for 269 war crimes. Although he had the book published a few days before President Barack Obama took the oath of office, Obama did not take any action to punish the perpetrators claiming his need to move forward. According to Haas, "the rest of the world is fully aware of the American lawlessness." [180]

Some of the war crimes committed by President Bush and his administration include, torture, murder, illegal war, the slaughter of thousands of innocents, and abuse of child prisoners. "These war crimes have been rolled over to the Obama administration on January 20, 2009, to haunt his presidency. Although President Obama signed executive orders to stop torture and close Guantánamo Bay, the war crimes have continued virtually unabated ever since. Indeed, the Times Square bomber specifically cited American war crimes as the reason for his action on May 1, 2010," Haas reports. On that day,

Faisal Shahzad attempted car bombing Times Square, but the bomb did not explode and he was arrested.

Haas also describes how the Georgian republic, Russia, and other countries have copied the American post-9/11 war crimes. "As a result, there is a new era of international barbarism that serves to aid anti-American terrorist recruitment while repudiating the advances achieved in humanizing warfare by President Abraham Lincoln during the Civil War, by the Red Cross, at the Hague Conventions, at the Nuremberg War Crimes Trials, and by the Geneva Convention," he reiterated. [180]

While the U.S. and its European allies have been silent about the war crimes committed since 2001, a War Crimes Tribunal was held in Kuala Lumpur, Indonesia. In November 2011, the Tribunal put former U.S. President George W. Bush and British ex-Prime Minister Tony Blair on trial *in absentia*. The trials were conducted according to the *Nuremberg Charter* as the format of the tribunal. According to the *Charter*, "Leaders, organizers, instigators, and accomplices participating in the formulation or execution of a common plan or conspiracy to commit war crimes are responsible for all acts performed by any person in execution of such a plan," said Professor Francis Boyle, war crimes expert, lawyer and, part of the prosecution team. The same model was previously used to try Chilean dictator Augustine Pinochet who was later arrested in Britain then extradited to Spain on Charges of war crimes. [181]

The Tribunal reports, "The evidence showed that the drums of wars were being beaten long before the invasion. The accused in their own memoirs have admitted their own intention to invade Iraq regardless of international law." [182] After a four-day hearing, Bush and Blair were found guilty of committing "crimes against peace" during the Iraq war.

While the Kuala Lumpur Tribunal tried and convicted ex-Prime Minister Blair as a war criminal, J.P. Morgan allegedly rewarded him with a $6 million a year for his conspiracy in invading Iraq [183] and allowing $20 billion to be looted from Iraq's central bank. [184]

Yvonne Ridley of *Foreign Policy Journal* reports that on May 12, 2012, President Bush and seven of his administration members including Dick Cheney, Donald Rumsfeld, and their legal advisors Alberto Gonzales, David Addington, William Haynes, Jay Bybee, and

John Yoo were also tried *in absentia* at the tribunal. At the end of a weeklong hearing, the five-panel tribunal delivered unanimous guilty verdicts for torture and cruel, inhumane, and degrading treatment. The Kuala Lumpur War Crimes Commission sent relevant trial material to the Chief Prosecutor of the International Criminal Court, the United Nations, and the Security Council. The Commission also requested entering and including in the Commission's Register of War Criminals for public record the names of Bush, Cheney, Rumsfeld, Gonzales, Yoo, Bybee, Addington, and Haynes. "The Tribunal recommends to the War Crimes Commission to give the widest international publicity to this conviction and grant of reparations, as these are universal crimes for which there is a responsibility upon nations to institute prosecutions if any of these accused persons may enter their jurisdictions," the Tribunal states. [181]

When asked about the difference between the Bush and Obama Administrations, Francis added, "If President Bush was the President of extra-judicial torture, then U.S. President Barack Obama is the President of extra-judicial killing through drone strikes. Our work has only just begun." [181]

Torture and human rights violations

*We have lost our souls; we mock our heritage; we flaunt
our laws; and some of our leaders and officials claim we
have known what we have been doing and are heroes for it.*
~ *Glenn L. Carle*~ [24]

The U.S. was once envied for its freedom and democracy. Today, while its leaders talk about democracy and the rule of law, images of torture from Guantánamo Bay and Abu Ghraib are shown all over the world. Some of these leaders also brag about committing illegal or immoral actions in their memoirs and public speeches. Jose A. Rodriguez, Jr., director of the National Clandestine Service of the CIA, was so proud of torturing that he wrote a book, *Hard Measures*, and boasted about his crimes on *60 Minutes*. On the other hand, he was so afraid of the consequences that he destroyed the records of his crimes. Surprisingly, the reaction to his crimes in most of the mainstream media was muted. [185]

If the crimes committed by the U.S. military at Guantánamo Bay or Abu Ghraib were perpetrated by a different dictator, the U.S. would have been calling for his arrest and trial in the International Court of Justice. In his comments on this American moral crisis, *Business Week*'s Joshua Kurlantzick says, "All those are not good signposts for the virtues of democracy. A [recent] public opinion survey revealed increasing skepticism among people everywhere about whether democracy is the form of government that can best improve their lives. Restoring faith in democracy requires the U.S. and other developed countries to fix what ails their political systems." [186]

In its warped thinking, the administration of George W. Bush believed that dehumanizing prisoners by calling them "unlawful enemy combatants" justified their being tortured. Some of these prisoners have been in Guantánamo Bay prison for more than 10 years. Only one trial has been held, that for a 15-year-old boy, Omar Khadr, who, it was claimed, killed an American soldier. Without his lawyer's plea bargain, he would have been given a death sentence. The U.S. made history by becoming the first so-called democratic country to put a child-soldier on trial.

The American leaders mock the concept of democracy and American values by supporting the dictators in the Middle East and other parts of the world, as long as they serve the interests of big oil companies and special interest groups. The U.S. justified the invasions of both Iraq and Afghanistan, as well as the use of depleted uranium in Iraq, Afghanistan, Pakistan, Libya, and Gaza. The radiation causes birth defects in offspring of exposed persons and lasting contamination to the soil, air, and water. They talk about human rights in Libya and Syria while supporting the oppression of the Palestinians and ignoring massacres committed in Yemen and Bahrain.

In 1953, the U.S. conspired, on behalf of British Petroleum, to overthrow the Iranian government led by Mohammad Mosaddeq, a democratically elected prime minister, and install Shah Mohammed Reza Pahlevi. After the Islamic Republic was proclaimed in February 1979, the U.S. has imposed economic sanctions on Iran.

The U.S. backed Saddam Hussein when he used chemical weapons against the Iraqi Kurds in March 1988 and against Iran during the Iran-Iraq War from September 1980 to August 1988.

Extraordinary rendition program

Extraordinary rendition is the practice of transporting suspected foreign terrorists, or other individuals suspected of crimes, to third countries for interrogation and imprisonment. The CIA established an extraordinary rendition program during the Reagan administration, together with internment of suspected terrorists. [187] The CIA has claimed that the program helps to gather intelligence information from suspects, who are then either sent to facilities maintained by the U.S. or put into the custody of foreign governments. Suspects are transported to countries where safeguards against torture and abusive treatment are looser than in the U.S. Extraordinary rendition thus permits the torture of detained suspects, despite the fact that torture is illegal under international law. Suspects have been interned and tortured in countries around the world, including Egypt, Jordan, Afghanistan, Morocco, and some Eastern European countries.

Extraordinary rendition was first used against suspected Muslims in the late 1990s. [188] In the words of former CIA agent Robert Baer, "If you want a serious interrogation, you send a prisoner to Jordan. If you want them to be tortured, you send them to Syria. If you want someone to disappear—never to see them again—you send them to Egypt." [188]

This tactic has always been used by tyrants who preferred to create fictitious conspiracies and plots to justify cruelty in punishing adversaries. Under torture, suspects will tell the investigators what they want to hear. Ironically, confessions made under torture are often false.

Since 2001, the CIA has captured an estimated 3,000 people and transported them around the world to countries known to use torture. The Secretary of State at that time, Condoleezza Rice, denied that she transferred them for the purposes of torture because, legally, that would be admitting that she contravened U.S. and international laws. [189]

The U.S. program prompted several official investigations in member states of the Council of Europe. On February 14, 2007, the European Parliament published a press release deploring the passivity of some member states in the face of illegal CIA operations of torture on European soil "at U.S. military bases." Between 2001 and 2005, the CIA conducted 1,245 flights, many of them to destinations where suspects could face torture, in violation of Article 3 of the *United Nations Convention Against Torture.* [190] So far, President Barack Obama has taken no action against those who committed these crimes, including Jose Rodriguez Jr.

On November 4, 2009, an Italian judge convicted 22 CIA agents of kidnapping an Italian-Egyptian cleric from Milan and sending him to Egypt. A U.S. Air Force colonel and two Italian secret agents were involved in the kidnapping. The Italian ruling was the first conviction in the world against those involved in the CIA's extraordinary renditions program. [191]

Another victim of torture by the CIA was Maher Arar, a Canadian-Syrian citizen who was detained at Kennedy International Airport on September 25, 2002 by U.S. Immigration and Naturalization Service officials. Arar was on his way to Canada, but was sent to Syria under the extraordinary rendition program to be interrogated and tortured by Syrian intelligence. On October 18, 2007, Maher received a public apology from the U.S. House of Representatives and $10.5 million in compensation from the Canadian government for his pain and suffering as well as a formal apology from Canada's Prime Minister, Stephen Harper. [189,192]

Our deafening silence regarding the extraordinary rendition program encouraged the government to step up their violations to reach the American people.

The National Defense Authorization Act – Section 1021

The *National Defense Authorization Act,* which was presented by Sen. Carl Levin (D, Michigan) and Sen. John McCain (R, Arizona), passed in 2012.

The Act enables the U.S. government to hold "alleged" terrorist suspects in military custody indefinitely, even when "proof beyond reasonable doubt" has not been provided. Under this act, anyone can be accused of terrorism without even knowing what he has done. It is very confusing to listen to what the U.S. authorities say and what they do.

The *Act* places investigations and interrogations with respect to domestic terror in the hands of the military, a practice that has been used in many authoritarian regimes and has been condemned by the United Nations. It opens the door for indefinite detention of any person, including American citizens, as long as the government says they are terrorists. Commenting on the law, Sen. Al Franken (D-Minn.) said that it "denigrates the very foundations of this country."[193] "It puts every single American citizen at risk," Senator Rand Paul (R-Kentucky) added. [194]

The authorities claimed that indefinite detention in terrorism cases would be limited to foreigners, but Professor Robert Chesney of the University of Texas, has said the law does include U.S. Citizens if they are accused of terrorism offenses. [195]

U.S. congressional representatives should have asked themselves these questions:

- What does the *NDAA* say about the U.S., which claims to be the leader of democracy in the world?
- How would this law affect world opinion of U.S. and the democracy it promotes?
- What is the difference between this *Act* and the actions taken by a Dictator?

Indefinite incarceration of "suspected prisoners" is a blow to the democratic ideal. As Erik Kain of *Forbes* Magazine said, "If that was the only achievement of Bin Laden, he won the war. He succeeded [in crushing] freedom and democracy in the United States." [196]

When the *NDAA* was signed, Americans did not speak out. Would they wait until the authorities took their sons, daughters, brothers, or friends away because someone claimed they might be terrorists? This is how dictatorships evolve. Fortunately, a group of activists called "Freedom Seven Group" filed a lawsuit against the Obama administration over the *NDAA*. The group includes Pulitzer Prize-winning journalist Chris Hedges, *Pentagon Papers* whistle-blower Daniel Ellsberg, and Massachusetts Institute of Technology professor Noam Chomsky.

The case was tried before Katherine B. Forrest, U.S. District Court Judge of the Southern District of New York. In her judgment in May

2012, Forrest ruled Section 1021 of the NDAA to be unconstitutional. She based her ruling on the First Amendment, as well as on the "due process" clause of the Fifth Amendment, and decided no American should be subject to indefinite detention.

Unfortunately, this judgment will not put an end to the trend of laws evolving since 2001 that deprive American citizens of their freedoms and liberties. This will not stop until the election is funded by the taxpayers and the wealthy elite are prevented from buying the congressional representatives.

Is standing on the sidelines a betrayal of your country?

In the past decade, individual freedoms in the U.S. have been restricted by laws ranging from George W. Bush's *USA Patriot Act* to Barack Obama's *National Defense Authorization Act*. Immediately after the 9/11 attack, the U.S. government claimed that Al-Qaeda was behind it and demanded that Osama bin Laden be extradited to the U.S. from Afghanistan. The Taliban government, following diplomatic protocols, first required the U.S. government to present them with proof of bin Laden's involvement in the attack. The U.S. did not have any evidence, so decided to invade Afghanistan and overthrow the Taliban government. However, in November 2001, Patrick Martin reported that the invasion of Afghanistan was planned prior to the 9/11 attack, which was then used as a pretext for invasion.[197]

The U.S. military chased Al-Qaeda and the Taliban to the Afghani-Pakistani border. Then it hired mercenaries from Pakistan's Inter-Services Intelligence (ISI) to continue the hunt in Pakistan. The more people the ISI arrested and sent to the CIA, the more money it made. The ISI arrested any foreigners found in the Pakistan/Afghanistan border area, including a British man who happened to be in Pakistan attending the wedding of a friend. U.S. Secretary of Defense Donald Rumsfeld used every maneuver possible to justify this illegal practice. He called the accused "unlawful enemy combatants" to excuse depriving them of their human rights, tortured them, and detained them for years without trial. The detainees were interrogated by torture in secret prisons operated by the CIA, including the one at Guantánamo Bay, which received 779 men. Nine men died in the camp, while 602 suspects have been released without charge or transferred to facilities in their home countries. Only Omar Khadr, a child soldier who was arrested in Afghanistan at 15, was tried, and sentenced to eight years in prison. The remaining 166 men have been in Guantánamo Bay without trial since 2001.

In his campaign for the presidency in 2008, Barack Obama promised to close Guantanamo Bay detention camp. So far, he has not delivered on his promise after five year as a president and according to The Rendition Project website, [189a] some serious issues still exist. The rendition itself has not been outlawed and secret detention and torture are only outlawed when the detainee is in the custody or under the effective control of a U.S. officer, employee, or in a facility owned, operated, or controlled by a U.S. agency.

These acts bring to mind the words of Martin Niemoller, the German pastor during the Nazi era, who said:

"When the Nazis came for the communists,
I remained silent;
I was not a communist.
When they locked up the social democrats,
I remained silent;
I was not a social democrat.
When they came for the trade unionists,
I did not speak out;
I was not a trade unionist.
When they came for the Jews,
I remained silent;
I was not a Jew.
When they came for me,
There was no one left to speak out."

We become accomplices when you remain silent to the atrocities the U.S. government commits. Our silence is a nod of approval and encouragement for it to continue to serve the interests of the Power Triad at the expense of ordinary Americans.

Cost of invading Iraq and Afghanistan

The aggressions against Iraq and Afghanistan crippled the American economy, caused major financial losses, cost tens of thousands of American lives, and damaged the U.S. reputation as a superpower. These wars cost the U.S. $5.4 trillion, [176] more than 50,000 dead and maimed American soldiers, and more than 300,000 brain-injured soldiers. Among the most horrific crimes the U.S. committed in Iraq was the use of illegal depleted uranium ammunition. Thousands of American soldiers became collateral damage as they would suffer from mysterious illnesses after contacting the ammunition or exposure to its explosion on the battlefield.

The *Daily Mail* ran a review of a 2011 report that describes the struggle of the U.S. veterans, "Today, one U.S. veteran of the war in Iraq and Afghanistan attempts suicide every 80 minutes. In a staggering indictment on the lack of mental health programmes in the U.S. military, the report reveals 1,868 veterans made suicide attempts in 2009 alone." [198]

The invasion of Iraq was based on lies the U.S. administration used to justify the war to the American people and the world as presented by the infamous speech of Collin Powell at the U.N.

During the illegal invasion, the U.S. violated the fundamental international laws as it:

- Killed more than one million innocent Iraqis;
- Destroyed the infrastructure of Iraq (water, sewers, roads, power generation, and government buildings);
- Polluted the country with radioactive material;
- Increased the incidence of cancer for future generations;
- Created more than four million refugees;
- Caused the migration or death of most of the professional class of the country;
- Divided the country along the racial and religious lines;
- Destabilized the country politically; and
- Destroyed the safety and security of the Iraqis.

As a result, the U.S. is feared and despised among developing countries in South America, Africa, and Asia. Invading the Muslim world has been very costly for the U.S. and one of the major blunders driven by the Israel Lobby and other Triad members.

The cost of wars to the U.S. include:

- Losing its credibility as a sole superpower because the war revealed that the U.S. could be defeated in asymmetric warfare;
- Driving the U.S. economy to the verge of economic collapse;
- Turning the U.S. into the most indebted country in the history;
- Losing the lives of thousands of its service men and women who were killed, maimed, or disabled in vain;
- Disregard of the health and safety of the American soldiers—exposing them to radioactive materials from ammunition inside their barracks and on the battlefield;
- Losing $5.4 trillion dollars in "The War on Terror;"
- Depriving the American people of their freedoms and liberties and turning the U.S. into a police state;
- Jeopardizing Americans' feeling of safety and security domestically and abroad;
- Potential social unrest due to widening inequality and high unemployment;
- Enraging millions of Muslims because of the misery and pain it inflicted upon them for nothing they have done; and
- Loss of confidence in the U.S. as an honest broker in addressing the world crises, especially those in the Middle East.

Strategic plan and accountability at the U.S. Department of Defense

The U.S. used borrowed money to fund the business of war, while these resources were needed urgently to maintain its deteriorating infrastructure, and fund social security, Medicare, and education. The Department of Defense has been a black hole where trillions of dollars disappear without trace. In 2001, Rumsfeld, the Secretary of Defense could not track $2.3 trillion dollars in transactions, money that could have been used to pay for Medicare for at least five years. Rumsfeld said, "Money wasted by the military poses a serious threat. According to some estimates, we cannot track $2.3 trillion dollars in transactions...as a matter of fact, it could be a matter of life and death." Today, one may wonder how much has this number swelled up to in the past 11 years.

Being patriotic is not just supporting the troops; it is also making moral judgments about why the U.S. would attack another country. If it is an attack driven by the interests of the wealthy elite and the strategic objectives of Israel, like those launched against the Muslim countries, therefore opposing such a waste of U.S. lives amounts to supporting the troops.

Government strategic planning

The U.S. government needs to optimize the use of its finite resources to define its strategic goals and in each sector of the economy. That means having a planning horizon that extends beyond the next election.

In the U.S., the legislature has elections every two years. [199] As soon as the elected officials are in office, they start raising funds, getting ready for the next election campaign. Consequently, long-term strategic planning is not part of the dialogue within the legislatures. Setting up long-term strategic plan makes politicians accountable to the people and the budget is allocated according to the plan, goals, and objectives. State departments need to set up goals that justify their budgets, and make their achievements measurable. Money allocated to a department without defining objectives, is money that goes into a black hole and we do not know the value added by spending this money.

In contrast, China has used 5-year strategic planning (2011 – 2015) for national economic and social development in the past six decades. Its 12th Five-year Plan, approved in October 2010, prescribes the broad guiding principles that define the direction of economic growth and social development objectives and optimizes the country use of its human, production, and material resources to satisfy the societal development and economic growth. The plan guaranteed continuity of the long-term integrated plan that is independent of changes of elected officials.

Turn the military away from the business of war

The U. S. administration uses advisors or consultants that have dual U.S./Israeli nationality, and as such, the government has a built in conflict of interest that does not serve the interests of the nation. Hence, it is impossible to find a rational "American" reason for the wasteful wars it has launched since the beginning of the 21st century. To protect themselves from future disasters, the Americans must prevent the Power Triad from interfering in the political process. This can be done in the following manner:

- Amending the *Constitution* to state that a corporation is not a natural person and that the unfettered spending of money is not free speech;
- Prohibiting retiring generals from working as consultants for defense contractors;
- Lowering the military budget to meet the demands of "defending" the U.S. within its borders;
- Selling some of the 1,077 foreign military bases and sites around the globe to pay down part of the debt;[200]
- Banning dual citizenship in the U.S. Administration;
- Making the Pentagon accountable for the billions of dollars that disappeared down the military black hole;
- Withdrawing from occupied lands in Afghanistan sooner, and dismantling the army of mercenary contractors it left behind in Iraq;
- Withdrawing from NATO, which was established in 1949 by Harry Truman to defend Western Europe as a

part of the Cold War. Today, Europe is not under threat, and is capable of defending itself.

- Turning the Department of Defense back to its original objective—protecting the American people; and
- Employing military personnel to rebuild America's crumbling infrastructure by paving roads and highways, maintaining bridges, building communication infrastructure, and providing medical services.

Rebuild support in the Muslim world

The U.S. needs to stop its aggressive policies towards Muslim countries, treat them with respect, and stop interfering in their internal affairs. In this way, the U.S. will restore its safety and security, do away with the laws that violated the *Constitution*, and restore peace, democracy, and prosperity to its people.

The U.S. does not have to protect Israel because it can take care of itself. It is the only nuclear power, and has the strongest army and air force in the Middle East.

The U.S. needs to be a fair broker of the Israeli-Palestinian peace,[201] because the Palestinian-Israeli conflict is a source of grievance and made the Muslim world distrust the U.S. because of its bias against the Palestinians. [202]

The U.S. must also stop providing billions of dollars in military aid to the Middle East (Egypt gets $1.7 billion and Israel $2.7 billion annually). It should limit its aid to the region to economic development.

If the U.S. stops its aggressive attitude towards the Muslim world and resolves the problems it created with these countries, the American people will stop the phony "War on Terror" without wasting a single life on either side. [203]

Know the enemy

It is important to be aware of mainstream media brainwashing programs, which are embedded in the news, political discussions, movies, comedies, and talk shows. Free citizens must do their own research to discover what is true and what is propaganda designed to mislead them.

You need to know that neither the Muslims nor the Communists are seeking to hurt you or your country. They are, like Americans, too busy making a living, and taking care of their families. They are not interested in invading your country, destroying your way of living, or converting you to Islam.

Do your own research and find out about those American Muslims who have been demonized by the media based on fiction and scare tactics. Discover on your own that Americans, whether they are Muslims or not have been sacrificed for the sake of achieving Israel's strategic objectives and multinational corporate profits.

We need to learn to be very careful in using our remaining resources because the economy has changed and the era of plenty has ended. Americans cannot afford another war and they need to use their resources in building their economy.

Egyptian President, Mohamed Morsi, in his interview, in September 2012, by David Kirkpatrick and Steven Erlanger of the *New York Times*, explains what the American administrations have done, "Successive American administrations essentially purchased with the American taxpayer money the dislike, if not the hatred, of the people of the region [the Middle East], by backing dictatorial governments over popular opposition and supporting Israel over the Palestinians."[204]

China, on the other hand, is gaining the hearts and minds in the Muslim world by helping them develop their economy, building their infrastructure, and creating a friendly relationship to purchase their resources.

Chapter 7

China – the upcoming world economic superpower

*American multinational corporations dug the United States'
economic grave using tools made in China*

Since the implementation of Deng Xiaoping's economic reforms in 1979, China has been the world's fastest-growing economy.[214] In 2010, it surpassed Japan to become the world's second-largest economy. Today, the U.S. and China are the world's leading economic powers, but while the U.S. has been stumbling since the 2008 economic crisis, China has been growing rapidly and, according to the International Monetary Fund, China will become the world leading economy by 2016. [2a,205] In the past four decades, the U.S. has significantly contributed to the success of the Chinese economic reforms. Since the beginning of the Reagan Administration, U.S. economic and foreign policies have facilitated the shipping of manufacturing operations and high paying jobs to China. Since the 9/11 attack, U.S. administrations obsessed with the business of war against the Muslim world and became distracted from the economy. This obsession with war impoverished millions of Americans and destroyed the lives of tens of thousands of American families. In addition, thousands of American soldiers were killed, maimed, or psychologically debilitated. The "War on Terror" turned the U.S. from the world's richest country into the most indebted. At the same time, the Chinese government was focusing on developing its manufacturing base and expanding global markets. Although China has the second-largest economy, it is the world's leading exporter and manufacturer. It has become the preferred partner for many African governments and the biggest trading partner of many emerging economic powers, such as Brazil, Iran, and South Africa.

While the U.S. is struggling with a heavy debt that amounts to more than $16 trillion and a stagnating economy, China is becoming the largest net creditor to the world, sitting on more than $3 trillion in cash and a market that can grow five times faster than that of the U.S.[206] Whereas the U.S. could not bail out Europe during its financial troubles, China used its financial power to purchase natural resources in the troubled Western economies, thereby achieving its military and foreign policy objectives.

After WWII, the U.S. led the global economy and dictated how it would function. In the early 1980s, the U.S. aggressively adopted free markets and globalization, outsourcing its manufacturing operations, with China benefiting the most by expanding its manufacture base and its markets in North America and Europe.

At the 1944 Bretton Woods Conference, the U.S. dollar became the world's reserve currency. [207] Today, that is what keeps the U.S. dollar afloat. However, China and other countries like Brazil, Russia, India, Iran, France, and Japan have already started to use their own currencies in mutual trades. [208,209-213] As China gradually assumes its leadership role, the yuan will replace the U.S. dollar as the world's reserve currency.

Since the end of the 20th century, America's standing in the world has been in steady decline both economically and militarily. Its involvement in a war against the Muslim world has exacerbated that decline. Although the U.S. managed to overthrow three governments in the Muslim world, it lost political ground and deepened Muslims' mistrust of its government.

This flourishing democracy went from focusing on the interest of its people to pursuing the strategic goals of the Power Triad. It exhausted its resources in futile wars in the Middle East and Asia, and in bullying China by arming Taiwan and increasing the American military presence in the China Sea.

Ironically, the U.S. government and U.S. multinational corporations have been indirectly helping China to build up its military through the sale of highly sophisticated technologies and American expertise. Today, China funds its military with the interest on its loans to the U.S. government.

This chapter presents a description of the Chinese industrial revolution and a brief comparison between the economic and political strategies of the U.S. and China, their policies in securing the natural resources to supply their manufacturing operations, the structure of their economy, and the effect of their strategic policies on the economy both locally and globally.

The Chinese Industrial revolution

Since the collapse of the U.S.S.R., the U.S. has become the sole superpower, in addition to being the world's largest economy until the beginning of the 21st century. It has been gradually losing its global economic leadership to China, and its superpower status has weakened due to its involvement in wars with the Muslim world, deteriorating economy, and escalating debt.

The Chinese economic reforms of 1978 marked a major turning point by improving living standards and putting China on the fast track to economic growth and technological development. At the same time, it continued to maintain its political independence and honor its cultural heritage. [214] Its economy grew at rate between 9 and 10 percent. [215] In 2011, the Chinese GDP real growth rate was 5.4 times that of the U.S. While the Chinese economy grew at a rate of 9.2 percent, the growth of the U.S. economy was a meager 1.7 percent. [216]

China is attractive to foreign investors because of its low taxes, lax environmental regulations, cheap and skilled workforce, and vast potential local market. Since 1979, massive foreign investment in hundreds of billions of dollars has flown in annually to hone China's competitive edge. The foreign investors recruited the best managerial talent and used the best manufacturing practices, the most sophisticated manufacturing machinery to enable China to develop local management and workers to improve worker productivity, increase the profit margins, and lower production costs enough to absorb future wage increases. In addition, investments by corporate America and lenient patent law enforcement enabled Chinese manufacturers to develop sophisticated products by reverse engineering.

As a result of outsourcing and transferring manufacturing operations to China, U.S. multinational corporations have significantly increased their profits at the expense of the American middle class. Adoption of free markets and globalization policies by President Reagan accelerated shipping of American manufacturing operations to China without any repercussions, although it cost the U.S. hundreds of thousands of high paying jobs, and billions of dollars in tax revenues.

The wages of the middle class stagnated and the American economy became sluggish. China used its trade surplus with the U.S. to purchase U.S. government bonds in order to maintain the growth of its U.S. market. In addition, the Chinese funds increased liquidity, kept the interest rate low, and enabled Wall Street banks to increase their profits significantly using derivative instruments. Although they harmed the American people, the multinational corporations continued to enjoy uninterrupted access to the U.S. market.

In joint ventures, American multinational corporations shared their expertise and intellectual property with their Chinese partners, and consequently expedited the economic and technological development of Chinese expertise, which would otherwise have taken many decades. The state maintained control of joint ventures with multinational corporations. In addition, the low cost of Chinese products gave China a competitive edge and enabled it to expand its market into North America, Europe, and other parts of the world.

Environmental regulations in developed countries are more stringent, but they help minimize waste generation, and improve productivity. However, tighter regulatory requirements become a disadvantage in the short-term because the production costs are lower where the environmental laws are less stringent and protection of the health and safety of the workers is lacking.

Control of foreign and local corporations

American multinational corporations control the political process in the U.S., but in China, the government controls local and foreign corporations. The Chinese government put several powerful corporations such as Yahoo, Google, and Microsoft in their place. Yahoo yielded to the Chinese government and collaborated to indict a Chinese dissident. In 2010, Google threatened to withdraw from China in protest over censorship, but it backed down in return for token concessions. [217]

The Chinese government does not allow private or public corporations to grow too big. It uses state-owned corporations to control the important sectors of the economy, including aviation, railways, steel, telecom, finance, energy, and electricity. At the 2011 World Economic conference in Davos, Switzerland, Western leaders acknowledged the success of the model of state-owned corporations.[141]

The Chinese government uses state-owned corporate profits to increase its services and grow the economy according to the state economic plan. In addition, state-owned corporations employ as many Chinese workers as possible in their operations abroad.

In the U.S., the relationship between the American multinational corporation and the U.S. government is parasitic. The government uses taxpayers' money to launch wars that cost hundreds of billions of dollars to benefit multinational corporations. However, the profits these corporations make do not benefit the average American or the U.S. economy because most of these "American" corporations divert these profits to their subsidiaries abroad to avoid paying taxes. As a result, the U.S. wastes taxpayer money to benefit corporate owners and the special interest groups.

China's strategy for mining and oil resources

Between the beginning of the 18th and the middle of the 20th century, imperial Europe used brutal force to subjugate developing countries that had non-renewable resources needed to run factories and to open new markets for its products. Nevertheless, by the end of the 19th century, colonization became too costly, and European governments gave many of their colonies independence, but continued to control them by imposing indigenous rulers to serve the interests of European corporations.

Since the beginning of the 20th century, the U.S. has been adopting this 19th-century European imperial practice. U.S. administrations have been subjugating and coercing developing countries that own non-renewable resources. It threatens to use economic sanctions, lead covert operations to overthrow their governments, and impose rulers who serve the interests of the American multinational corporations and special interest groups. Then, these multinationals "purchase" the natural resources from the developing countries for pennies on the dollar. The corporations accumulate wealth for their shareholders at the expense of the people of the invaded country, and American taxpayers, who sacrifice the lives of their young men and women (under the banner of protecting the national security) to pay for the cost of wars of aggression.

On the other hand, for China to continue its high rate of economic growth, it has to secure its future needs of raw materials, minerals, oil, and natural gas for its manufacturing operations. It learned from the European and American experience that it is too costly and inhumane to coerce the developing world to sell their resources at a discount to Chinese corporations. Instead, it uses its profits from the global markets to purchase these resources at a fair market price, and win the hearts and minds of the local people by helping them to grow their economy. It initiates infrastructure projects and offers technical and financial assistance to secure funding. As a result, China has become the preferred partner of many African governments.

Today, China is the gatekeeper of world resources. It controls metals from aluminum needed for soft drinks, to lithium for hybrid car batteries and titanium for airplane manufacturing. Its control of global strategic resources will enable it to control American corporations, and indirectly control the government of the U.S.

The U.S. government needs to learn from China's experience. It has neither to sacrifice the lives of its soldiers nor to use borrowed money to launch wars in order to improve the bottom line of the American multinational corporations. Instead, these "American" corporations should purchase the rights for oil and gas exploration and mining operations for fair market prices, saving the U.S. government the cost of war and the sacrifice of the lives of its soldiers. Most importantly, from a humane perspective, American administrations would spare the lives of millions of innocent people from being killed in unnecessary wars.

Despite the sacrifice of the American people in these wars, the "American" multinationals transferred their manufacturing operations to China to increase their profits and stashed most of these profits in tax havens to avoid paying taxes in the U.S. In the process, they helped China to enhance its technological development and economic growth. As a result, China accumulated huge trade surplus and locked up emerging markets using the American technology. In fact, the profits the Chinese government made with the help of the American companies is currently used to buy non-renewable resources from Canada, the U.S., South America, Africa, and Europe.

China has proven that piracy does not pay. The wars launched by the U.S. to control the resources cost the taxpayers hundreds of times the price they could have paid to purchase these resources and could have created a win-win situation for all, except for the Military contractors. Even if the U.S. military is successful in securing oil and other resources for the American corporations, they will not help the American economy because they divert their profits to subsidiaries abroad in order to avoid paying taxes.

Chinese rare earth metals

China tends to leverage its national resources to get the most benefit for the Chinese economy. For example, it controls the global market of rare earth metals needed in the manufacture of hybrid vehicles. It produces 95 percent of the world's rare earth metals and limits the export quota of these metals based on its local needs.

Currently, Japan dominates the manufacturing of batteries needed for hybrid vehicles. However, because of the limited supply of the rare earth metals outside China, the Japanese vehicle manufacturers may have to transfer their factories to China in order to have an unconstrained supply of these metals at a cheaper price, despite the risk of having to reveal their valuable patents to a Chinese manufacturer.

Moving Japanese auto manufacturers to China will lead then to revealing the technology behind Japan's strategic high-tech production including sophisticated magnets used in hybrid cars, now produced by only three companies in Japan. As required by Chinese law, these companies have to establish joint ventures with Chinese firms, a move that could damage Japan's technological supremacy in this sector. [218] In addition, moving the Japanese factories to China will make it the major consumer of these metals, significantly decreasing the demand abroad. Consequently, China will have worldwide control of these metals because any new mining company that produces these metals will lack the demand for its products outside China, making the mine easy for the Chinese to buy.

China's approach to becoming the world superpower

To protect its technological and economic development, China had to become a superpower capable of deterring U.S. hegemony. In the past decade, according to Peter Navarro and Greg Autry, authors of *Death by China: Controlling the Dragon*, "The buildup of the Chinese Red Army has been accelerating and its military budget has been growing twice as fast as its economy. It modernized its largest standing army, constructed deep water navy to challenge the U.S. on the high seas, and built advanced nuclear submarines capable of striking U.S. cities with nuclear weapons. It equipped its force with the most advanced fighters and bombers available from the Russians." [219]

China Domination of the world markets

Since 1979, the Chinese economy has grown in two stages. In the first stage, China competed effectively in the global market because its cheap prices were so low that importers did not pay much attention to product quality. China created a dominant market position in everything from autos, furniture, refrigerators, computers, and machines to jeans and underwear. In the second stage, which started in 2005, economic growth became more dependent on domestic consumption.

The first stage started in the late-1970s, when China gradually became a preferred outsourcing destination for American corporations. Its cheap, well-educated, and well-disciplined workforce is more productive than that of other emerging markets, such as Bangladesh, Pakistan, Burma, Cambodia, or Vietnam. This workforce, combined with the use of superior manufacturing methods, has enabled China's manufacturers to flood the U.S. market with low-priced consumer products that helped Americans sustain their standard of living despite decreasing wages. Although oil prices have almost tripled, prices of Chinese goods have not increased proportionately. Indeed, prices continued to fall at the beginning of the 21st century because China had been subsidizing its exports indirectly by allowing its labor force to work under severe conditions for dismal wages. Chinese workers had to live in the factory's dormitories where they were on call 24 hours a day.

Because of outsourcing to China, the structure of the U.S. economy has gradually changed from a manufacturing to a service-oriented economy. Dependence on Chinese manufacturing increased the trade deficit with China and devalued the U.S. dollar. To maintain its price advantage and enhance economic growth, China pegged the yuan to the U.S. dollar instead of allowing it to float. Under pressure from the U.S., it reluctantly began to increase the value of the yuan. Economists in the U.S. believe that the yuan is undervalued by as much as 40 percent. However, under the current economic circumstances, a floating yuan would cause the trade deficit of the U.S. to balloon, sending the dollar into steep decline, and the U.S. into a deep recession.

China has used its trade surplus to purchase U.S. treasury bills, enabling the U.S. Federal Reserve to keep interest rates low and the fragile U.S. economy to function. According to *The Economist*: "The U.S. trade deficit was due mainly to excessive spending and inadequate saving, not to the unfair Chinese competition. If China has contributed to America's deficit, it is not through its undervalued exchange rate, but by holding down bond yields and so fuelling excessive household borrowing and spending. From this point of view, global monetary policy is now made in Beijing, not Washington." [220]

In the second stage, China planned to increase its dependence on domestic consumption in order to maintain its economic growth. It has been gradually increasing wages to increase workers' purchasing power. In such a populous country, this approach would significantly increase the demand for Chinese products, so increased wages combined with increased demand would cause a sharp rise in commodity prices. As a result, inflation in the U.S. and other developed countries would skyrocket. While these economies will slow down, China's economy will continue to grow because the increase in domestic consumption will balance any decrease in exports.

In the past, the wage of the Chinese workers was about $2 for a workday of eight to 16 hours ($0.13 to $0.25 per hour). In 2005, the minimum monthly wage was increased to $80 ($0.33 per hour) in order to boost domestic consumption and to narrow the inequality gap that was a source of growing discontent. The number of hours in a workday was not limited to eight hours and workers were not compensated for working overtime. However, by 2008, the Chinese government required overtime pay for workers who put in more than eight hours in a day or more than 40 hours a week. [221]

During the five-year strategic plan (from 2011 to 2015), the Chinese government raised the minimum wage by at least 13 percent annually.[221] By September 2011, Chinese minimum wages rose by 21.7 percent, [222] and in 2012, the minimum wage increased to $240 a month. [223]

Today, it is evident that the U.S. has less power to pressure China and as the Chinese economy strengthens, its resistance to the American demands will gradually increase. When the second stage reaches a point where the growth of the Chinese economy becomes more dependent on domestic consumption and exports to other emerging markets, China will have more power over the global market and more influence on the U.S.'s economic future.

Since the beginning of the second stage, China has also become less dependent on the U.S. dollar as a reserve currency. It has been bartering or using its own currency in international trade. In the near future, when the U.S. dollar loses its privilege as world trade currency, the U.S. will not be able to bully China because the Chinese can destabilize the U.S. economy by dumping the U.S. government bonds (more than US$1.3 trillion) on the world markets. As a result, the value of the dollar will plummet, interest and mortgage rates will soar, inflation will rise, the housing market will further collapse, and the U.S. financial market will plunge into chaos.

Other consequences of shipping America's manufacturing plants to China

America's multinational corporations shipped to China the American manufacturing operations, transferred their patents and their most advanced technologies to their Chinese partners, and helped train Chinese factory operators and scientists. As a result, China has succeeded in developing its own technologies, developed its space program, and expanded its research and development programs in order to support its manufacturing operations and products.

The transfer of the manufacturing operations has created tens of thousands of wealthy investors. They diversified their investments by purchasing real estate in the international cities in the developed countries causing the prices to rise beyond the reach of the local residents. This section discusses the Chinese space program, research and development in China, and the Chinese real estate investments in developed countries.

China's Space Program

U.S. tax revenue has been decreasing because American manufacturing operations and high paying jobs have been shipped to China. Consequently, the U.S. government has had to cut its budget and cancel some programs, including space programs. At the same time, the Chinese economy has enabled China, according to Navarro and Autry, to "aggressively move with plans for permanent space stations, implement a very sophisticated space program, and roll out a massive space-related powerful satellite network and a global positioning system capable of tracking U.S. military assets." [219]

On August 21, 2012, at the opening ceremony of the 28th General Assembly of the International Astronomical Union (IAU), China announced that it would launch its first space telescope (Hard x-ray modulation) in 2014. "China's technology has advanced markedly, and some of its buildings are really world-class. The fact that we are meeting here is an indication that China has emerged in a short period of time to be competitive on the world stage in the science of astronomy," said Robert Williams, IAU president. [224]

Research & development

Research and development, and technological innovations helped the U.S. to expand its economy and save it from several recessions over the past century. Nevertheless, innovations do not come from a vacuum. Manufacturing and research & development go hand in hand. Transferring manufacturing operations to China will lead China to outpace the U.S. in innovation. China's factories and research centers have been equipped with the most advanced manufacturing equipment. In a few years, the U.S. will lose its lead in technology, and its research centers and education institutions will become second to those of China.

Sharp increase in the price of real estate in international cities

Shipping the operations of the American multinationals to China has created tens of thousands of wealthy Chinese. To diversify their investments, they use part of their accumulated wealth to speculate on real estate in cities, such as Vancouver, Canada, that have a hot real estate market. The objective of the purchase is to make a quick profit but this has made real estate unaffordable for local residents. In February 2012, real-estate consultants Colliers International reported that the mainland Chinese account for 20 to 40 percent of foreign property investors in Vancouver, Toronto, and London. In Singapore, Chinese investors currently own nearly 30 percent of Singapore's private residences. [225] In central London, mainland Chinese and Hong Kong investors bought 20 percent of the newly built properties up to the end of 2011.

While there is a campaign to curb real estate speculation in China by preventing multiple home purchases, governments at all levels in the developed world, such as Canada, the U.S., and the United Kingdom are encouraging Chinese investors to speculate in their real estate markets, a practice that will lead to another real estate bubble. Speculation where land is limited, real estate prices skyrocketed beyond the reach of the middle class.

Several countries like Australia, Thailand, and Switzerland have banned real-estate speculation. Diane Francis of the *National Post* reports that in Toronto, for example, "a deluge of hot money from abroad …is creating an artificial and potentially dangerous real estate bubble." To avoid such a bubble, Australia banned non-resident foreigners from buying homes or investment properties. [226]

Governments allow speculation in the real-estate market in order to cater to the wealthy elite. However, it is an unwise, shortsighted government policy. It may temporarily enrich the wealthy, local developers, and foreign Chinese investors, and improve the real-estate sector, but at the end, it will inflate the prices to make life unaffordable for the residents, create a real-state bubble that might cause another recession. The outcome is that both the foreign Chinese speculators and the wealthy elite make profits from speculation at the expense of the middle class and working people who are struggling to make ends meet.

Recommendations

Use of the U.S. military and economic power

It is time for the U.S. to realize that its status as the sole superpower will not last forever. It can continue to bully the world for a short while and create a world of chaos, or use its power and remaining influence to create a peaceful prosperous world and be a role model for other nations to follow.

Securing raw materials for the American markets

U.S. multinationals should start to secure their supply of resources without firing one single bullet. The U.S. government can win the hearts and minds of the people in the Muslim countries, not by killing their people and destroying their infrastructure, but by using the Chinese strategy of offering technical and financial support to help them improve their economy, and maintain a long-term friendship.

The U.S. should extend friendship to the Muslim world instead of pursuing the strategic interests of Israel and consequently jeopardizing the U.S. national security and interests.

Real estate ownership

As the number of wealthy Chinese increases, speculation on real estate severely affect the local residents in metropolitan areas in the developed world, especially in the U.S., Canada, Australia, and the United Kingdom. Today, in Vancouver, Canada, a modest condominium is unaffordable for the middle class Vancouverites, while foreigners are purchasing most of the newly built real estate. To protect the local residents and allow them to own their own residence, we should learn from other countries' experience—ban selling real estate to non-resident investors and restrict local real estate ownership to only one mortgaged unit per family, as it is the case in China and Hong Kong. [226]

Chapter 8

The financial crisis

*Power corrupts, and the financial market power has
completely corrupted the financial markets.*
~ Professor Simon Johnson ~ [227]

The economic crisis of 2008 was a manifestation of a Ponzi
scheme that created the biggest financial collapse since the
stock market crash of 1929 and the subsequent Great
Depression. The political institutions allowed it to happen, and neither
punished the culprits nor took measures to prevent it from recurring.

The crisis was devastating for many Americans. On July 10, 2012, in
his testimony to the Committee on Financial Services Subcommittee
on Capital Markets and Government Sponsored Enterprises, Dennis
Kelleher, CEO of Better Markets, reported [228] that the costs of the
financial crisis comprised:

- Gross domestic product (GDP) had fallen dramatically.
  It has not been expected to return to normal levels until
  at least 2018. At that time, the cumulative shortfall in
  GDP is expected to reach $5.7 trillion.
- The October 2009 unemployment rate represented 15.4
  million workers, many of whom may have become
  permanently unemployed.
- Government expenditures were well in excess of a
  trillion dollars. The value of the government's total
  commitment provided through some 50 separate
  programs is estimated at $23.7 trillion.
- The national debt is expected to increase by $8 trillion
  by 2018.

- Between October 2007 and March 2009, the stock market fell by more than 50 percent, representing a paper loss of $11 trillion.
- From 2007 to 2010, median family income fell by 7.7 percent, and median family net worth fell by 38.8 percent, a total of more than $7 trillion, erasing almost two decades of accumulated prosperity.
- Since 2008, home values have declined 33 percent, representing $7 trillion in lost value.
- Over 11 million homeowners own homes worth less than their mortgages, or about 22.8 percent of all owners of mortgaged residential properties.
- An estimated 3.6 to 5 million homes have been lost to foreclosure since the crisis began, with millions of additional foreclosures expected.
- The number of families falling below the poverty line has climbed steadily since 2007, rising from 12.5 to 15.1 percent, representing over 46.3 million individuals, and increased to 47.8 million in 2012. [229]
- The human anguish caused by the crisis has been enormous and incalculable, encompassing all of the psychological and physical health effects that come with unemployment, poverty, homelessness, delayed retirement, abandoned college education, increased crime rates, and lost health care.
- Faith in the American Dream, which holds that the U.S. is the land of opportunity—everyone gets a fair shot, and the next generation will have it better than the last, has dropped at an alarming rate, undermining the spirit of the American people.

The U.S. government dealt with the symptoms of the financial crisis by increasing the money supply and bailing out the banks. Democratic pollster and political scientist Stanley Greenberg, Chief Executive of Greenberg Quinlan Rosner wrote regarding the bailout of Wall Street bankers:

"Our research shows that the growth of self-identified conservatives began in the fall of 2008 with the Wall Street bailout, well before Mr. Obama embarked on his recovery and spending program. The public watched the elite and leaders of both parties rush to the rescue [of Wall Street]. The government saved irresponsible executives who bankrupted their own companies, hurt many people, and threatened the welfare of the country. When Mr. Obama championed the bailout of the auto companies and allowed senior executives at bailed-out companies to take bonuses, voters concluded that he was part of the operating elite consensus. If you owned a small business that was in trouble or a home or investments that lost much of its value, you were on your own." [230]

There was no difference between the Bush Republicans and the Obama Democrats when it came to addressing the financial crisis. Both presidents dealt with the symptoms of the financial crisis by increasing the money supply and bailing out the banks. Obama rewarded the culprit bankers, who kept their jobs and continued to draw their exorbitant bonuses, even after they drove their organizations to the verge of bankruptcy.

The Federal Reserve cut interest rates from one percent to 0.25 percent and to resolve the liquidity crisis, the government set up a scheme called "quantitative easing"—buying assets such as treasury bonds and the now-worthless derivatives and mortgage backed securities, from the banks to increase the money supply. All this did was, harm the American taxpayer further.

- Homeowners watched the value of their assets deteriorate;
- The elderly, who depend on pensions and fixed-income investments, were hurt because the interest rate fell below the inflation rate, decreasing their incomes and the value of their investments:
- Increasing federal government debt devalued the U.S. dollar and led to a decline in the standard of living of the American people; and
- Loss of confidence in U.S. financial markets and Wall Street became even more powerful, without effective

regulations, making the U.S. more vulnerable to another crisis.

The U.S. was once a global destination for international investors because of confidence in its financial markets. This confidence has been deteriorating.

The Impact on the Economy

"The Great Recession," which began in December 2007, caused severe global economic problems, characterized by high unemployment, especially among marginalized young people in the developed countries, including the U.S., U.K., Spain, Greece and France, as well as emerging markets such as Tunisia, Morocco, Egypt, Bahrain, and Saudi Arabia. It even caused political unrest in Morocco and Egypt.

Today, the U.S. is drowning in debt and the dollar is falling as a result. In the future, investors will demand higher rates of interest, putting more pressure on the debt, triggering a vicious cycle. At the same time, Congress is inclined to pursue austerity measures that target the poor and the middle class the most, while continuing to spend lavishly on self-destructive military adventures in the Middle East and Asia.

This situation brings to mind the story of the Egyptian farmer who has just opened a checking account. The bank manager tells him he can now pay for his seeds and other goods by check instead of cash, but the farmer misunderstands the process. Very excited, he goes on a spending spree. His checks bounce. The bank manager calls him to his office and tells him, "You have overspent your credit by 500 pounds." The farmer immediately responds, "No problem! Here is a check for 500 pounds."

U.S. overcame previous recessions because it could create new jobs through its powerful manufacturing base and leadership in technology and research and development. However, over the past four decades, corporate America has largely moved its manufacturing base to China, and to a lesser extent India.

The U.S. and China are in a symbiotic economic relationship: U.S. corporations move their manufacturing operations to take advantage of China's cheap labor force. China then exports cheap products back to the U.S. and uses its trade surplus to buy U.S. treasury bonds, which in turn helps the U.S. maintain low interest rates and increase the money supply.

At first, the loss of high-paying jobs to China was not noticeable, but gradually it reached the tipping point and was fully revealed by the 2008 economic crisis.

A main source of wealth for Americans used to be the increasing value of their homes, which encouraged them increase their spending and live on credit. Today, the value of their homes has fallen sharply, and these people are up to their necks in debt. They can no longer maintain their high standard on credit because many of the high-paying jobs that made it possible have disappeared. Today, more than 47.8 million Americans rely on food stamps, [107] and the current policy of keeping the interest rates artificially low is hurting the elderly—a further 35 million who depend on their savings to support themselves and fund their retirement. The government is impoverishing them further by continuing quantitative easing in order to bail out the banks. [229] Quantitative easing is a government monetary policy, which is used when lowering the interest rate close to zero percent fails to stimulate the economy. The central bank buys government securities or other securities from commercial banks in order to help them increase lending and liquidity. Nevertheless, quantitative easing exposes the economy to the risk of high inflation. [232]

Despite injections of hundreds of billions of dollars to increase liquidity, high unemployment and a lack of high-paying jobs have discouraged consumers from spending, thus keeping the U.S. from rebounding. According to the Federal Reserve Board of Governors, at the beginning of 2010, outstanding consumer credit declined for the first time since 1942. [231] As a result, China has been forced to inject huge amounts of money into its system to drive growth.

The U.S. labor market will not recover until the U.S. repeals laws that give corporations control of the political process. Even if the unemployment rate stays stable or decreases slightly, any new jobs generated in the U.S. will continue to be low-paying service-sector jobs. The official unemployment rate will continue to be in the high single digits (8.2 percent in May 2012), but government statistics do not account for the unemployed who have stopped looking for work.[231]

Use of the U.S. dollar as the world reserve currency

For more than 50 years, the U.S. dollar has been the chief currency used for trade. However, since the beginning of the U.S.' fabricated "war on terror," the dollar's use as a global reserve currency by central banks fell from 70.1 percent in 1999 to 62 percent in 2011. [233] If the U.S. dollar continues to be used as the reserve currency, it will cause inflation to rise and could lead to another global recession.

Currently, China has about $3.2 trillion in treasury bills, while Japan holds approximately $1.3 trillion. Since 2008, both countries have started to diversify their reserves. China signed a 1.3-trillion yuan currency-swap agreement with 15 countries and regions, including South Korea, Malaysia, Hong Kong, Belarus, and Argentina. Some of these agreements also promote bilateral trade and investment. [234] Charles Kupchan, professor of international affairs at Georgetown University says that the current swap agreements are a sign that China is headed in the direction of internationalizing the yuan. [208]

The first national leader to stop using the U.S. dollar as a reserve currency was former Iraqi president, Saddam Hussein. When the U.S. imposed economic sanctions on Iraq, he switched to the euro for oil trading. In November 2000, Iraq received United Nations approval to sell oil through the oil-for-food program for euros, although this move cost Iraq millions of dollars in currency conversion fees. [235]

More recently, Iran replaced the dollar with the euro in response to U.S.-imposed sanctions. When trading with other countries, Iran either barters or uses local currencies, like the yuan, rupee, the rial, or gold. [209] This was another blow to the status of the U.S. dollar as a reserve currency.

In his article, "The Demise of the Dollar," in October 2009, Robert Fisk reports that the Gulf Arabs made agreements with China, Russia Japan, and France to stop using the American dollar for oil trading. These agreements possibly explain the sudden rise in gold prices, but they also suggest an extraordinary transition from dollar markets. [210]

In November 2010, China and Russia decided to renounce the dollar and use their own currencies in bilateral trade. [211]

In February 2011, the International Monetary Fund issued a report about the possible replacement of the dollar as the world's reserve currency by using Special Drawing Rights (SDRs) that were created in 1969 and can be converted into any currency at exchange rates based on a weighted basket of international currencies. [212]

In December 2011, China and Japan signed an agreement to begin direct trading of their currencies. Japan applied to buy Chinese bonds in 2012, allowing it to accumulate more yuan in its foreign-exchange reserve. [208]

In January 2012, China's central bank signed a 35-billion yuan currency-swap agreement with the bank of the United Arab Emirates. Then, in March 2012, the BRICS countries (Brazil, Russia, India, China, and South Africa) signed two key accords to promote trade among them using their local currencies and to explore setting up a development bank for mobilizing resources for infrastructure and sustainable development projects. [213]

When this move away from the dollar is complete, the American empire will fade into the background, as did the British, Islamic, and Roman empires.

Are financial crises deliberately created?

The history of U.S. financial crises since the beginning of the 20th century shows that American administrations have repeated the same mistakes—deregulation and cutting government oversight of the banking industry. These mistakes triggered the 1929 crash and the bank failures that caused Great Depression and the financial crises in the 1980s, 1990s, and 2008.

According to the Law Library, "In the early 1900s, commercial banks established investment affiliates that floated bond issues and underwrote corporate stock issues. The expansion of commercial banks into securities underwriting was substantial until the 1929 stock market crash and the subsequent depression. In 1930, the Bank of the U.S. failed, because of the activities of its security affiliates, which created artificial conditions in the market. In 1933, all of the U.S. banks closed for four days and 4,000 banks closed permanently. This closure, along with the already devastated economy, caused the public to lose confidence." [236a]

Of more than 25,000 banks in business in 1929, fewer than 15,000 survived to 1933. To restore confidence in the financial markets, Congress enacted the *Glass-Steagall Act* (*The Banking Act*), in 1933, as part of President Franklin D. Roosevelt's New Deal, which became a permanent measure in 1945. The act prohibited commercial banks from engaging in the investment business and forced a separation of commercial and investment banks. [236,236a]

The Glass-Steagall Act created the Federal Deposit Insurance Corporation, an insurance program to guarantee the safety of deposits in member banks. The FDIC also examines and supervises financial institutions for safety and soundness, performs certain consumer-protection functions, and manages banks in receivership. This brought stability to a financial industry that had been on the verge of collapse and restored public confidence in the banking system.

Unfortunately, for Americans, President Ronald Reagan ended the era of FDR's New Deal and put the U.S. on the path to the 2008 Great Recession. In his 1980 campaign speeches, Reagan presented his economic proposals as merely a return to free-enterprise principles, not mentioning that these same principles had caused the Great Depression. These policies were a return to corporate control of the political system, which had existed before the New Deal era.

Reagan embraced neo-liberalism and deregulated Savings and Loans (S&Ls) operations. Deregulation allowed S&Ls to offer a wide array of savings products, significantly expand their lending authority, authorize the use of more lenient accounting rules to report their financial condition and eliminate restrictions on the minimum number of stockholders. These policies, combined with an overall decline in the regulatory oversight, were among the factors that caused the financial crisis of the 1980s and 1990s. Commonly known as the S&Ls crisis, it caused the collapse of 747 institutions and cost the taxpayers $87.9 billion. [237a]

In 1982, the FDIC violated the *Glass-Steagall Act*, approving the affiliation of state-chartered, non-Federal Reserve banks with securities firms, even if they had FDIC insurance. In 1983, the Federal Reserve authorized Bank of America to buy Charles Schwab (the largest brokerage firm) and in 1987, it allowed Bankers Trust,

Citigroup, and J.P. Morgan to trade mortgage-backed securities and commercial paper. [237]

In his book, *Radical Conservatism, The Right's Political Religion*, [126] Robert Brent Toplin, professor of history at the University of North Carolina, says: "... admirers [of Ronald Reagan] rarely acknowledge how central Reagan's ideas are to the market difficulties troubling us today. As the country's greatest modern champion of deregulation, perhaps Ronald Reagan contributed more to today's unstable business climate than any other American did. His long-standing campaign against the role of government in American life, a crusade he often stretched to extremes, produced conditions that ultimately proved bad for business. The main problem with Reagan's outlook was a failure to recognize that government regulation can serve business interests quite effectively."

In 1999, the Clinton Administration completed deregulation of the banking system, led by Secretary of Treasury Lawrence Summer and encouraged by Alan Greenspan, then the Chairman of the Federal Reserve. That year, President Bill Clinton signed into law the *Financial Services Modernization Act* (*The Gramm-Leach-Bliley Act*), which repealed the *Glass-Steagall Act*. During the debate in the House of Representatives regarding the *Gramm-Leach-Bliley Act*, John Dingell (Democrat, Michigan) reminded the representatives of the S&Ls crisis and argued that the bill would result in banks becoming "too big to fail" and require them to be bailed out by the Federal Government. [238] Senator Byron Dorgan (North Dakota) expressed his opposition to repealing the *Act*, saying:

"We are, with this piece of legislation [Financial Services Modernization Act], moving towards greater risk. Substantial new concentration of the financial services industry that is not in the interest of the consumer and we are deliberately with this legislation moving towards inherently much greater risk in the financial service industry. I regret that I cannot support the legislation. We will look back in 10 years' time and say we should not have done that because we forgot the lessons of the past." [238a]

Obviously, Congress knew the consequences of voting for the *Act*, but it was passed by both the Republicans (205 votes for and 16 against) and the Democrats (129 vote for and 69 against). The only independent senator, Bernie Sanders, voted against it. [239a]

Were President Clinton, Summers and those who voted for the act deliberately negligent? Was Alan Greenspan (Chairman of the Federal Reserve from 1987-2006) aware that deregulation had caused many crises in the past and would create an environment similar to that of the 1920s? On October 12, 2005, he said: "…recent regulatory reforms, coupled with innovative technologies, have stimulated the development of financial products, such as asset-backed securities, collateral-loan obligations, and credit-default swaps that facilitate the dispersion of risk. These increasingly complex financial instruments have contributed to the development of a far more flexible, efficient, and hence resilient financial system than the one that existed just a quarter-century ago." [239]

Instead, deregulation, innovative technologies, and the development of "complex financial products" turned the U.S. financial markets into a global casino and led to the collapse of the U.S. economy.

Greenspan played a major role in creating the 2008 economic crisis. He discouraged the regulation of derivatives and supported the privatization of Social Security. He encouraged tax cuts that increased the deficit and led the way for the easy-money lending policies, which caused the sub-prime mortgage crisis that led to the financial crisis. Was it a coincidence that the crisis erupted within months of his departure from the Federal Reserve? [240]

After the 2008 financial crisis, the U.S. government did not take serious steps to regulate the financial industry and oversee the banking sector. Wall Street bankers supported this lack of action because the system had always worked well for them. Although the sale of derivatives contributed to the collapse of the financial market, Wall Street increased its share of that high-risk asset. On May 2012, J.P. Morgan suffered a loss of $6 billion in derivatives. [241]

Executives of financial corporations have been winning whether their companies go bankrupt or increase in value. After serving as Governor of New Jersey, Jon S. Corzine worked as Chief Executive Officer at M.F. Global Holdings. Although under his leadership, the company went bankrupt, he received an $8 million pay package in the year it went into bankruptcy and faced a loss of $1.6 billion. Despite the financial losses, not to mention job losses at M.F. Global, Corzine netted $3 million in cash compensation, including a $1.25 million bonus. [242,244]

Corzine is not the only executive who earned exorbitant amounts in return for very poor performance. The Wall Street Journal reports that, "In 2011, Bank of America CEO Brian Moynihan made six times what he made in 2010, even though the bank's stock price was cut in half. Goldman Sachs CEO Lloyd Blankfein's pay increased 13.7 percent to $19 million in 2011, even though shareholder return declined 45.6 percent. Wells Fargo CEO John Stumpf received a 2.1 percent bump in pay to $17.9 million, although the company's shareholders saw their returns decline by 9.5 percent." [243] Waldron Travis of Think Progress reported that in the past three years, Citigroup CEO Vikram Pandit was paid $43 million while the company's share value dropped 44 percent in 2011 and 27 percent over the past three years. [244]

Economy and the national debt

Gross Domestic Product (GDP) is the total value of all goods and services produced within a nation in a given year. Although the U.S. represents 4.4 percent of the world population, it generates approximately a quarter of global Gross Domestic Product (GDP) and accounts for a fifth of the globe's purchasing power. Its economy maintains a very high level of output per capita, amounting to $49,600 in 2012, the sixth highest in the world. [245]

Nevertheless, because of its war against the Muslim world, the U.S. government has accumulated a public debt that ballooned from $5.75 trillion in 2000 to $16.2 trillion by the end of 2012. Since President Bush started the "war on terror," the public debt has increased by over $500 billion each year, with increases of $4.6 trillion in three fiscal years (2008, 2009, and 2010). [246]

The debt continues to grow at a rate of about $5.48 billion each day. Today, the federal debt exceeds GDP, and the total public and private debt was a staggering $56.9 trillion at the end of the second quarter of 2012, or 3.70 times GDP. [247,248]

In December 2007, the U.S. economy experienced a recession caused by the derivatives market, the sub-prime mortgage crisis, and a declining dollar. [249] The White House estimates that the government's cost for servicing the debt will exceed $700 billion a year in 2019, [250] up from $202 billion in 2009. [251] China will be receiving interest on this debt in an amount equal to two times its military budget. [245]

By February 2012, the U.S. owed $5.1 trillion to foreign investors, the largest of which were China, Japan, Brazil, Taiwan, Switzerland, Russia, and the United Kingdom, with China holding 26 percent of all foreign-held U.S. treasury securities. [252] In 1945, just after World War II, debt as a share of the U.S. economy reached a peak of 112.7 percent of GDP, but then gradually fell and reached its lowest level in 1974, thanks to post-war economic growth. [251]

In the 1980s, President Ronald Reagan pursued free market and globalization policies, increased military spending and lowered tax rates. Because of this, as well as corporations' outsourcing of jobs, the debt continued to rise during George Bush's presidency.

During the Clinton years, the debt fell somewhat because of the decrease in military spending after the end of the Cold War and the increased tax revenue that resulted from the dot-com bubble. Various budget controls, as well as economic growth, contributed to budget surpluses and lower debt. Nevertheless, the debt escalated again during the presidency of George W. Bush because of the tax cut and increase of military spending to fund his "war on terror."

Wars were once seen as a way to improve the U.S. economy. The government used to be able to recover the cost of wars because of its industrial and technological strength. The costs were absorbed due to the ability of the U.S. economy to generate wealth and increase tax revenues that enabled the federal government to repay its debts. Things changed since the 1980s when the U.S. began sending manufacturing operations to China and other emerging markets. Today, the beneficiaries of the wars against the Muslim world are not Americans, but the Power Triad.

The recovery from the 2008 financial crisis will be painfully slow because the corporations that now benefit from wars have established subsidiaries abroad to avoid paying taxes to the U.S. and have relocated their manufacturing operations and high-paying jobs overseas. As a result, tax revenues continue to decrease and the budget deficit continues to increase to pay the cost of wars.

As the economy fails, investors will demand higher interest rates on the debt as they anticipate further dollar devaluation. Higher interest rates will slow domestic growth and increase inflation, leading to recession. In addition, wages will continue to fall because most of the new jobs generated will be in the low-paid service sector. As a result, tax revenues will decrease and the vicious cycle will continue unless U.S. brings its military spending in line with that of other nations.

The U.S. financial market—a casino

If a company needs to raise money for any reason, it can either sell bonds or issue stock to the public. In return for a bond, investors receive a fixed interest rate, paid to them periodically. In return for a stock purchase, an investor can receive an appreciating asset if the stock does well, and some companies may pay a dividend, usually every quarter. With the proceeds from the bond sale or stock offering, the company is expected to enhance its profitability by, for example, expanding productive capacity or developing new products or services.

In contrast to this rational model, the U.S. financial market bears more of a resemblance to a casino selling derivatives, and commodity futures speculation, day trading, high frequency trading, flash trading, and super-fast computer trading. These practices, described below, have enriched a small group of bankers at the expense of an enormous number of investors, not to mention the world economy.

Derivatives

A derivative is a financial contract "derived" from a traditional security (a stock or bond), an asset (commodity), or a market index. Futures contracts, forward contracts, options, mortgage-backed securities, and swaps are the most common types of derivatives. Derivatives are speculative tools that expose world markets to unacceptable levels of risk. Warren Buffett described derivatives in his 2002 letter to Berkshire Shareholders as "financial weapons of mass destruction, carrying dangers that, while now latent, are potentially lethal." [253]

For example, the changing value of crude-oil futures depends primarily on the upward or downward movement of oil prices. By purchasing a derivative, the buyer or seller is gambling that the price of crude oil will rise or fall.

Wall Street bankers turned to high-risk derivatives because their policy had changed from protecting the bank from risks to generating profits at any cost. Today, the global value of the derivatives market is estimated at $1,200 trillion. This sum is 20 times larger than the global economy, which ranges between $50 trillion and $60 trillion.[254,255] According to Gary Gensler, Chairman of the Commodity Futures Trading Commission, "both the financial system and the financial regulatory system failed the American public." [256]

Unlike stocks or bonds, derivatives have little direct connection to tangible assets and are not subject to industry regulation and oversight. In the case of a bond, a bondholder can buy financial guaranty insurance to guarantee scheduled payments of interest and principal on the bond in the event of a default by the issuer. As compensation, the insurance company is paid a premium (a lump sum or in installments) by the issuer or owner of the bond. On the other hand, a "credit default swap" (CDS) is a type of derivative bought as insurance for a bond the purchaser does not own. It is buying default insurance on somebody else's investment, and gambling that that investment will fail! For example, a person can gamble that the Greek government will default on its debt payments by buying an $1,100 CDS from an investment bank for each million dollars of debt. If Greece defaults, the holder gets $1 million for each CDS. If Greece does not default, the CDS is lost. In this example, the bank is exposed to a $1 million loss against a relatively small bet of $1,100. Evidently, the initial "investment" is very small amount compared to the potential gain, but if the insurance company erred, the losses would be huge.

CDSs are speculative, high-risk products that should be sold at a casino in Las Vegas, not at a financial institution. However, as early as 1997, Federal Reserve Chairman Alan Greenspan fought to keep the derivatives market unregulated. Based on the advice of the President's Working Group on Financial Markets, the Congress and the President allowed over-the-counter derivatives market to regulate itself by passing the *Commodity Futures Modernization Act* in 2000. From 1998 to 2008, the volume of credit default swaps increased 100-fold. By November 2008, the volume ranged from $33 to $47 trillion, an amount two to three times that of the 2012 U.S.'s GDP of about $15.8 trillion. [245,257]

During the 2008 economic crisis, banks failed, but this time the taxpayer bailed them out. Bankers should have learned their lesson and stopped gambling. On the contrary, in May 2012, J.P. Morgan

Chase & Co declared that the firm suffered a $6 billion trading loss after an "egregious failure" in a unit managing risk. [241,258]

Super-fast computer trading

The purpose of the stock market is to encourage people to invest in the economy, but recent progress in computer technology has enabled bankers, trading houses and hedge-fund managers to use super-fast computers in what is known as "high-frequency trading." Using supercomputers, Wall Street and hedge fund traders have turned the stock market into a casino where the average holding period for a stock is minutes, not days or years.

"[High-frequency traders] are parasites who exploit a technological advantage to suck money out of the market and add no value," says *60 Minutes.* [259] The trading scheme has taken over much of Wall Street in the past few years. They use computers, which are programmed to scan the stock market extremely fast, decide in fractions of a second, which stocks to buy and sell, jump in ahead of rallies to buy the stock and then sell it off before a decline. If a stock is rising, the computer gets to the front, buys the stock, then sells it to the buyer. The trade makes a small profit, but if done say, 40 million times a day, the money adds up. In 2006, high frequency trading in the U.S. increased from 30 percent of stock trades to as much as 70 percent in 2010. According to Manoj Narang of Tradeworx, the microseconds add up to billions of dollars a year. [259] For this reason, traders are willing to pay very high lease rate to place their computers at the stock exchange.

Joe Saluzzi, an institutional trader for Themis Trading LLC, believes that the investment game is rigged. He says that high frequency trading causes small investors to lose confidence, and consequently leads to the deterioration of financial markets. Since the spring of 2009, for example, small investors pulled $70 billion out of mutual funds. [259]

Unfortunately, the stock exchanges, which are supposed to offer an honest venue for trading, are siding with these traders. For example, the "New York Stock Exchange floor was once the center of the financial world. Today, however, fewer than 30 percent of trades are conducted on the Exchange floor. The remaining 70 percent has been replaced with high frequency trading," says 60 Minutes. [259]

Even though this trading takes advantage of small investors, the New York Stock Exchange is encouraging this practice by leasing space in Mahwah, New Jersey to high-frequency traders.

High-frequency traders could cause a meltdown of the market if a computer algorithm goes wrong. For example, a mini-crash occurred on May 6, 2010, when the Dow Jones Industrial plunged 600 points in 20 minutes. In that time, a computer at a mutual fund company dumped $4.1 billion worth of securities on the market. The securities had been picked by high-frequency traders' computers and sold almost immediately, triggering other computers and traders to dump their holdings. In 2012, the same practice was behind the failure of BATS (a U.S. Stock Exchange Company) and Facebook's Initial Public Offering. [259]

The Security Exchange Commission did not address the root of the problem. Instead, it dealt with a symptom of this problem by placing circuit breakers to halt trading automatically when a stock moves more than 10 percent in a five-minute period.

Senator Ted Kaufman (Democrat, Delaware) has tried to bring fairness and confidence back to the stock market, but he did not have much support from Congress. In his farewell speech from the Senate in 2010, Kaufman made his case:

"The rise in high frequency trading has come to dominate the equity markets and now accounts for well over half of all daily trading volume. There is a real perceptual risk that retail investors will no longer believe that the markets are operating fairly, that there is simply not a level playing field. If investors do not believe the markets are fair, they will not invest in them. And if that happens, Mr. President, we can all agree our economy will be in serious trouble. Where there is no transparency and therefore no effective regulation, we have a prescription for disaster. We had a disaster in the fall of 2008, when the credit markets suddenly dried up and our markets collapsed. We had a near-disaster on May 6, 2010." [260]

Short selling

This instrument is another "legal," speculative tool designed by professional traders to make millions of dollars at the expense of small investors. Short selling increases volatility in the stock market, and adds no value to it. Short selling allows traders to sell shares they do not own in the expectation that the price of the company's stock will fall. They then buy the stock back at a lower price and pocket the difference. For example, if a professional trader thinks that your company's stock price will drop, he can borrow shares from your broker without your knowledge, and sell them. In this way, he increases the supply of the shares in the stock market, causing the price to fall further. If the price goes down enough, he buys the stock back to return it to your broker and pockets the difference.

This tool has been used by hedge funds to drive the stock price of small- and medium-sized companies into the ground and make millions of dollars at the expense of the owners of these stocks. On the other hand, if the short-seller guesses wrong, and the stock rises, his losses could be enormous.

Speculation in commodity futures

Today, global population growth is outstripping the world's non-renewable resources. Increasing demand for resources of all kinds is coming from the most populated emerging markets, including India and China. In addition, Wall Street and hedge fund traders have billions of dollars with which to speculate on commodity futures, thereby manipulating the market, and leading to inflated prices, especially for specific commodities in short supply. As the supply of commodities is expected to decrease relative to actual demand, prices of commodity futures will become extremely volatile.

The commodity futures market has created a layer of parasitic traders whose business is to skim profits from the consumers without adding value to the economy. Commodity futures trading was one of the issues that contributed to the Crash of 1929. In the aftermath, President Franklin Roosevelt regulated the futures and securities markets to guard against fraud and manipulation and to ensure transparency.

Subprime mortgages and the 2008 financial crisis

The 2008 financial crisis was triggered by what is known as sub-prime mortgages, collateralized debt obligations (CDOs) and credit default swaps.

Subprime mortgage scheme

In the past, investors from pension funds, insurance companies, sovereign and mutual funds, who were seeking a safe place to put their money, would buy treasury bills, the safest investment, with an AAA rating.

However, after the dot-com bubble bust and the 9/11 attack, Allan Greenspan lowered the interest rate to one percent in order to increase liquidity. This interest rate was too low for investors but very good for the banks, which could borrow money at this low rate from the Federal Reserve and other sources such as Japan, China and the Middle East.

The low interest rate encouraged banks to increase their borrowing. For example, if a bank's client deposited $10,000, the bank could then borrow, $90,000 and buy a product for $100,000, then sell, it, for $110,000. The bank's gross profit is $10,000. The bank then pays back the $90,000 and keeps the $10,000 profit on its original $10,000 capital (clients' money). In other words, the bank makes a 100 percent gross profit on its deposits.

In the past, homebuyers borrowed money from a bank or other lending institution, which ensured that the borrower could afford to pay back the mortgage. The lender charged a fair interest on the loan and the family got its dream home. Then, every month, the lender received mortgage payments, from those whose mortgages they held, and used the funds to pay back their investors.

Before the financial crisis, real estate in the U.S. was booming and the banks wanted to partake of what they saw as easy money. They came up with some new financial products, like asset-backed mortgages. For instance, a bank bought a mortgage from a lender for a fee and took over the risk from a borrower it did not know. In this scenario, the bank borrowed billions of dollars at a very low rate (one percent) and bought more mortgages, then sold them as bonds with a higher interest rate than that set by the Federal Reserve.

The banks divided mortgages into three groups: safe, moderately safe, and risky. For example, investors who bought the safe bonds got a four percent return. Investors in the second group of bonds got six percent, and investors who purchased risky bonds got nine percent.

The three kinds of bonds together were called Collateralized Debt Obligations (CDOs).

As the mortgage money was repaid, it was given to the first group of bondholders. Then, whatever was left went to the second tier, and any overflow from the second tier went to the final group of bondholders. If some homeowners did not pay their mortgages, less money came in and less money went to the third group.

To make the first tier of bonds even safer, banks insured it with Credit Default Swap (CDS), which was invented by Blythe Masters of J.P. Morgan in 1994. [261] The CDS guarantees that the buyer of a bond will receive a payoff if the bank defaults. Because these bonds were insured, credit rating agencies gave the first group of bonds an AAA rating, the second group a BBB rating and left the third group unrated. The first and safest portion was sold to those who wanted a low-risk investment, the second to those who did not mind some risk and the third to hedge-fund managers.

Notice that the risk has been moved away from the lending institution and given to the insurance companies and the investors. The investment bankers made billions of dollars in profits. They paid their loans back to the Federal Reserve. The investors got better interest than one percent treasury bills. And because they believed the investment was safe, they demanded more mortgage bonds.

Because of the boom in the housing sector before the 2008 crisis, home prices were rising. When a homeowner defaulted, the lender got the house and sold it to the next buyer. This system worked well as long as housing prices continued to rise and homeowners could pay their monthly mortgage. However, at a specific point, almost all qualified homebuyers in the U.S. already owned homes and the mortgage brokers were desperately looking for new buyers.

The Wall Street bankers realized they could make more profit by finding more would-be borrowers, regardless of their ability to pay back their mortgage. In their new scheme, bankers had already transferred the risk to the investors and the insurance company.

Nevertheless, greed blinded the bankers. They convinced themselves that housing prices would continue to rise forever and, even if the homeowner defaulted, the brokers would sell the house to the next buyer and the bankers would continue to make billions. If the economy collapses, they will not be hurt. Consequently, Wall Street bankers decided to waive any need for a down payment or proof of income. Instead of lending to people who could afford to pay mortgages—these were known as prime mortgage—the bankers started to lend to people who had no down payment and could not pay back the loan. These were known as *sub-prime* mortgages.

As the number of homeowners with sub-prime mortgages increased, more monthly mortgage payments were not paid. The banks got these houses, but the supply of houses grew much higher than the demand. The real-estate boom ended and the price of houses started to fall. This created a problem for those homeowners who were able to pay their mortgages. As the houses in the neighborhood went up for sale, the value of their homes, financed with prime mortgages, went down, and gradually the values dropped to less than the mortgage they owed. Those with prime mortgages started to wonder why they were paying back a mortgage for a house that was worth much less than the mortgage. These owners began to walk away from their homes, although they could still afford to pay their mortgages. Default rates skyrocketed, making housing prices plummet.

The investment bankers who had been selling CDOs found they were now worthless. Investors refused to buy, and the banks could not sell the bonds, which had originally been purchased with borrowed money. The financial system froze. [262]

Mortgage brokers, the lending institutions, and the bankers made billions of dollars at the expense of the investors and the insurance companies. However, the Wall Street banks did not have enough money to continue with regular business. The whole system had been corrupted.

This is how the Wall Street banks drove the global financial system to its biggest crisis since the Great Depression. Surely, any reasonable person would have seen that this scheme would end with a catastrophe when the market reached a saturation point for prime mortgages. However, they must have been sure it would not hurt them. And they were right. The government did not put one single Wall Street banker on trial for this crime. They also still had the power to "persuade" the government not to reenact the *Glass-Steagall Act*.

The banking system

The U.S. Federal Reserve

> *Once a nation parts with the control of its currency and credit, it matters not who makes the nation's laws. Usury, once in control, will wreck any nation. Until the control of the issue of currency and credit is restored to government and recognized as its most sacred responsibility, all talk of the sovereignty of parliament and of democracy is idle and futile.*
> *~ William Lyon Mackenzie King, former Prime Minister of Canada ~*

The Federal Reserve System was created on Dec. 23, 1913, under the *Federal Reserve Act*. The Federal Reserve is not owned by the U.S. government. It is owned by private banks and generates profits for its shareholders. The president has no authority over it beyond appointing the Board of the Governors.

The original objectives of the Federal Reserve (known as the Fed) were to establish monetary policy for maximum employment and stable prices, and to moderate long-term interest rates. Its duties today are to set the nation's monetary policy, supervise and regulate banking institutions, and maintain the stability of the financial system, as well as to provide financial services to depository institutions such as banks, the U.S. government, and foreign official institutions.

The Federal Reserve comprises 12 Federal Reserve Banks (FRB), each responsible for its own district. Under the 1913 Act, each regional FRB has its own board of directors of nine people, divided into three "classes."

- Class A directors, elected by banks to represent banks;
- Class B directors, elected by banks to represent the public; and
- Class C directors, appointed by the board of governors to represent the public

In this system, bankers, particularly those based on Wall Street, are over-represented on boards, decreasing the Fed's credibility and creating a conflict of interest. The Hon. Louis McFadden, Chairman of the House Banking and Currency Committee in the 1930s, put it this way: "Some people think that the Federal Reserve Banks are U.S. Government institutions. They are private monopolies which prey upon the people of these U.S. for the benefit of themselves and their foreign customers, foreign and domestic speculators and swindlers, and rich and predatory money lenders." [263]

On June 12, 2012, in the aftermath of the 2008 financial collapse, Sen. Bernie Sanders made the records of the Government Accountability Office available to the public for the first time. The records indicate that more than $4 trillion in near zero-interest Federal Reserve loans and other financial assistance went to the banks and businesses of at least 18 current and former Federal Reserve regional bank directors. "This report reveals the inherent conflict of interest that exists at the Federal Reserve. At a time when small businesses could not get affordable loans to create jobs, the Fed was providing trillions in secret loans to some of the largest banks and corporations in America that were well represented on the boards of the Federal Reserve Banks. These conflicts must end," Sanders said. [264]

Sanders gave a few examples about the conflicts of interest between the Fed and its board members, including Jamie Dimon of J.P. Morgan Chase, Stephen Friedman of Goldman Sachs and Jeffrey Immelt of General Electric. While Dimon was a member of the board, his bank received some $391 billion of the $4 trillion in emergency Fed funds and served as a clearing house for emergency lending programs. In March of 2008, the Fed provided J.P. Morgan Chase with $29 billion in financing to acquire Bear Stearns. Dimon also got the Fed to provide J.P. Morgan Chase with an 18-month exemption from risk-based leverage and capital requirements. He also convinced the Fed to take risky mortgage-related assets off Bear Stearns' balance sheet before J.P. Morgan Chase acquired the troubled investment bank.

"Another high-profile conflict involved Stephen Friedman, the former Chairman of the New York Fed's board of directors," said Sanders. "In 2008, the New York Fed approved an application from Goldman Sachs to become a bank holding company, giving it access to cheap loans from the Federal Reserve. During that period, Friedman sat on the Goldman Sachs board. He also owned Goldman stock, something that was prohibited by the Federal Reserve's conflict of interest regulations. Although it was not publicly disclosed at the time, Friedman received a waiver from the Fed's conflict of interest rules in late 2008. Unbeknownst to the Fed, Friedman continued to purchase shares in Goldman from November 2008 through January 2009." [266]

"In another case, Jeffrey Immelt, CEO of General Electric, was a New York Fed board member at the same time that GE helped create a commercial paper funding facility during the financial crisis. Later, the Fed provided $16 billion in financing to GE under this emergency lending program." [266]

The Federal Reserve Bank of New York is one of the bodies designed to act as a watchdog. Interestingly, while Dimon sits on the board of directors, Ann Darby, the wife of New York Fed president William Dudley, who used to work at J.P. Morgan Chase, is still getting "deferred-income" checks for the work she did there in the amount of $190,000 a year. This income will not cease until 2021. Alexander Eichler of the *Huffington Post* said: "The fact that Darby gets regular checks from J.P. Morgan Chase while her husband presides over a major financial regulator underscores the trouble with regulating complex and interwoven financial institutions." [265]

On May 22, 2012, Sanders introduced legislation to prohibit banking industry and business executives from serving as directors of the 12 Federal Reserve regional banks. [266,267]

Members of the Federal Reserve Boards will always be in favor of policies or decisions that serve the interests of their private banks. For example, Alan Greenspan acted in favor of the financial sector's interests, at the expense of the American people, when he supported deregulation of the financial system and repeal of *Glass-Steagall Act*.

In an article in the *New York Times*, economics reporter and author of *Busted: Life Inside the Great Mortgage Meltdown*, Edmund L. Andrews stated: "Critics, including many economists, now blame the former Fed chairman for the financial crisis that is tipping the economy into a potentially deep recession. Mr. Greenspan's critics say that he encouraged the bubble in housing prices by keeping interest rates too low for too long and that he failed to rein in the explosive growth of risky and often fraudulent mortgage lending." [268]

Although the Fed's board members are appointed by the president and confirmed by Congress, it is independent, as it says on its website: "its decisions do not have to be ratified by the President or anyone else in the executive or legislative branch of government." [269]

In the past century, the Federal Reserve has failed the American people. The economy has gone through 18 recessions and three deep financial crises, including the 1929 Great Depression, the Savings and Loan crises, and the 2008 Great Recession. [270]

Wall Street banks

Wall Street banks became Too Big to Fail (TBTF) because their failure could threaten the solvency of other institutions that rely upon them and their creditors to fulfill their obligations, creating a domino effect that can cripple the national economy. Consequently, during the 2008 economic crisis, the government had to bail out these banks to prevent an economic catastrophe. This government insurance of bailing out TBTF banks combined with deregulation of the financial sector created a moral hazard in which a bank tends to take undue risks because the costs are not borne by it. If it loses, it will be bailed out. At the same time, bank creditors of wealthy investors, have little incentive to monitor the bank's behavior because their money in these banks is insured by the government. [271a]

The most significant change undertaken to reduce the moral hazard problem was the *1991 Federal Deposit Insurance Corporation Improvement Act* (FDICIA). The act improved the supervision and regulation of banks and formally limited the Federal Reserve's ability to make loans to faltering banks to keep them afloat. However, Gary H. Stern, president of the Bank of Minneapolis Fed, and his vice-president, Ron J. Feldman state that in reality the FDICIA has done little to change existing policy towards the big banks. [271]

Stern and Feldman recommend that policymakers use stress testing and contingency planning to identify the likely effects of a major bank's failure on the economy. In addition, the government would close faltering banks before they can impose large losses on their creditors, require deposit coinsurance, and alter existing payment systems to limit the amount that banks owe each other throughout the system. Others, such as Alan Greenspan, suggested in 2012 that if a bank is too big to fail, then it should be broken up. [272]

After the 2008 economic collapse, the U.S. government used hundreds of billions of dollars to bail out the big banks rather than purchasing them to prevent future failures. Since then, the big banks have grown even bigger. By the end of 2011, the five big banks (J.P. Morgan Chase, Bank of America, Citigroup, Wells Fargo, and Goldman Sachs) held more than $8.5 trillion in assets, equal to 56 percent of the U.S. economy. [273]

Being one of the big five offers a huge advantage. In July 2012, Brendan Greeley of *Business Week* reported that major banks receive an unfair subsidy. [273] Greeley noted that, between 2007 and 2010, these banks cost taxpayers a combined $120 billion in lower borrowing costs. Citigroup, Bank of America, J.P. Morgan Chase, Wells Fargo, and AIG saved $53 billion, $32 billion, $10 billion, $8 billion, and $4 billion, respectively. Borrowing–cost savings, according to Greely, may make the banks more inclined to take high-risk projects because they can use these extra profits to make even more money. Another cost to the taxpayer, according to Greeley, is that the implicit guarantee of a bailout makes government bonds slightly riskier and therefore raises borrowing costs.

Interest rate, which is currently hovering around zero, significantly benefits the banks, but hurts pensioners, both in their income and their capital, because net interest rate on their savings is negative (interest rate is lower than inflation). In addition, devalued U.S. dollar, decreased the purchasing power of ordinary Americans, and increased the cost of living.

Bank lobbyists claim that setting the rate close to zero improves the economy, but Professor Joseph Stiglitz of Columbia University, the Noble Laureate economist disagrees. He suggests that low interest rates have repercussions worldwide, "including currency misalignment." "The risks of an asset price bubble due to "the flood of liquidity is going abroad and causing problems all over the world," Stiglitz says. [274]

The stock market after the financial crisis

As we have seen, several factors contributed to the global financial crisis. These included deregulation, derivatives, TBTF banks, and a lack of transparency in the financial market. Despite the 2008 crippling crisis, Wall Street bankers are still using the same products that caused the financial crisis and are lobbying to hinder regulation of the industry.

Obama's new regulations are not sufficient to prevent another crisis. Sales of derivatives, which were at the root of the economic crisis, have increased significantly since 2008, and the financial markets, which were expected to be more transparent, have become even murkier—especially for the small investor. Stock trading in the U.S. used to be done on public exchanges regulated by the Securities Exchange Commission (SEC). Today, numerous trades are executed off public exchanges, and are not subject to SEC regulations or taxed. These trades account for 32 percent of the shares trading on NASDAQ and the New York Stock Exchanges (NYSE), where derivative trading now accounts for 29 percent of its net revenue. [275]

The increasing number of trades being executed "off exchange" is done at wholesale brokerages or at private-trading venues known as "dark pools." These pools include Crossfinder of Credit Suisse and Sigma X of Goldman Sachs, the largest among 40 such pools in the U.S.[275] Dark-pool trading is virtually unregulated and allows traders to avoid paying taxes, whereas public exchanges must file extensive data on trading activity to the SEC. Since 2008, dark-pool trading has more than tripled, increasing from four percent to 14 percent by the end of 2011. [275]

Recommendations

How to restore the health of U.S. financial market

The financial crisis was a Ponzi scheme developed by Wall Street banks to enrich their executives and owners. When Bernard Madoff ran his Ponzi scheme that cost investors $50 billion, he was sentenced to 150 years in jail. But when Wall Street bankers caused the worst financial crisis through fraudulent investments that crippled the global economy and cost the world economy trillions of dollars, nobody was held responsible. In fact, the Obama administration bailed out these banks and allowed them to continue business as usual. Bankers who gained billions of dollars in compensations and bonuses and caused the crisis were allowed to continue on the job and even claim that, without them, the banks would never be able to recover.

Several measures can be taken to restore the health of the financial market including:

- Tax capital gains and dividends at the taxpayers' marginal tax rate.
- Put a limit on the ratio of compensation of executives to that of the average employee of the company.
- Return the financial markets back to their original purpose—investing. Ban speculative financial instruments such as short selling, commodity futures, and other derivatives.
- Increase the government's ability and resources to oversee financial markets.
- Force the banking system to play its role in economic development.
- Create tax rules to stop speculation in the stock market, such as a "Robin Hood tax" on stock market transactions to discourage parasitic behavior of Wall Street bankers and hedge funds, and make the financial markets a level playing field for all (see p. 201).
- Restore the Glass-Steagall Act

   Deregulation helped Wall Street banks introduce unregulated derivatives, based on the advice of Alan Greenspan. The U.S. must put an end to Wall Street's murky operations, which allow bankers to accumulate billions of dollars for themselves, increase risk to the investors and could well bring on another crisis.

- Break up Wall Street banks into smaller commercial and investment banks to prevent them from becoming "too big to fail."

   Richard Fisher, Dallas Federal Reserve Board President, has advocated breaking up the top five U.S. banks because of his concern about their risk management, size, and scope. [276]

Bank profits

The relationship between banks and their depositors is a win-lose transaction. Although banks use their clients' deposits to run their business, the profits are kept by the bank, of course, and the depositors end up, after paying the bank fees, with less money in their bank account.

Banks and their depositors need a new relationship based on sharing their profits, rather than interest. Commercial banks provide deposit and savings accounts, money market accounts and term deposits. They are extremely profitable organizations and make their profits by using other people's money.

A U.S. commercial bank uses its depositors' money to borrow from the Federal Reserve up to 10 times the value of its deposits at close to a zero interest rate, and then lends it to borrowers at a much higher interest rate. The profits go to the bank and a very meager part, if any, is given to the depositors.

Banks should lend money to borrowers based on profit sharing. That way, the bank would not lend its money at a fixed interest rate; instead, it would become a financial partner with borrowers' projects. The profits would then be divided among the depositor, the bank, and the borrower, each according to their contribution to the project. This model would force the bank to be more selective in its lending practices and ensure due diligence in using depositors' money.

This system has several advantages over the fixed interest rate system.

- Profits are shared fairly among the depositors, the bank, and the borrower.
- The bank would have to perform a serious feasibility study to ensure that the project's risk-reward ratio is acceptable, and pick only the most profitable projects.
- The bank would have to hire more technical people to evaluate feasibility studies and deal with bank's joint projects.
- Depositors would get better returns on their deposits if returns were based on the profitability of the bank projects.

- All parties would share the risks and rewards equally.
- Competition between banks, based on the net return offered on deposits, would increase.

White-collar criminals

The U.S. needs tougher laws to deter corporate executives who make risky decisions to take advantage of investors. When an executive commits a crime and his company is fined "without admitting guilt," this encourages criminal acts, and does not make the perpetrators criminally responsible. In addition, when a company pays a penalty for mistakes made by its executives, investors are punished twice, once for the executive's mistake and a second time when they pay to mitigate that mistake. The financial penalty should be paid by the executives who made the mistake, and they should be tried in court, like anybody else who commits such a crime.

Politicians

A course should be offered to elected officials to educate them about the history of the U.S., with a focus on decisions made by politicians in the past century. Advisors should be available to help politicians identify relevant historical events and their outcomes. In cases of repeating a wrong decision, the politician should be held accountable, and be subject to recall by their constituents.

Derivatives, short selling, and commodity futures

Derivatives, short selling, speculation on commodity futures, short term trading and high-frequency trading with super-fast computers are harmful, parasitic practices. They increase market volatility, increase cost for small investors, decrease confidence in the financial markets, and add no value to the economy.

Regulations must be introduced to restore the integrity and fairness of financial markets, and put an end to Wall Street's most harmful practices. To restore trust in the market so that investors will continue to put their hard-earned money into stocks and bonds, regulations must be enacted to stop derivatives, short selling, and speculation in commodity futures.

Profit margin in high frequency trading may amount to a few cents per stock. A transaction tax or so-called "Robin Hood tax" at, just 0.5 percent could be imposed on stock trading in order to discourage Wall Street from predatory practices by making the profit from trading too difficult to warrant the risk. The tax could be used to provide funding for the SEC to increase its effectiveness in overseeing the financial markets. In addition, "off exchange" trades done at wholesale brokerages or at private-trading "dark pools" should be prohibited to provide a level playing field for the investors and the brokerages.

Derivatives

Derivatives have helped cause the collapse of global markets, which may take decades to recover. After the crisis, the U.S. government did not make enough regulatory changes to prevent the 2008 crisis from recurring. The financial markets must return to their main goal, investing, and those speculative tools that turn financial markets into casinos should be outlawed.

Short selling

Short selling should be banned. It is speculative, manipulative and unethical, as well as predatory. It increases market volatility, hurts small investors whose shares have been borrowed, and undermines the broad objectives of financial markets.

Commodity futures

People who trade in a commodity should own a licensed business and physical facilities with the intention of accepting deliveries of the commodities they trade in. For example, future traders of gasoline should own a business that supplies gas stations or distributes gas to its clients. Traders should be required to show that they own a legitimate wholesale or retail business to bid on the price, and they are not just speculating to raise the price of gas for their own benefit.

Federal Reserve

The Federal Reserve is a private bank that decides the future of the economy of the U.S. Federal Reserve board has a private monopoly that holds so much power over the future of the U.S. As James A Garfield, 20th president of the U.S. said: "Whoever controls the volume of money in our country is absolute master of all industry and commerce. When you realize that the entire system is very easily controlled, one way or another, by a few powerful men at the top, you will not have to be told how periods of inflation and depression originate."

Democratically elected officials, without interference from private banks, should control monetary policies; otherwise, the severe, erratic economic cycles that have been so noticeable in the past three decades will continue. The Federal Reserve should be owned and operated by the American people. The U.S. government should take over the role of the Federal Reserve, which should be turned into a public bank. As Abraham Lincoln pointed out, "The U.S. government should create, issue, and circulate all the currency and credit needed to satisfy the spending power of the government and the buying power of consumers .... The privilege of creating and issuing money is not only the supreme prerogative of Government, but it is the Government's greatest creative opportunity. By the adoption of these principles, the long-felt want for a uniform medium will be satisfied. The taxpayers will be saved immense sums of interest, discounts, and exchanges. The financing of all public enterprises, the maintenance of stable government and ordered progress, and the conduct of the Treasury will become matters of practical administration. The people can and will be furnished with a currency as safe as their own government. Money will cease to be the master and become the servant of humanity. Democracy will rise superior to the money power."

The idea of having public banks, which work for the public interests and owned by the people through their representative government is not new. An example of a public bank is the Bank of North Dakota. It was established by the state legislature in 1919. It is overseen by the state Industrial Commission, which consists of the Governor, the Attorney General, and the Commissioner of Agriculture. All bank deposits are guaranteed by the State. Its primary deposit base is the State funds, State institutions, and private citizens. [277]

The Federal Reserve profits will be returned to the public purse and be used to lower taxes and provide public services. It will not pay interest on government projects lowering the cost by 50 percent. It will be able to decrease the volatility in the stock market and assure the long-term prosperity of the nation. [278]

Chapter 9

Income inequality

Remove the secondary causes that have produced the great convulsions of the world and you will almost always find the principle of inequality at the bottom. Either the poor have attempted to plunder the rich, or the rich to enslave the poor. If, then, a state of society can ever be founded in which every man shall have something to keep and little to take from others, much will have been done for the peace of the world.
~ Alexis de Tocqueville, Democracy in America ~

This chapter discusses the impact of excessive executive compensation, globalization, and offshore tax havens on the widening inequality gap. Inequality breeds instability, and almost all revolutions have been triggered by income inequality. Revolutions occur when the inequality gap widens and the number of people who suffer from it reaches a tipping point. In the U.S., years of grooming the population for aggression may backfire if democratic processes and equality are not restored.

Some politicians advocate that wealth trickles down by cutting taxes for the wealthy, claiming that this would revive the economy, enhance growth, and increase job opportunities. In reality, only corruption and moral degradation trickle down.

With globalization and the availability of tax havens, inequality has been increasing. In the past four decades, the wage gap has widened and income inequality has increased, not only in the U.S. but also in a majority of the countries that belong to the Organization for Economic Cooperation and Development (OECD). What happens in the U.S. resonates in other parts of the world because the U.S.

economic model has been adopted by the developed world and some of the emerging market countries.

In 2011, the OECD prepared a report titled, *An Overview of Growing Income Inequalities in OECD Countries,* [279] which analyzed the major underlying forces behind the development of inequality. Secretary-General Angel Gurría warned of the need for governments to tackle it:

"Growing inequality is divisive. It polarizes societies, it divides regions within countries, and it carves up the world between rich and poor. Greater income inequality stifles upward mobility between generations, making it harder for talented and hard-working people to get the rewards they deserve. Ignoring increasing inequality is not an option."

The report pointed out that a key driver of income inequality has been the increasing number of low-skilled and poorly educated people who cannot find work, as well as those who live alone or in single-parent households. It also pointed to the increase in child poverty (Children living in a household with less than half the nation's median income).

"Children and young adults are now 25 percent more likely to be poorer than the population as a whole. Single-parent households are three times more likely to be poorer than the population average." [279]

Conservative governments are keen on decreasing taxes and spending less on social benefits, but this widens the inequality gap. As Gurría explains:

"Although the role of the tax and benefit system in redistributing incomes and in curbing poverty remains important in many OECD countries, our data confirm that its effectiveness has gone down in the past 10 years. Trying to patch the gaps in income distribution solely through more social spending is like treating the symptoms instead of the disease. The largest part of the increase in inequality comes from changes in the labour markets. This is where governments must act. Low-skilled workers are having ever-greater problems in finding jobs. Increasing employment is the best way of reducing poverty."

As the report indicates, affordable education is a powerful tool for economic growth that benefits all. Coupled with a government strategic plan, education helps to create high paying jobs to boost middle-class income.

In the past two decades, the U.S. has suffered from two stock market bubbles followed by two crashes, as well as a series of crises in housing and energy. During these market upheavals, Wall Street banks, hedge fund managers, and institutional investors made billions of dollars at the expense of small investors.

The 2008 economic crisis has been devastating for millions of people. According to the U.S. Census Bureau, the median household income in 2010 was equal to that of 1989 and declined by 7.1 percent below the median household income peak of 1999. [280]

U.S. government policies that favor the wealthy are the prime reason for inequality. Nobel laureate economist Joseph Stiglitz described the U.S. government as being "of the one percent, by the one percent, for the one percent." [281]

"In 1974, the top 0.1 percent of American families earned 2.7 percent of all income in the country," writes Eric Alterman at the Centre for American Progress. [282] "By 2007, this same tiny slice of the population had increased its holdings to fully 12.3 percent—roughly five times greater than it had enjoyed just three decades earlier. Half the U.S. population owns barely two percent of its wealth, putting the U.S. near Rwanda and Uganda and below such nations as pre-Arab Spring Tunisia and Egypt when measured by degrees of income inequality," he added. [282]

In an interview on Bill Moyers' program, Moyers and Company, on February 10, 2012, Bruce Bartlett indicated that "between 1979 and 2007, 36 percent of all income growth (post-tax) accrued to the upper one percent. But in just five years, between 2002 and 2007, 66 percent of the growth went to the top one percent, with the vast bulk of the gains made by the top 0.1 percent. During the same period, inequality within the remaining 99 percent has not changed. [283] However, taxes have been decreasing for the wealthy over the past five decades, from a marginal tax of 91 percent in 1964 to 35 percent in 2003." [283]

According to Tomas Piketty and Emmanuel Saez, the U.S. federal tax system has undergone three changes, making the federal tax system less progressive. In 1960s, the marginal tax rate was 91 percent. It was decreased to 28 percent by 1988, increased significantly to 39.6 percent in 1993, and fell to 35 percent as of 2003. President Ronald Reagan's 1981 cut in the top regular tax rate reduced the maximum capital gains rate to only 20%—its lowest level since the Hoover administration. [284] On the other hand, corporate taxes have decreased from four percent of the GDP in early 1960s to less than 2 percent of GDP in the early 2000s.

Sabrina Tavernise reports in *The New York Times* that, according to "2010 Census Bureau statistics, the number of Americans living below the official poverty line reached 46.2 million. This was the highest number in the past 52 years." In 2010, more than one in five American children was living in poverty, amounting to 16.4 million, and the number has been rising. In 2012, the number of people under the poverty line increased to 47.8 million. [107] On the other hand, by the end of 2010, corporate profits had risen by 61.5 percent from the low reached in the fourth quarter of 2008—the highest jump since 1947. [285] But the share going to workers' wages dropped to its lowest level for the first time, below 50 percent of national income. This discrepancy is due to the policy of corporations to increase executive compensation, while keeping workers' wages stagnant despite an increase in profits, causing the inequality gap to widen. [286]

History of inequality

Income distribution between the top one percent and the remaining 99 percent has varied widely between 1913 and 2008, but there was a correlation between inequality and economic crises. [287] Clearly, as equality increased, the majority prospered and the economy grew. Sir Anthony Atkinson of the London School of Economics, Professor Thomas Piketty of the Paris School of Economics, and Professor Emmanuel Saez of the University of California, Berkeley [288] indicate that inequality prior to the Great Depression (1917 to 1929) followed the same pattern as that prior to the 2008 financial crisis (from 1994 to 2007). During these two periods, the income of the top 10 percent increased from around 40 percent to about 50 percent of the total income in the U.S. Similarly, the income of the 1 percent followed the same pattern. Prior to the Great Depression and the 2008 Great Recession, inequality peaked and the income of the top one percent reached more than 23.5 percent. Following the Great Depression, it took 14 years for the economy to recover, when the income of the top 10 percent decreased to about 33 percent of the total income. [287]

Franklin Roosevelt's New Deal improved equality and the top one percent's income continued to decrease relative to the 99 percent. By 1978, it had reached a low of 8.9 percent. However, Ronald Reagan initiated the Great Regression, which refers to the trend of the reversal of gains made in wages, pensions, unemployment insurance, and welfare benefits in the U.S. since 1981. He rolled back the gains won by the New Deal and adopted the policies that prevailed prior to and caused the Great Depression. Since the beginning of Reagan's presidency, the gap between the rich and poor continued to widen and the top one percent's share of total income continued to increase, reaching a peak of 23.5 percent in 2007, and triggering the 2008 Great Recession.

Between 1942 and 1982, the New Deal stabilized the income of the top 10 percent earners at below 35 percent of the total income. Reagan's economic policies increased the share of the top 10 percent earners, reaching its peak of 50 percent in 2007.

The economic recovery in 2010 only benefited the wealthiest one percent, who captured 93 percent of the gains. Their income grew by 11.6 percent. In dollar value, the income of the top one percent increased by $104,637, while the bottom 99 percent saw an increase of only $80. [288]

Growing inequality has severed the link between the economy's overall growth and its benefits in reducing poverty. Anthony Atkinson *et al.* [289] reported that if the relationship between overall GDP growth and poverty that prevailed between 1948 and 1982 had continued, poverty would have been eradicated by the late 1980s. Instead, economic growth was not shared broadly after 1982 due to outsourcing and government policies, which reversed the gains achieved by the New Deal.

Executive compensation packages

Executive compensation packages typically include a base salary, and bonuses and incentives such as stocks and stock options, based on the increase of the share price in the stock market. As a result, executives are keen on taking any measures to increase the stock price because their compensation increases in value as the stock price rises. However, market forces beyond the control of executives determine the stock price increase and may not be a reflection of executive performance, which is demonstrated in innovations, and increase in productivity, sales, and profitability.

Some companies have established a stock buy-back program to work in association with stock options granted to the senior executives. Investment bankers developed the buy-back program so that corporations could buy back their own stocks after executives sold their stock options.

This compensation structure is designed to benefit both the executives and the investment banks at the expense of the shareholders. Executives prefer stock options because of the preferential treatment of stocks and stock options in income tax.

The investment bankers benefit from this compensation structure because it increases their revenues of consulting fees for preparing the buyback program and commissions for purchasing the corporate securities from the stock market. However, the program works against the interest of the investor for several reasons:

- It adds cost to set up the buyback program.
- It distracts the company executives from doing their job—paying attention to increasing the productivity of the company and its profits, instead of focusing on watching the stock market and orienting their activities to influence the stock price.
- When the stock price rises, the executives sell their stock options. Then, the corporation usually repurchases its stocks at a high price and tends to raise funds for investment in its operations when the price is low leading to dilution of the profits and lowering the value for the investors.

The sale of stock options increases the number of a company's shares in the stock market. Consequently, the company earnings per share are diluted. For example, if the company has 100 million shares and issued new 10 million shares (in stock options), its profit per share is diluted (the total profits divided by 110 million instead of 100 million shares). The company buys back these stocks to keep the overall share count stable. Consequently, the price of the stock becomes artificially high and the earnings per share inflate, leading to an increase of the stock price. The new increase in the stock price rewards the executives even more.

Such remuneration structures make it appear as if the CEO is the one who makes the company profitable. This cannot be further from the truth. For the corporation to be profitable, it takes the efforts and collaboration of everyone in the organization, from the janitors to the CEO.

Contrary to the common belief, executives are well compensated whether their companies do well, underperform, or even go bankrupt. This was demonstrated in the case of Jon Corzine of MF Global Holdings and other Wall Street bank executives, [242] Brian Moynihan, Bank of America CEO, and Goldman Sachs CEO Lloyd Blankfein, Wells Fargo CEO John Stumpf, [243] and Citigroup CEO Vikram Pandit (see p. 153). [244]

Effect of executive compensation on inequality

A major cause of inequality is executives' net income, represented in both the disparity between executive compensation and their preferential treatment in taxes over that of ordinary working people. In 1965, CEOs' total direct compensation was 24 times that of an average worker. In 14 years (1965 to 1979), executive compensation increased by 44 percent, but during the eight years of Ronald Reagan's presidency, this ratio increased drastically by 100 percent, and continued to rise exponentially. The ratio peaked in 2000 to 298.5, but decreased slightly in 2002, when the technology bubble burst. However, the ratio has since then resumed its rise to reach a peak of 277.3 times in 2007. It then decreased to 185.3 in 2009, but resumed its rise in 2010. According to Roger Lowenstein of the Bloomberg *Businessweek,* "the average pay of the highest paid 50 CEOs had skyrocketed to 255 times the pay of the average worker."[290]

By 2011, CEO compensation bounced back to 380 times that of the average worker. That year, the average CEO pay in Standard & Poor 500 companies rose to $12.94 million. This average increased by 13.9 percent in 2011, following a 22.8 percent increase in 2010. On the other hand, average workers' income in 2011, increased just 2.8 percent to $34,053. [291] At this rate, the inequality gap will continue to widen. [292] The poor will get poorer and the rich will get richer with very slim possibility for talented people to move up the income scale.

Globalization, free markets, and American jobs

Labor costs represent a significant portion of the cost of products and services. Since the mid-1970s, workers have increased their productivity that reached a ceiling beyond which corporate management could not squeeze any more money from employees. Consequently, the corporations considered outsourcing jobs overseas, where cheap skilled labor was abundant. If corporations could get work done by workers for a wage of just two dollars a day, why would they pay $30 per hour for U.S. workers? The threat of losing their jobs to overseas helped to keep wages of North American workers stagnant. Gradually moving the manufacturing operations overseas, loss of high-paying jobs of American workers became more pronounced.

The Reagan administration economic policies promoted outsourcing because it increased corporate profits. At the same time, it kept the labor unions under control by the threat of more outsourcing. In the 1970s, when a company outsourced part or all of its products or services overseas, it did not significantly affect the economy because only a small number of companies followed that practice. However, when outsourcing reached the tipping point, the practice began to affect the economy and U.S. tax revenues. Consequently, both the U.S. government and the Americans are unable to pay their accumulated debts.

Because of globalization, multinationals enabled China to conquer the West without a single bullet. Today, we are all dependent on Chinese products. The wealth transferred to China has been returning to buy American resources and control our major metropolitan areas, and the economy.

Globalization combined with progress in technology created a huge international skilled labor force with very low wage expectations and opened global markets for corporate products or services. Consequently, the profits of American multinational corporations skyrocketed and so did executive remuneration. For example, Apple paid Tim Cook, in his first year as CEO, a package worth $378 million. This amounts to $189,000 per hour. Assuming that Cook, as a human being, spends 20 minutes in the washroom each working day, this trip costs shareholders $14.3 million per year.

These exorbitant compensation packages come from the exploitation of the people by underpaying the workers and overcharging the customers, under the watch of the U.S. government. Apple products are made by Foxconn Technology Group, a Chinese manufacturer whose employees live in congested company barracks, work under unsafe conditions, and earn less than $17 a day. [293] Although its workers are overworked and underpaid, Apple products are extremely overpriced and their high profit margin is unprecedented.

Inequality and the wealthy tax evasion

Why are governments at all levels unable to provide the services they used to offer without increasing taxes? This section presents answers to this question and explains that most government debt results from tax evasion at offshore tax havens, which facilitate under-regulated, cross-border lending, as well as hedge funds and insurance operations.

Tax havens contributed significantly to inequality, aggravated the financial crisis, hindered the recovery of world economy, and divided the world community into two groups. The first is for the wealthy elite who are above the law, and another for the rest of us, who must abide by the law or face severe consequences.

"Secrecy at tax havens undermines law and order and forces average citizens to pay higher taxes to make up for revenues that vanish offshore," report Gerard Ryle, Marina Walker Guevara, Michael Hudson, Nicky Hager, Duncan Campbell, and Stefan Candea of The International Consortium of Investigative Journalists (ICIJ). They indicate that the Greek fiscal disaster and the banking meltdown in Cyprus were attributed to tax havens. In the ICIJ's 15-month investigation, they found that, "[offshore tax havens] allow fraud, tax dodging and political corruption to thrive," they add.[294] It is estimated that, "cross-border flows of global proceeds of financial crimes total between $1 trillion and $1.6 trillion a year."

James S. Henry, former chief economist at McKinsey & Company, is currently a member of the board of directors of the Tax Justice Network (TJN). The Network maps, analyzes, and explains the role of taxation and the harmful impacts of tax evasion, tax avoidance, tax competition and tax havens, with the objective of encouraging reform of laws at the global and national levels. [295] Henry describes in his report, *The Price of Offshore Revisited* [296] that trillions of dollars worldwide have been hidden by a relatively few individuals (0.001 percent of the world population), who evade taxes in the countries where the wealth is generated. In his rigorous and comprehensive research, Henry has uncovered a well-hidden sector of the global economy and estimates the wealth accumulated offshore to range from $21 trillion to $32 trillion, invested virtually tax-free in the world's quickly expanding black hole of more than 80 secret offshore jurisdictions. His estimate does not account for the real estate, yachts, racehorses, physical gold, and many other properties that count as non-financial wealth.

These offshore fortunes are owned through complex structures designed to ensure that the wealthy remain anonymous. For example, a bank account may be located inside Switzerland's borders but owned by an anonymous offshore company owned by a trust in another jurisdiction, whose trustees live in still other jurisdictions. This makes it almost impossible to identify the owners.

The owners of these accounts use a tiny portion of their money to control global politics through campaign funding and other illegal and immoral activities to pay off authorities. Ironically, they invest in the big five banks, thought to be "too big to fail," which were bailed out by hundreds of billions of dollars of the taxpayers' money at the expense of small investors who have lost more than 43 percent of net assets since the 2008 financial crisis.

According to Henry, "In 2010, the wealthy elite accumulated $7.3 to $9.3 trillion of unrecorded offshore wealth. At the same time, many of their countries of origin were borrowing themselves into bankruptcy, enduring agonizing austerities and netted an aggregate gross external debt of $4.08 trillion." [296] In fact, "These indebted source countries, including all developing countries, are not really debtors—they are net lenders to the tune of $10.1 to $13.1 trillion," he adds. The problem is that a small number of wealthy individuals send the assets of these countries to offshore havens, while the nations' debts are shouldered by the people of these countries.

The missing fortunes

Economists interested in studying inequality usually review data regarding individual income, but do not check the cumulative income and total assets of members of a society. For those who earn a very high income, net assets in the long term will be proportionate to the cumulative value of that income. However, studies show that the assets of the top one percent of the population were much lower than their cumulative income. Sam Pizzigati, associate Fellow at the Institute for Policy Studies (IPS) in Washington, DC, and editor of the *IPS* newsletter on inequality, titled *Too Much*, [297] notes: "There is a huge paradox in the data—a disconnect between the data on income inequality and the data on wealth inequality."

Although the income data indicate a huge disparity between the top one percent and 0.1 percent and everyone else, the wealth data show no great growth in the wealth of the top earners. Apparently, the income of the rich has not been accumulating in their declared net assets. Does it go underground in offshore secrecy? Several researchers suggest so.

Professor Thomas Piketty of the Paris School of Economics and Professor Emmanuel Saez of the University of California, Berkeley, have shown that the income of the top one percent of the U.S. population more than doubled from 1980 to 2010 (2.4 times), while that of the top 0.1 percent trebled (3.3 times) and that of the top 0.01 percent quadrupled (4.3 times). [298] Comparing wealth data shows a completely different picture from income data. According to Sylvia Allegretto, co-chair of the Center on Wage and Employment Dynamics of the University of California, Berkeley, the top one percent of households owned 33.8 percent of all wealth in 1983, while 26 years later, in 2009, the top one percent owned 35.6 percent, a tiny increase. Pizzigati concludes that the increase in incomes has to go somewhere and suggests that missing fortunes are likely to be stashed offshore in tax havens. [298]

What are offshore tax havens?

You may think that "offshore" refers to a geographic location of private assets. Not so, it is a secretive, intricate investment system, specializes in tax evasion for the wealthy as well as money laundering of proceeds from illegal activities. In this system, multi-jurisdictional networks of legal and quasi-legal entities manage and control the wealth of world's wealthiest individuals and corporations to avoid paying taxes, and keep the owners anonymous. The owners are indifferent to the interests of working people and national interests.

There are about 80 front-line offshore and offshore havens. The offshore havens include Bermuda, the Cayman Islands, Nauru, St. Kitts, Antigua and Tortola, in addition to European havens such as the Channel Islands, Monaco, Cyprus, Gibraltar and Liechtenstein. These residential havens provide secure low-tax physical residences and offer highly secure storage facilities for private collections of art, gold, jewels, classic cars, yachts and planes. Onshore tax evasion includes jurisdictions such as Delaware, Alaska, Nevada (limited liability companies), South Dakota, Switzerland, Mauritius, and the Bahamas. Onshore-offshore tax havens can be traced in Luxembourg, Hong Kong, Singapore, Jersey, the United Kingdom, Canada, and Ireland. [296]

Henry reports that "The offshore system offers residential havens to more than 60 million people, more than 3.5 million companies, thousands of shell banks and insurance companies and more than half of the world's registered commercial ships above 100 tons, as well as thousands of shell subsidiaries for the world's largest banks, accounting firms and energy, software, drug and defense companies."[296]

Who manages Offshore investments

The offshore industry is a very lucrative global industry managed by the world's largest financial institutions, as well as leading law and accounting firms. All these institutions are located in the developed world in financial capitals like New York, London, Geneva, Frankfurt, and Singapore. The offshore investments are mostly managed by the top 50 multinational banks. Some of the major players in the U.S. are Morgan Stanley, Goldman Sachs, J.P. Morgan Chase, Bank of America/Merrill Lynch, UBS, Credit Suisse, Deutsche Bank, HSBC, and Barclays. [296]

Banks in the developed world encourage the wealthy of both rich and poor countries to shelter their wealth offshore tax-free. In many cases, they lend their stashed money to the governments and banks of their own countries. In the past 26 years, the global offshore industry has more than quadrupled in size. Meanwhile, the U.S. government, and international organizations such as Bank for International Settlements, the International Monetary Fund, the World Bank, the OECD, and the G20 have ignored them. [296] Ironically, when Wall Street banks failed and their offshore clients were about to lose some money, they were saved by taxpayers' money during the 2008 - 2012 period. In effect, ordinary taxpayers have been subsidizing the world's largest banks to keep them afloat, even as they help their wealthiest clients evade taxes. These banks received hundreds of billions of dollars of bailout money. Without these subsidies, several banks would have disappeared.

Who owns tax havens' accounts

Offshore money is not limited to wealthy individuals and corporation from the developed countries. Individual account owners range from 30-year-old Chinese real estate speculators and Silicon-Valley software tycoons to Dubai oil sheiks, politicians, presidents, mineral-rich African dictators, and Mexican drug lords.

Henry [296] estimates that between 25 and 30 percent of offshore funds come from emerging market countries, such as Russia, Saudi Arabia, and other Middle Eastern oil producers; while China accounts for nearly $1.2 trillion or 13 percent. The money goes in a round-trip—is taken offshore, then returned back home as foreign investment in order to evade taxes and take advantage of tax breaks and exchange rates only available to foreigners.

Leonce Ndikumana, research director of the African Development Bank, and James Boyce, professor of economics at the University of Massachusetts, Amherst reported that, in Africa between 1970 and 2008, an estimated $944 billion in accumulated capital left 33 African countries, compared to just $177 billion in external debts, making Africa a net creditor to the world. [299] However, the assets accumulated by means of capital flight are private while the external debts are public, owed to creditors by the people of Africa through their governments. In other words, "capital is looted from African countries and ordinary people are left with the burden of the debt," Boyce and Ndikumana report. [299]

Offshore private wealth from Venezuela, Mexico and Brazil has been going on round-trips through U.S. bank deposits. Top U.S. banks play a major role in helping clients of Latin America and some Asian countries move their liquid capital to offshore accounts under the cover of shell companies and trusts. They also help them invest their wealth, manage it, and spend it. [296]

The offshore investment community never questions the sources of the client's investments. Consequently, it empowers criminals to protect the proceeds from fraud, bribery, money laundering, illegal gambling, and other illegal activities such as trafficking in drugs, arms trading, running sweatshops, endangered species trading, and other for-profit crimes. [296]

Despite their diverse backgrounds, offshore investors have many things in common:

- They share similar needs and interests from the standpoint of financial secrecy, banking services, taxes, and regulations.
- They have their own virtual country—a place with no physical boundaries that offers escape from their financial and moral responsibilities towards society.
- They are interested in weakening income and wealth taxation laws.
- They press governments for deregulation of the financial sector, open markets and globalization, and they want to get rid of restrictions on election campaign funding and political influence.

Why financial regulators allow these dubious activities to continue

The system of tax evasion is designed for America's wealthiest individuals, and corporate executives who control the elected politicians and lobby to enact laws that serve their interests. They created this secretive system which is operated by highly paid, sophisticated specialists from the world's largest private banks (led by UBS, Credit Suisse, and Goldman Sachs), law offices, and accounting firms. The investment system shelters and manages the wealth

America's wealthiest and powerful individuals, politicians, well-paid medical doctors, lawyers, dentists, mainstream banks, and major American corporations including shipping companies, insurance companies and accounting and law firms.

Governments talk about ending the offshore tax evasion, but are they serious about it? Elected representatives from both sides of the isle tend to ignore this subject as it could harm them or the wealthy they represent. Consider an elected representative who owns an offshore account, or has his or her election campaign funds paid by someone who owns such an account. Would he or she seriously want to stop this corruption? Of course not.

Amazingly, North Americans seem to accept such corruption from elected representatives. Mitt Romney was not the first to run as a presidential candidate while having an offshore account. Paul Martin was elected as a Member of Parliament, then as a Prime Minister of Canada, although Canadians knew that he had his own shipping company based in Barbados, where it was subject to a 2.5 percent tax rate based on a tax treaty with Canada. It was legal. Indeed, under the double-tax treaty, Martin's company has to pay only 2.5 percent tax to Barbados and no Canadian corporate tax. [300]

At its 2009 London summit, the G20 declared, "[We] will take action against non-cooperative jurisdictions, including tax havens. We stand ready to deploy sanctions to protect our public finances and financial systems. The era of banking secrecy is over. We note that the OECD [The Organization for Economic Co-operation and Development] has today published a list of countries assessed by the Global Forum against the international standard for exchange of tax information." [301]

The G20 did not create rules for regular, automatic exchange of information or reduce the financial flows to tax havens. Instead, they created new rules that made it practically impossible for governments to get information about those who stash their money in tax havens. [302] By July 2012, 89 countries had implemented internationally agreed tax standards and have signed more than 800 agreements on exchanging information with authorities of other countries. [303]

In 2010, the U.S. passed the *Foreign Account Tax Compliance Act*, which will be phased in by 2018. It requires foreign financial firms to identify account-holders and investors who might be American; otherwise, 30 percent income tax is withheld in the U.S. The U.S.

government has signed bilateral agreements with 50 countries in exchange for information about the foreign citizens, but it did not address the tax havens.

The U.S. model has been endorsed by the European Union and by developing countries such as India. [302] The G20 can find out the size and growth of unrecorded cross-border private wealth, which might be concentrated in a few countries including the U.S., United Kingdom, Switzerland, the Netherlands, Belgium, Luxembourg, and Germany through its major investment banks, accounting and legal services. [304]

That may not be enough. Henry uncovers the existence of a highly lucrative banking business that has not been disclosed in any bank's annual reports, treasury or Federal Reserve databases, or congressional inquiries, even though, according to Henry, "this has become the big banks' most lucrative business." [296] This is the offshore business of international private banking, whose core mission is to be reliable, secure, top-tier and "too big to fail."

During the past decade, the Tax Justice Network has been advocating for change, but the efforts did not seriously address the root of the problem. As Reuters reported on July 26, 2012, tax haven clampdown yields cash, but secrecy still thrives.

Although G20 governments declared the end of secrecy in 2009, they implicitly support the offshore industry. If they have the will to put an end to tax havens, they can do so by pursuing the organizations involved in tax-haven operations, including:

- Private bankers, haven lawyers, and accountants who hide their clients' assets and maintain their own influential lobbyists;
- Bank regulators and central banks of most individual countries that view private banks as important clients; and
- Multilateral institutions like the Bank for International Settlements (BIS), the IMF, the World Bank and the OECD, which have never required financial institutions

to report their cross-border customer liabilities, deposits and customer assets.

As of December 2010, "the top 50 global private banks alone had $12.06 trillion of private cross-border financial wealth under their management with an annual growth rate of about 16 percent since 2005. The top banks in this group grew faster than the financial industry as a whole and increased their share of assets under management from 42 percent in 2005 to more than 51 percent in 2010," Henry reports. He emphasizes that, "the debt of the developing world is due to unrecorded wealth that is now offshore in the hands of private bankers and their agents. That means the debt problem of the developing countries has really become a fair tax problem, which the developed countries have a responsibility as well as the capacity to resolve." [296]

In April 2013, ICIJ received 2.5 million files of a list of more than 120,000 offshore companies and trusts, exposing those who are evading paying taxes in more than 170 countries and territories. The tax evaders include American doctors and dentists, as well as politicians and Wall Street swindlers. The files reveal details regarding incorporation and cash transfers dates over the past 30 years. ICIJ has been collaborating with 80 journalists from 46 countries to analyze the data. Some of the reporters are from The Guardian and the BBC in the U.K., Le Monde in France, Süddeutsche Zeitung and Norddeutscher Rundfunk in Germany, The Washington Post, the Canadian Broadcasting Corporation (CBC), and 31 other media partners around the world. [294] Let us see what actions the government of the U.S. will take to identify those tax evaders and whether they will be taxed fairly.

Recommendation

Put an end to tax havens

In order to recover the economy, the world community must put an end to tax havens, ensure transparency in the financial markets, and make those who have stashed billions of dollars in offshore accounts pay their fair share of taxes retroactively. Those assets have been accumulated without paying taxes to society and should be taxed at least at 50 percent of their value.

Owners of tax haven accounts could be identified if Wall Street banks, major international financial institutions, and offshore jurisdictions change their policies to allow information to become known regarding these anonymous investors.

Ending offshore secrecy starts with onshore secrecy. The U.S. offers more than 21 percent of the global market for offshore financial services in the states of Delaware (asset protection trusts), Alaska, Nevada (limited liability companies) and South Dakota. Henry emphasizes that "These limited liability corporations and asset protection trusts offer secrecy, protection against creditors and tax advantages that rival those of the world's traditional offshore havens. The widespread use of onshore havens undermines the ability to stop offshore jurisdictions from establishing their tax havens." [296]

If wealthy individuals paid their fair share of tax, the burden on middle- and low-income people would be significantly reduced without affecting government services. Therefore, it must be made illegal for investment banks to deal with offshore investments if the names of the investors are not revealed and to permit them to be taxed in their original source of wealth. This law will also help us to win the battle against money laundering, which is a byproduct of offshore secrecy.

Second, jurisdictions and investment banks that allow the creation of trusts, corporations, and foundations established for offshore investing must be subject to economic sanctions. The same applies to jurisdictions that put up barriers to cooperation and information exchange, whether explicitly or by establishing bureaucratic barriers.

Putting an end to tax havens worldwide is of utmost importance to tackle poverty, government debt, and unpaid taxes.

Recover lost taxes from the stashed untaxed wealth

The lost tax revenue from offshore accounts is large enough to make a difference in the global economy and address the world's economic woes. Taxing the wealth in the tax havens would allow the economy to recover and governments to pay off their debts. Since assets in offshore accounts have not been taxed and assuming the owners have a marginal tax bracket of just 50 percent, members of the wealthy elite owe the rest of the world at least $10.5 to $16 trillion, which would double if their non-financial assets were taken into account.

Reform executive compensation

Executives enjoy a preferential tax that their employees do not have because most of their compensation is treated as capital gains. As a result, and according to Warren Buffett, their tax rates are much lower than that of their secretaries.

- Executive compensation should be treated as income and taxed accordingly. For clarity purposes, executives should be paid a fixed salary and bonuses should be in cash not stocks or stock options.
- Executive salaries should be capped at 24 times that of the average worker as it was in 1960s.
- Executive compensation should be based on their company's performance, not on the performance of stock in the stock market. If the corporation's performance is excellent, a performance bonus should be determined as a percentage of the corporation's profits, and be equally distributed amongst all employees, regardless of salary or position. This says to employees that the efforts of every individual are as important as the CEO's in making the corporation successful.

Chapter 10

Individual and corporate taxes

The U.S. personal tax code has undergone several changes since 1963 regarding income, capital gains, estate, and inheritance taxes. Since 1964, under President Lyndon Johnson, marginal income taxes have been reduced from 91 percent for the wealthiest Americans to 35 percent in 2003 under the Bush Administration. In addition, estate and inheritance taxes have declined steadily since the 1990s. The conservative economist Bruce Bartlett reports that, during the Reagan Administration (1986), the top tax rate was 50 percent and America's top earning one percent had an effective federal income tax rate of 33.1 percent (total federal income tax owed divided by the adjusted gross income). This fell to just 23.3 percent in 2008 when the top marginal tax rate was lowered from 50 percent to 35 percent. Had the top one percent kept paying at the 1986 rate, the federal debt today would have been some $1.7 trillion lower. [305]

Policy makers claimed that by decreasing taxes, wealth would trickle down to the poor because lower taxes for the wealthy would encourage them to expand their businesses and increase job opportunities. This assumption contradicts historical facts about taxes in the U.S. During the 1950s and early 1960s, when the top income tax bracket was over 90 percent, the economy was growing, the middle-class was prospering, and the stock market was booming. [306] In fact, lower taxes benefited the wealthy and increased inequality.

Today, the U.S. national debt is soaring while the rich are not paying their share of taxes, as we saw in Chapter 9. Despite their low tax margins, they avoid paying taxes altogether by stashing their wealth in tax havens.

George W. Bush's tax cuts have added at least $3 trillion to the debt. When Bush took office, budget projections showed a $6 trillion surplus, enough to pay off the pending $6 trillion national debt. Nevertheless, by the time Bush left office, the national debt had ballooned to over $10 trillion. Yet, tax cuts are beloved by conservatives. Grover Norquist, the champion of tax cutting, famously said he wanted to shrink the federal government "down to the size where we can drown it in the bathtub." Surely, that would mean the end of the U.S., as we know it. [305] A smaller government means no oversight of corporations and no provision of services to the poor, sick and elderly.

Between 1979 and 2007, 36 percent of all post-tax-income growth accrued to the upper one percent. However, in just five years, between 2002 and 2007, 66 percent of the growth went to the top one percent. The vast bulk of the gains made by the one percent were by the top 0.1 percent—a tiny group of people numbering in the hundreds. They have managed to acquire a huge share of the gains that the U.S. has made in terms of income and wealth. During the same period, inequality among the 99 percent has not changed. [305]

Tax revenues and GDP

The U.S. has been the world's sole superpower and largest economy with a GDP of approximately $15 trillion, or about 25 percent of world GDP. However, the economy has been deteriorating since the mid-1970s and the standard of living for the middle class and working people has been sustained only by borrowing. While President Clinton was in power, technological development and growth brought in higher tax revenues, enabling the U.S. to balance its budget. In 2001, U.S. government spending amounted to 18.2 percent of GDP. By 2009, it had risen to 24.6 percent. [307]

George W. Bush initiated a large budget deficit by increased spending to fund "The War on Terror," invading Iraq and Afghanistan, combined with tax cuts for the wealthy. The deficit accelerated under Obama when he bailed out the banks that were supposedly "too big to fail."

Transfers of technology, jobs, and manufacturing operations to China decreased the number of high paying jobs, and increased unemployment. The new jobs created are mostly in the service industry. As a result, tax revenues have decreased from a peak of 20.35 percent of GDP in 2000 to just 14.9 percent in 2009—the lowest since 1944. [308]

By 2020, the baby boomers will be consuming huge amounts of public resources, principally health care and pensions. In his book, *Grey Dawn*, former Chairman of the Federal Reserve of New York and co-founder of the Blackstone Group, Pete Peterson, argues that the greatest crisis faced by the U.S. in the 21st century is the aging population, characterized by the unprecedented growth in the elderly and the decline in youth. He noted that today there are three workers for every pensioner, but that this will decline to 1.5 to one or even one to one. [309]

The U.S. situation appears even worse when the unfunded liabilities of Social Security, Medicare, and Medicaid are included. These collectively account for 44 percent of total federal spending and are steadily rising. [310] Although this situation is clearly unsustainable, the wealthy continue to ask for major cuts to social programs in the U.S. while the economy deteriorates and jobs are lost from the class targeted for austerity measures.

The U.S. federal debt has to be paid by either cutting services or increasing revenues through tax hikes. However, current circumstances, from the aging population and retiring baby boomers to deteriorating infrastructure, require increasing spending, not decreasing it. Clearly, the U.S. will have to make taxation more equitable by reversing the tax breaks given to the wealthy in the past 60 years and tax the money stashed in tax havens.

Warren Buffett, an opponent of lowering taxes for the wealthy, wrote an article in *The New York Times* urging U.S. lawmakers to raise taxes to pay for Washington's huge budget deficit. He proposes an increase on Americans who make at least $1 million per year and an additional increase on those making $10 million or more. "Our leaders have asked for 'shared sacrifice,' but when they did the asking, they spared me. I checked with my mega-rich friends to learn what pain they were expecting. They, too, were left untouched," Buffett wrote. "While the poor and the middle class fight for us in Afghanistan, and while most Americans struggle to make ends meet, we mega-rich continue to get our extraordinary tax breaks."

Buffett's federal tax rate was 17.4 percent in 2010, while some investment managers were taxed just 15 percent on income reaching into the billions. The income of Mitt Romney, the 2012 Republican Presidential candidate, was $21.5 million in 2010 and his effective tax rate was only 14 percent, while the middle class is taxed up to 25 percent, along with heavy payroll taxes.

Buffett recalled far higher tax rates for the rich in the 1980s and 1990s, and yet nearly 40 million jobs were added from 1980 to 2000. "You know what's happened since then: lower tax rates and far lower job creation," he said. "Most of the income of the rich is invested globally where there are more profitable opportunities in the developing countries such as China and other countries with cheap labor." Then he concluded, "My friends and I have been coddled long enough by a billionaire-friendly Congress...It's time for our government to get serious about shared sacrifice." [311]

Capital gains preferential treatment

In the late '70s, the capital gains tax peaked at 39.9 percent, and then in the *Tax Reform Act* of 1986, capital gains was taxed as income for assets held for less than a year and ranged from 15 percent to 39.6 percent, depending on the marginal tax rate. For capital gains from assets held for more than a year, the tax rate ranged from 10 percent to 20 percent, a much lower rate than hard-earned wages are taxed because the wealthy realize most of their income as capital gains. It is unfair to give a favorable tax treatment of capital gains over a person who trades his time for wage and work so hard to contribute to the economy.

The tax code also favors frequent stock trading and speculating rather than investing for the long-term. It makes it more rewarding to seek short-term investment than to invest for long term. Those who invest to generate income are discouraged because their income is taxed twice: once through taxing corporate profits, and again by taxing the dividends in the hands of the investor. Lower taxes for short-term investments have turned the stock market into a gambling casino, with the financial service sector becoming the primary beneficiary because the more you trade, the more fees the brokers collect.

In Canada, ordinary people who work hard to improve the economy (outside the financial sector) are taxed much more than those who use their money to gamble in the stock market. Those "investors" are taxed at a rate of 50 percent of their marginal tax rate on realized capital gains.

Taxing the dividends

A dividend is money paid (annually, quarterly or monthly) to shareholders from a company's profits after being taxed at a median rate of about 39.5 percent. The dividend is taxed for the second time in the hands of the shareholders, based on their marginal tax rate. This policy punishes those who invest for income and encourages unnecessary trading in the financial markets.

In Australia, for example, double taxation of dividends has been eliminated. Dividends are distributed to shareholders with tax imputations attached to them. Shareholders' taxes are reduced by an amount equal to the tax imputation credits (the tax paid by the company issuing the dividend).

There are several benefits for this taxation arrangement:

- Stopping double taxation;
- Encouraging companies to distribute their profits as dividends;
- Improving the income of retirees who are dependent on fixed incomes;
- Encouraging payment of fair taxes, based on investors' marginal tax rate;
- Decreasing volatility in the stock market will discourage frequent trading or "churning"; because investors will seek long-term investments;
- Eliminating speculation and parasitic practices in the stock market as stock market volatility decreases;
- Forcing companies to reveal their actual financial situation in their financial statements; and
- Increasing tax revenues because most corporations will be motivated to increase their dividends.

Taxing the wealthy

The tax law has favored the rich since mid-1940s when the marginal tax rate was 94 percent. Since then, it has been lowered to a level that has not been seen since the Great Depression. In 1918, the marginal tax rate was increased to 77 percent (on income over $1,000,000) to finance the First World War. Gradually, the top marginal tax rate was reduced, and just before the Great Depression, it reached 25 percent in 1925 on income over $100,000. It had gradually increased in 1932 to reach 94 percent on income over $2.5 (in 2013 dollar) in 1945 under President Harry Truman to rebuild the nation. It was maintained at 91 percent from 1950 to 1963, until it was lowered to 70 percent in 1965 under Lyndon Johnson. Ronald Reagan lowered it to 50 percent and George H.W. Bush to 28 percent. It increased to 40 percent under Clinton, and further decreased under George W. Bush to 35 percent, the lowest marginal tax rate since 1932. [312a]

The Great Depression and the 2008 Great Recession were associated with a low marginal tax rate for the wealthy. When wealth is concentrated at the top, the spending power of the rest of the population shrinks and the economy is crippled. This phenomenon contributed to both the Great Depression and the Great Recession.

Since the 2008 Great Recession, the federal debt has surpassed the GDP. Tax revenues have reached a level that has not been seen since the 1950s. In 2012, President Barack Obama proposed the *Paying a Fair Share Act* to create a minimum tax rate for high-income taxpayers, regardless of whether their income was derived from long-term capital gains, dividends, wages, or salary. Americans earning over $2 million a year would be required to pay a tax rate equal to 30 percent of their total income. Americans earning between $1 million and $2 million would pay a graduated rate approaching 30 percent. However, it seems that *Act* will not make much difference, but has been floated just to appease the masses. Andrew Leonard of *Salon* reports that the *Act* would add up to $160 billion over 10 years, while removing tax cuts on Americans earning over $250,000 a year would raise $800 billion over the next 10 years. [312] Clearly, this act would not go far enough. If taxes were rolled back to 1963 rates, someone who makes $3 million would pay $2.4 million—80 percent of his or her income.

Financial market transactions

Investing in the stock market is very important to provide liquidity and improve the economy. Because of day trading, the average holding period of stocks has fallen steadily to a level not seen since the Great Depression. [313] Moreover, the financial service industry encourages such trading activities because it makes more commission from a high turnover or churning. They have sold to the public the idea that the "buy and hold" practice is dead and in order to make a profit, the market must be "timed." Pump and dump practices used by stock market gurus and traders keep small investors chasing the latest stock in vogue and cause huge market volatility.

In 1936, John Maynard Keynes advocated the use of financial transaction taxes on dealings on Wall Street to curb the excessive speculation by uninformed financial traders. Since 2010, a "Robin Hood Tax" has been advocated by a coalition of non-governmental organizations in the U.K. and Canada, echoed by the "Occupy" movement. [314] For economists, this idea is known as the "Tobin tax," named after the Nobel Laureate James Tobin who advocated for imposing a tax on all spot conversions of one currency into another to put a penalty on short-term financial round-trip excursions into another currency. Tobin suggested his currency transaction tax in 1972, shortly after the Bretton Woods system of monetary management ended in 1971.

Today, many factors encourage parasitic behavior in the financial markets by both individuals and financial institutions. These factors include:

- New technologies that enable anyone with access to the Internet to trade securities at a very low fee, and financial institutions to do billions of trades a day using superfast computers;
- New financial instruments such as derivatives, which drove the global financial markets to collapse; and
- The availability of cheap money.

This environment destabilized the financial markets and took advantage of small investors. Such a tax would remove speculation and improve the image of the financial markets, raise large revenues for governments, and protect uninformed investors.

The financial institutions and the media have led people to believe that they can make a living from speculation in the stock market in day trading and swing trading. A study to determine how day traders perform in the market indicates that heavy day traders earn gross profits, but their profits are not sufficient to cover transaction costs. Moreover, in a typical six-month period, more than eight out of 10 day traders lost money. Despite these bleak findings, a relatively small group of day traders may make profits because the stocks they buy outperform those they sell by 62 basis points, the difference between the sell and buy prices that is sufficiently large to cover transaction costs. [315]

In January 2012, then-French President Nicolas Sarkozy announced that he would introduce a 0.1 percent tax as part of a package of measures to promote growth and create jobs. He predicted that the tax would generate one billion Euros ($1.3 billion), which would be used to cut the budget deficit. Expectedly, this tax was opposed by the French Banking Association, as well as U.K. Prime Minister David Cameron, who argued that such a tax would penalize the City of London, where 75 percent of European financial transactions take place. [316]

Democracy and taxes

Not long ago, an inventor who invented something useful, like the car or the telephone, spent a lifetime becoming wealthy. Today, with rapid technological development and the Internet, a young entrepreneur with very little life and professional experience can become a multibillionaire within months. Some of them may become wealthier than their own nations. They can buy the political system by funding election campaigns and dictate their will on the nation. For this reason, we should have a mechanism to prevent those who have money from having the power to control the political process and decide our destiny.

History teaches us that a major threat to democracy occurs when individuals or corporations become more powerful than the state. They can drive the country into fascism and threaten social and political stability. It happened in Germany in the 1930s and sparked

World War II. It almost happened in the U.S. when the wealthy conspired to overthrow President Franklin Roosevelt. However, the wealthy can indirectly achieve their objective by funding election campaigns to buy elected officials, and then change the laws to serve their interests and those of the corporations. In this manner, they can continue to take advantage of the poor and facilitate the transfer of wealth from the poor to the rich, increasing inequality and their control, and enhancing their false feelings of security. An outstanding example is the way the elites have changed democracy in the U.S.

Today, the business environment is so corrupt that a project's financial value seems to be inversely proportionate to its benefits to society. For example, a singer can become a multimillionaire overnight from a meaningless song. The same can be said of a social network such as Facebook, which has negatively affected the young, added to their sense of isolation, is used by the company to harvest personal information to its own benefit, and does not seem to add value to the society. Facebook, owned by a man of 28, was recently valued at $100 billion. In the past, it would have taken someone a century to reach that degree of wealth. At the same time, that person would have had gained the wisdom to spend his money on something that benefits society and the economy.

Those who have accumulated so much wealth for so little work, with little intellectual depth or life experience, have confused fantasy with reality. They are willing to spend billions of dollars on dreams, such as space exploration for mining purposes. They have blurred the line between movies and real life.

Mark Zuckerberg, CEO of Facebook, paid $1 billion for a company called Instagram, in operation for only 18 months, had 13 employees, no revenues, and distributed its product for free. Such a transaction diminishes the value of real work. [317] This would have not happened if we had a functional economy that based prices on benefit to society and has a tax structure to prevent a few individuals from controlling the nation's economy. Taxes should curb the rich from controlling the state. Had the income of the rich been taxed at the rates existing in the 1960s, their income would have been curtailed to an acceptable level.

The Founding Fathers were aware of this problem and, in the early days of the Republic, made sure to rein in corporations. Laws prevented corporations from buying one another in order to protect society from corporations that become a source of threat to freedom and liberty.

Taxing the wealthy

As we saw in Chapter 5, to create more jobs in the U.S., the states competed amongst each other to attract more business by giving corporations more privileges and power. Today, corporations control the political process and are capable of enacting laws that serve their own interests.

When Europe started to descend into recession in 2008, the idea of raising taxes on high-income earners began. In 2009, the U.K. government increased its top marginal income-tax rate to 50 percent from 40 percent. During the most recent French presidential election campaign, François Hollande suggested raising the marginal tax for those who make over $1.35 million a year to 75 percent from 41 percent. "It is a message of social cohesion … a matter of patriotism," he told journalists. He also planned to increase the marginal rate of those who earn over $202,000 from 41 percent to 45 percent. [318]

Now, competition between countries around the globe has renewed. Again, those who are competing to attract the wealthy by giving tax breaks and other privileges are betraying their own people's trust and forgetting the common good. The U.K. Prime Minister, David Cameron, recently invited France's wealthy to move to England to escape the proposed 75 percent tax rate. Unfortunately, the same thing is happening in the U.S. Top executives of Johnson & Johnson, Merck and other multinationals commute from their homes in Pennsylvania to offices in New Jersey, thus saving roughly two-thirds of their state income tax bill and costing New Jersey's treasury $50 million, by one estimate. [319] A progressive tax code can mitigate the effect of recessions by taking a smaller percentage of income from lower-income consumers than from higher-income consumers, enabling them spend more of their disposable income on consumption and restore economic equilibrium.

Recommendation

Taxing capital gains and dividends

Today, with baby boomers retiring in large numbers, income from dividends will become very important. Taxing dividends should be reconsidered. They should be taxed once in the hands of the shareholder, and both capital gains and dividends should be taxed as income.

Robin Hood tax

As shown in Chapter 8, Wall Street created new financial instruments such as derivatives and other speculative trading instruments. In addition, new high-speed computers have facilitated day trading, swing trading, and other parasitic practices. A transfer tax on equity transactions (or transaction tax) should be imposed in order to discourage these activities and protect the small investors and the integrity of the financial markets. A transfer tax on equities is the oldest tax in existence in the U.K. It was first implemented in 1694 at the London Stock Exchange as a fee payable by share buyers. [320]

A Robin Hood tax would also apply to financial institutions, which use super-fast computers to jump ahead of the small investor to buy or sell and get a few pennies on each stock, which add up because they trade in billions of dollars every day. This tax would increase confidence in the financial markets because small investors would then trust that there are no hedge funds or financial institutions using superfast computers to rig the market.

Taxation of executive compensation

To make taxation fair, the proceeds from current executive compensation packages should be taxed as income like the earnings of any other employee of the corporation.

Executive compensation packages typically include a base salary, bonuses, and incentives, such as stock options and stocks. This compensation is structured to lower executives' taxes significantly because stocks and stock options are preferentially taxed and profits from selling stocks and stock options are considered capital gains.

When the tax law treats capital gains as income, corporations may stop this practice and resort to a fixed salary instead.

Taxing the wealthy

Today, similar to the situation after World War I and World War II, the U.S. federal government is deep in debt, infrastructures are deteriorating, the economy stumbling and the spending power of the middle class diminishing. At the same time, wealth has accumulated at the top and the tax rate paid by the rich, although seemingly in the teens, is actually much lower if wealth stashed in tax havens was considered. To revive the economy, the U.S. government has no other choice but return to the high tax rates implemented after World War I and World War II to increase its spending on infrastructure, rather than taking austerity measures.

Graduated tax rates are very healthy for society and prevent the wealthy from becoming stronger than the state. Rolling back to the tax structure of 1963 would restore equality to the U.S. because the tax cuts since 1963 have mainly benefited the rich and increased inequality.

Wealth Tax

Imposing a wealth tax of 2.5 percent on those who own more than $5 million in net assets will also help create equality and the increase the contributions of the wealthy to society. Such a tax, on individual global assets would prevent the wealthy from scattering their assets globally or hiding them in tax havens. This tax should be collected and paid to the governments in proportion to the individual's assets in each country. Such a tax would make those who own large unproductive assets put them to use to generate new jobs and more income.

Estate tax

Estate tax is an effective tool for preventing the concentration of wealth in the hands of a relatively few powerful families. In the U.S., the estate tax was created by *The Revenue Act* of 1916. An exemption of $50,000 was allowed. The tax rate was graduated from one percent on the first $50,000 to 10 percent on the portion exceeding $5 million. Between the late 1920s and 1940s, the taxes were used as a way to redistribute income. The top rate of 77 percent and an exemption of $40,000 ($625,000 in 2013 dollar) were reached in 1941. Since then, the estate tax exemption continued to increase and the top estate rate to decrease and in 2001, it was eventually repealed by the *Tax Relief Reconciliation Act* in 2010. By 2011, the estate tax reverted to the 1997 law with a top rate of 55 percent. In 2013, exemption reached $5,250,000 and top rate reached 40 percent. [321]

Estate tax plays a role in decreasing inequality and affects the top five percent of earners. In today's economic environment where inequality is extremely high, an estate tax would stop wealth from being inherited intact and creating a new class of extremely wealthy families who become richer and more powerful than the state and could eventually threaten society. The U.S. should restore the 1975 estate tax.

The estate tax has many benefits for the people and the economy including:

- Breaking up large concentrations of wealth;
- Raising a large amount of revenue; and
- Increasing charitable giving, due to allowable deductions from estate tax liability.

The estate tax should be applied to all personal assets, which are assumed to be sold on the day of death, and be taxed according to the deceased individual's tax rate.

Corporate taxes

Combined federal and state corporate taxes

Scott A. Hodge, president of the Tax Foundation, reports that the U.S. corporate tax is the highest among the OECD countries. Currently, the average combined federal and state corporate tax rate in the U.S. is 39.3 percent, while the median corporate tax in the OECD countries is 26.3 percent. The U.K. has lowered its combined tax rate from 26 percent to 24 percent in April 2012 and to 23 percent in 2013. [322]

Despite the apparent high taxes in the U.S., loopholes in the taxation system enable the multinationals to pay minimal or no taxes. To improve its competitiveness among OECD countries, the U.S. should close the loopholes in the corporate tax laws and make lower its combined federal and state corporate taxes to 26.3 percent. [322] Rupert Neate of The Guardian report that Apple's corporate tax rate in 2011 on overseas profits was 1.9 percent. The Guardian analysts fount that Google, Amazon, Starbucks, and Facebook have paid less than one percent in corporate taxes. [323a]

State corporate tax

The relationship between U.S. states and corporations in the past century shows that, when states competed among each other to attract businesses by giving privileges to the corporations, it harmed the society, increased inequality and corrupted the democratic process. Corporations controlled state legislatures, which enacted laws to serve corporate interests and erode democracy. To make a level playing field among the states, the total federal and state corporate taxes should add up to 26.3 percent (the average among the OECD countries). The state corporate tax rate should be changed to the median of seven percent. The federal tax will then be 19.3 percent (26.3 percent − 7.0 percent). If a state such as Nevada does not want to increase its tax to seven percent, then the federal tax for corporations in that state should be 26.3 percent.

The new tax will make the U.S. more attractive to businesses from abroad and the increase in individual tax (due to reverting to 1963 tax rates and taxing both dividend and capital gains as income at the marginal tax rate of the owner) would balance the loss due to decreasing the corporate federal tax. In addition, dividends would be taxed only once in the hands of recipients by giving the owner a credit for the tax paid by the corporation. In this way, the U.S. would become more competitive and attract more business from many of the OECD countries.

Taxes of American subsidiaries abroad

Taxes on the earnings of subsidiaries controlled by U.S. corporations are deferred until the earnings are brought back to the U.S., and are then paid at a rate of 35 percent. This is clearly the work of lobbyists.

Of course, corporations would not bring their profits back to the U.S. to lose more than one third of it. They would invest it abroad where there are better opportunities. Accordingly, U.S. multinationals are currently holding more than $1.5 trillion in foreign profits, [323] while the U.S. federal debt is skyrocketing.

This law should be repealed and American corporations should pay the accumulated taxes they owe on the earnings of their subsidiaries. However, to settle this situation, American corporations may be required to pay the suggested tax rate of 26.3 percent instead.

Country by country accounting

Multinationals report their total profits worldwide in aggregated financial statements, not on a country-by-country basis. This approach allows them to hide some information from the public and avoid paying a fair tax. [324]

The Tax Justice Network, an independent organization in the British Houses of Parliament, [325] together with the "Publish What You Pay Coalition," are leading an international campaign to require multinationals to report their financial statements on a country-by-country basis. Richard Murphy, founder of the Tax Justice Network and a columnist for The Guardian, considers accounting country by country to be part of corporations' obligation to society in exchange for the limited liability of their subsidiaries. [324] This practice defines risk a community faces for allowing the operations of the multinational and enables state politicians, regulators, and society to assess the risk and form the basis for state's economic decision-making. It also allows investors to evaluate the risks of these operations, especially in mining, oil and gas, financial, and manufacturing sectors.

Benefits of country-by-country reporting include:

- Uncovering offshore subsidiaries used for tax evasion;
- Limiting corruption;
- Improving transparency regarding accounting, corporate activities, accountability, trade within and across national boundaries, employees' remunerations, and taxes;

- Providing resources for local governments where these multinationals operate; and
- Insisting that multinationals reveal the stability of the countries in which they operate and whether they are subject to sanctions.

According to the Tax Justice Network, multinational corporations account for nearly two thirds of global trade. By shifting profits between subsidiaries in different jurisdictions, they can allocate their costs to high-tax jurisdictions for tax reduction, and shift their profits to tax havens, where they pay little or no tax. Details of these practices are not documented in their annual reports, however; under current international accounting rules, multinationals are allowed to total all their results—profits, tax payments, borrowings, and so on—into a single figure or set of regional figures. Accordingly, a set of results for "Africa" or "Europe" is impossible to break down in order to explain what has happened in each country.

Country-by-country reporting would make multinational corporations provide financial results for each country. A multinational corporation would disclose in its annual financial statements the names of its subsidiaries in each country and its sales, purchases, labor costs, employee numbers, financing costs, pre-tax profits, tax charges, and capital assets. This practice would be an extremely cost-effective way to improve global corporate transparency for the benefit of local citizens, tax authorities, investors, and economists. The World Bank, for instance, agrees that the benefits would outweigh the costs, and strongly supports the initiative. [324]

Chapter 11

The New Era Community Clubs
A Call to action

Americans are divided into two distinct classes. The First Class is the one percent, represented by the Power Triad. The Second Class consists of the rest of the population, defined by the Occupy Movement as the 99 percent.

In this chapter, I compare these classes and present a pragmatic idea of how to overcome the power discrepancy between them.

The First Class (the Power Triad)

This class is a relatively small group of Americans with diverse backgrounds, but its members seem to work in unison because they have similar objectives. They use the American people as stepping-stones to achieve their self-serving goals using lawmakers, large accounting and law firms, Wall Street bankers, lobbyists, key government personnel, and other career politicians. These people are indifferent to the interests of the 99 percent or the common good. They may be Americans, but they would not hesitate to sacrifice the American people, the national interests, and the national security if that would help them achieve their goals. They also have common interests with foreign superrich individuals, and they collaborate to serve their mutual interests in both the developed and emerging market countries. They use the international organizations, such as WTO, the Bank of International Settlements (BIS), the IMF, the World Bank, and OECD, to secure wealth, power, and global control (see Chapter 5).

The one percent includes wealthy heirs, owners of hedge fund companies, executives of Wall Street banks, arms dealers, media moguls, and technology entrepreneurs as well as securities industry professionals, many executives and managers who work outside the financial sector, and those who accumulated wealth through illegal means. They enjoy the privileges that society offers, but they feel no responsibility toward it. They avoid paying taxes, violate human rights, and subvert the democratic process. To control the nation, they create conflicts among Americans using religion, race, color, or sexual orientation. These people are interested in weakening tax laws, deregulating the financial sector, promoting globalization, and controlling the government and public opinion.

Fortunes of the one percent are protected even when everyone else's is at risk, as we have seen during the financial crisis. Their money was safe when Wall Street banks were on the brink of bankruptcy. The government was there to rescue them using the 99 percent's taxes. The same practice occurs in other countries. The European Union recently extended this policy even further during the Cyprus banking crisis. The government confiscated 40 percent of the small depositors' money to rescue the banks, but gave the opportunity to those at the top of the food chain to withdraw their deposits in full. [326] In 2013, the government of Canada considered the Cyprus solution if the Canadian banks would fall in trouble and this scheme would become the rule rather than the exception. [327]

Strategies and plans of the First Class

The main strategy of the First Class is to fund the election of candidates who can serve their interests, and then get them to work on executing them, whether it is a tax break, loophole to evade corporate responsibilities, or new war.

They use many tools to control the economy and both local and foreign policies, including:

- Undermining democracy;
- Buying lawmakers through campaign funding (electioneering) and lobbying;
- Influencing the selection of the Supreme Court judges;
- Influencing foreign policy and leading the business of war;
- Weakening income and wealth taxation laws;

- Deregulating the financial sector, and promoting globalization;
- Eliminating restrictions on election campaign funding and political influence;
- Deindustrialization of the U.S. – Exporting jobs to China and other emerging market countries to increase their profits; and
- Using the media to control the 99 percent.

Organizational structure to control the 99 percent

The U.S. has more than 22,000 special interest groups but they are not equal. The few that work on behalf of the Power Triad are well funded, well organized and have the means to control the political process.

They establish:

- Professional, well-funded organizations, such as ALEC, AIPAC and other lobby firms;
- Grass-roots groups such as ACT! for America and Christians United for Israel;
- Think tanks, such as the Project for a New American Century and the Center for Strategic and International Studies (CSIS); [19] and
- Networks of media, journalists, and professionals, such as Bernard Lewis, Foad Ajami, and Fareed Zakaria. [19]

They spend billions of dollars annually and dedicate plenty of professional services to restore the power and control they had before President Roosevelt brought in The New Deal. They reached an important milestone in 2010, when the Supreme Court granted the corporation personhood and enabled the Power Triad to spend unlimited amounts of money to fund the election campaigns and consequently have full control over who will be elected to the Congress and the White House. [3]

As President James Madison pointed out 200 years ago, democracy does not work when groups that focus on their own self-interest are allowed to assume such a dominant role. [328]

The Second Class (The 99 Percent)

This class represents the middle class and the poor, which reached a staggering number of more than 47.8 million in 2012. [107] They are used to fuel and pay for the wars launched for the benefits of the First Class. They are targeted by propaganda to sway their opinion in support of policies that serve the interests of the First Class.

A myth among the Second Class members is that if you get an education, find a good job, and work hard, you will make it. This belief ignores the fact that elected representatives can enact laws that undermine your opportunities. For example, you may have spent many years to get a good education and develop your expertise, and then lawmakers have created a loophole that allows corporations to replace local experts with low-paid foreign employees on Intra-company Transfer visas (L-1 Visa). Another example is that, while you were working hard to raise your standard of living, the government has cut taxes for the wealthy and consequently, affected your standard of living by decreasing public services.

Organizational structure of the 99 percent

The efforts of the 99 percent to influence the political process are scattered over thousands of diverse advocacy groups that are underfunded, understaffed, and lack the resources to tilt the balance in their favor. They advocate on various issues concerning wages, prices, and profits; environmental interests; equal rights; and consumer interests. Each group works on its own, and as a result, important causes do not get the attention they need.

Because career politicians have to look out for themselves, they cater to the First Class groups. Therefore, those who belong to the 99 percent do not get equal hearing from the lawmakers and are ignored if their demands conflict with the interests of the Power Triad.

Lack of continuity

Currently, participation of the 99 percent in the political process is reactive and transient. If the government wants to make a decision against the will of the Second Class, such as going to war, all the people do is to demonstrate for a few hours, and then go home and continue with their daily activities.

A demonstration against a political decision helps vent frustrations, but has rarely succeeded in bringing about change. Demonstrations of millions of people against the war in Iraq, Gaza, or Afghanistan did not end the wars. The politicians continued with their decision despite popular opposition.

Evidently, the 99 percent do not have an organizational structure that poses a direct challenge to the decision makers. Politicians will continue to make decisions against the interest of the people knowing that the public will forget by the next election. Even if they remember and vote for the opposing candidate, the losing candidate will have his/her own interests taken care of by the Power Triad.

The people will not be heard unless they have a powerful permanent organization that uses the power of the people to make politicians recognize that there will be personal and career repercussions if they fail the electorate.

The New Era Community Clubs (NECCs)

Despite the significant deficiencies of the 99 percent' advocacy groups, they have more power than all the special interest groups that work for the Power Triad. It is the collective power of the 99 percent, which can be used to force Congress to bow to their will, if it is used effectively.

The lack of success is due to two main issues. First, the Triad is able to control of the Congress through funding elections using corporate personhood. Second, laws have been enacted to allow individuals and corporations to spend unlimited amounts of money on the elections. If the people can focus on resolving these two issues to start with, they will be able to rein in the Power Triad, restore their democracy, and control the economy.

To reach this tipping point advocacy groups need to work under the umbrella of one group within a community in what I call "New Era Community Clubs," which will focus on achieving the aforementioned goals. After they succeed, other causes will be placed in priority sequence based on their importance and benefits to the society.

The NECC will be non-partisan with focus on serving the interests of the community at the local, state, and the national levels.

The NECC will inform its members using alternative media and the services of the Prometheus Radio Project to establish local non-commercial radio stations. NECCs and their members will use social media to connect and interact with each other to exchange information, integrate their operations, and spread knowledge about the current issues.

NECC and Continuity

The 99 percent need to have a mechanism by which to hold their elected representatives accountable, and expect them to report regularly what they have been doing so that they could not pass laws that support the Power Triad.

The people need to run the political system like a business. In a corporation, the shareholders hire a management team to oversee the operations and a board of directors to hold the management team accountable. The board requests corporate plans and progress reports, evaluates the management performance, and takes measures to ensure compliance of the management team with the objectives of the corporation.

In today's political system, the people (shareholders) hire career politicians to work on the people's behalf, but they give these politicians a free hand to do whatever they see fit. They enact laws and make decisions that deeply affect the people's lives and the future of the nation. Gradually, these politicians get a sense of entitlement to power and authority over their electorate.

The political system does not have a board of directors in its structure to hold the representatives accountable. Following the elections, we mind our own personal lives and ignore that these representatives work for us until the next elections.

Imagine if the people had a board of directors that holds regular monthly meetings to examine what the representatives have been doing in the legislature, their activities to serve the community, and their achievements. The people will realize that their representatives are not their masters, they are their "public servants." In addition, politicians will realize that their political future depends on satisfying the board of directors' requirements. As a result, the representatives will put their electorate's interests ahead of that of the Power Triad.

In this organizational structure, every voter, who is a member of a New Era Community Club, will become a member of the board of directors.

It is no longer possible to be bystanders. Everyone must either make a difference in their community, or allow their freedoms, liberties, and wealth to be lost to the Power Triad. To become engaged in the political process, we need to start at the community level and establish "New Era Community Clubs" (NECCs). The local NECC will take advantage of the social media to connect with other national NECCs.

The NECCs will be a consistent, long term, citizens' groups around the country to educate, inform, and take action to protect themselves and their interests from the First Class, the Power Triad.

NECC and political awareness

To restore democracy and transfer power to ordinary people using non-violent means, we need to increase awareness of the importance of popular participation. NECC meetings can arm members with knowledge and understanding of what needs to be done and how to do it.

We have the right to vote, but we misuse this right when we vote without fully understanding the issues. Before we go to vote locally, we must have studied the issues that concern us and our communities, examined the qualifications of the candidates, talked to them and asked them what they will do to address our concerns. Then, we can make up our minds and vote wisely.

We must not just depend on mainstream media to be our source of information. We must do our own research and find out more about the issues by talking to other community members at regular NECC meetings. We can listen to what the corporate media report, but verify its validity, accuracy, and importance through our own research channels on the Internet and other alternative media.

With the advent of the Internet, we are so interconnected that we do ourselves a disservice if we do not expand our knowledge to understand what is happening in other parts of the world.

We need to engage the young in the political process because they are the future of the nation. Their knowledge, understanding, and participation are crucial for our future.

We can use multicultural and diversified community as a divisive tool to polarize the nation, or use it to enrich us intellectually and culturally, and broaden our understanding of the world around us. We can use NECC meetings to promote mutual understanding, to unite and strengthen the community, and to improve the relationship between various faiths, cultures, and races.

When the community works together, politicians pay attention. Our active participation in the political process is the only way we can save our democracy and maintain our freedoms. And when we are united, we can change the world.

NECC and leadership

Occupy Wall Street started on Sept. 17, 2011, by taking over Manhattan's Zuccotti Park and soon activists spread the Occupy movement to cities across North America. It protested inequality and the oppressive power of corporations, and then broadened to express the grievances of the ordinary Americans with various issues such as the economy, global warming, health care, and education.

Occupy did not have a clear agenda, objectives, or leadership. It did not try to engage the mainstream Americans or have a plan to pursue a defined political agenda to the end. It frightened the political establishment, but it did not take long for the local, state, and federal authorities to coordinate their efforts and disperse the gatherings. The authorities physically abused and arrested innocent, peaceful protesters, making them an example to others who contemplated to follow.

All NECCs will start in unison to advocate for one issue at a time. They will seek support from the public, and persist in their demands while refusing to be drawn into a violent confrontation. Non-violent resistance requires tremendous courage, self-control, and perseverance.

NECC and elections

Soliciting membership in a NECC is very important, and it should be easy for the NECC to reach a critical mass in its community to affect the outcome of elections. An individual may not belong to a political party because The NECC will gradually substitute the political parties because it will be able to serve the needs of the community effectively. In addition, it will have stronger influence on the political process and be able to decide who will be elected to office.

Most Americans do not vote. Accordingly, a very small proportion of highly motivated and mobilized citizens can have a disproportionate impact. According to the U.S. Census Bureau, on average, only 41.6 percent of the population votes in congressional elections. [329]

For a candidate to win, he or she has to get 50 percent plus one. That is only 22 votes out of each 100 eligible voters. If NECC membership reaches 25 percent of the population, the NECC members will be able to decide who wins the elections.

NECC Structure

The NECCs will start with a central office that provides research and guidance regarding the issues that faces the nation and coordinate campaigns to promote among local NECCs issues of common national or global concern, as well as local issues. At the beginning, the most pressing issues will be building memberships, and educational program about the subjects presented in this book, but it will make its first priority funding the elections fully from the public purse and ban individuals, corporations, and other special interest groups from using their money to interfere in the election process.

A board of 12 individuals will be selected based on their knowledge and experience to evaluate and prioritize issues based on their impact on the democratic process and promote them among the local NECCs. Board members will be volunteers, independent thinkers who are interested in the common good and should have no aspirations to political office.

Interested individuals can submit ideas that complement the work in this book. You can build a better future for yourself and your family, and your country by joining or establishing a New Era Community Club in your neighborhood. Visit http://www.TheNewEraClubs.org.

References

1   Lincoln, Abraham, November 19, 1863, The Gettysburg
    Address, delivered during the American Civil War,
    Gettysburg, Pennsylvania.

2a Moulds, Josephine, November 9, 2012, China's economy to
    overtake US in the Next four years, sys OECD, The Guardian,
    http://goo.gl/izgpA.

2   Gibran, Khalil, 1938, The Prophet

3   Citizens United v. Federal Election Commission – 08-205
    (2010), 558 U.S. 310, January 21, 2010, http://goo.gl/imsQs.

4   Wikipedia, Defense Contractor, http://goo.gl/QCMj7.

5   Perble, Christopher A., November 29, 2012, The Military-
    Industrial Complex's waning political influence, CATO
    Institute, http://goo.gl/PLqHe.

6   Matt, Grossman, The Not-So-Special Interest: Interest Groups,
    Public Representation, and American Governance.

7   Mearsheimer, John, and Stephen Walt, 2007, The Israel Lobby
    and U.S. Foreign Policy.
    John Mearsheimer and Stephen Walt, The Israel Lobby,
    London Review of Books, Vol. 28 No. 6. 23 March 2006,
    London Review of Books, http://goo.gl/kESAt.

8   Stiglitz, Joseph E., and Linda J. Bilmes, September 5, 2010,
    The true cost of the Iraq war: $3 trillion and beyond, The
    Washington Post, http://goo.gl/eKTV. Also in The Iraq War
    will cost us $3 trillion, and much more, March 9, 2008,
    http://goo.gl/kDOt, and their book, The Three Trillion Dollar
    War, February 17, 2008, http://goo.gl/pGcYd.

9   Rebuilding America's Defenses: Strategies, Forces, and
    Resources For a New Century, September 2000,
    http://goo.gl/Mhuns.

10 Verma, Sonia, May 20, 2008, Iraq could have largest oil
    reserves in the world, The Times Natural resources,
    http://goo.gl/9eRli.

11 Business Pundit, July 22, 2008, The 25 Most Vicious Iraq war
    Profiteers, The http://goo.gl/MqJkQ.

12 Rubin, Robert E., Times Topics, The New York Times,
    August 12, 2010, http://goo.gl/uNw6F.

13   Alterman, Eric, May 2011, Think Again: The Era of the 'One Percent', Vanity Fair, http://goo.gl/4cfLf.

14   Levitt, Steven, and Stephen Dubner, Freakonomics.

15   Savage, Gus, March 29, 1990, Speech to the House of Representatives, Congressional Record, 101st Congress (1989-1990), http://goo.gl/FbtCe.

16   U.S. Human Rights Network, August 2010, The United States of America: Summary Submission to the UN Universal Periodic Review, *Universal Periodic Review Joint Reports: United States of America.* p. 8.

17   Pew Center for People and the Press, September 9, 2009, Muslims Widely Seen As Facing Discrimination, http://goo.gl/mO86i.

18   U.S. Department of Labor, Myth Busting the pay gap, June 7, 2012, http://goo.gl/5O5nc.

19   Sheehi, Stephen, 2011, Islamophobia, The Ideological Campaign Against Muslims, Clarity Press, http://goo.gl/22KQ0.

20   Ali, Wajahat, Eli Clifton, Matthew Duss, Lee Fang, Scott Keyes, and Faiz Shakir, August 2011, Fear, Inc., The Roots of the Islamophobia Network in America, American Progress, http://goo.gl/Pg2yt.
      Shakir, Faiz, August 26, 2011, $42 Million From Seven Foundations Helped Fuel The Rise Of Islamophobia In America, http://goo.gl/lOeN1.

21   Department of Justice, Confronting Discrimination in the Post-9/11 Era: Challenges and Opportunities Ten Years Later, A Report on the Civil Rights Division's Post-9/11 Civil Rights Summit Hosted by George Washington University Law School, October 19, 2011, http://goo.gl/gFG67.

22   Markets & Finance, November 7-13, 2011, Jon Corzine comes up snake eyes, p44, Bloomberg Business Week.

23   Bloomberg Business Week, July 30 – August 5, 2012, Florida's GOP Governor Goes Rogue.

24   Carle, Glenn L., May 1, 2012, Hard Measures: Torture Is Humane, The Huffington Post, http://goo.gl/LT9vT, Author of The Interrogator.

25   Wikipedia, Political party, http://goo.gl/j3YIF.

26   Wikipedia, Term Limits in the United States, http://goo.gl/knnBo.

27   National Conference of State Legislatures, June 6, 2012,
      Recall of State Officials, http://goo.gl/Z3MB9.
28   Hedges, Chris, 2010, Empire of Illusions, The End of Literacy
      and the Triumph of Spectacle.
29   CNN, CNN Poll: Americans believe Iran has nuclear weapons,
      http://goo.gl/wC2ZQ.
30   Gonzalez, Juan, and Joseph Torres, News for All the People:
      The Epic Story of Race and the American Media.
31   Associated Press' history, http://goo.gl/D6Or2.
32   Fog, Agner, May 20, 2004, The supposed and the real role of
      mass media in modern democracy, Working paper,
      http://goo.gl/Ix0BM.
33   Rather, Dan, 2012, Rather Outspoken, My Life in the News.
34   Plunkett, John, and Lisa O'Carroll, 28 May 2012, Leveson
      Inquiry: Blair says newspapers used as 'instruments of
      political power, The Guardian, http://goo.gl/2ewiD.
35   Associated Press, 15 June 2012, Blair aide: Murdoch pressed
      UK chief over the Iraq war, http://goo.gl/7ZRPl.
36   Conroy, Scott, April 12, 2012, Gingrich unloads on Fox News
      in private meeting, Real Clear Politics, http://goo.gl/IrVHI.
37   Mimms, December 22, 2011, Sarah, Ron Paul Ignored by the
      Media? Not So Much, The National Journal.
38   Cook, Jonathan, Rubert Murdoch's Bid to persuade Gen.
      David Petraeus to run as Republican Candidate in the 2012
      Presidential Election, http://goo.gl/Cpw7J.
39   Bagdikian, Ben, May 15, 2004, The New Media Monopoly,
      retrieved September 1, 2012, http://goo.gl/XiGb9.
40   Kasser, Tim, 2002, *The High Price of Materialism*, MIT Press,
      Cambridge, Mass. and, London, England.
41   Patten, Dominic, May 30, 2012, CNN hits 20-year monthly
      rating low in May, Deadline.com, http://goo.gl/zk9Fa.
42   Coulter, Ann, September 13, 2001, This is War, National
      Review, http://goo.gl/UO8jo.
43   Danios, May 18, 2011, Evolutionary Psychologist says black
      women are scientifically ugly, advocates Muslim holocaust,
      Loonwatch.com, http://goo.gl/7v2cf.
45   Secret Cooperation, June 3, 2012, Israel deploys nuclear
      weapons on German-built submarines, Spiegel,
      http://goo.gl/Hjr6v.
46   Samandar, Issa, May 19, 2005, Israel's silent nuclear attack

revealed, The Electronic Intifada, http://goo.gl/os2yQ.

47   Wikipedia, Prometheus Radio Project, http://goo.gl/PsCJH.

48   Wikipedia, Propaganda model, Retrieved September 1, 2012, http://goo.gl/bkqrI.

49   Website Monitoring, YouTube Facts & Figures history & Statistics, http://goo.gl/xmcV.

50   YouTube, Statistics, Retrieved on September 1, 2012, http://goo.gl/mceKw.

51   Linde, Steve, 28 November 2006, Israel's newest PR weapon: The Internet Megaphone, Jerusalem Post, http://goo.gl/zhkgs.

52   Wikipedia, Megaphone desktop tool, Retrieved September 1, 2012, http://goo.gl/m3KR.

53   GIYUS.ORG, Retrieved September 1, 2012, http://goo.gl/KRwDw, http://goo.gl/KRwDw.

54   Wong, Brad, January 3, 2009, Hundreds march in Seattle to protest Israeli attacks on Gaza, The Seattle Post Intelligencer, http://goo.gl/dn6cD.

55   Silverstein, Richard, January 9, 2009, Hasbara spam alert, With Israel's foreign ministry organising volunteers to flood news websites with pro-Israeli comments, Propaganda 2.0 is here, The Guardian, http://goo.gl/iOa2K.

56   Linde, Steve, November 28, 2006, "Israel's newest PR weapon: The Internet Megaphone," Jerusalem: Jerusalem Post, http://goo.gl/zhkgs.

57   The Register, Retrieved September 1, 2012, http://goo.gl/m88Q.

58   Williams, Chris, September 8, 2006, Pro-Israel lobby targets BBC online poll, London: The Register, http://goo.gl/dBxwN.

59   Washingtons Blog, January 9, 2009, Does The Government Manipulate Social Media?, http://goo.gl/IrU9V.

60   Miller, Laura, The Victory of Spin, The Center for Media and Democracy's PR Watch, http://goo.gl/lMHTW, Retrieved September 1, 2012.

61   Mazzetti, Mark, and Borzou Daragahi, November 30, 2005, U.S. Military covertly pays to run stories in Iraqi press, The Los Angeles Times, http://goo.gl/1tS6N.

62   Jarvis, Jeff, March 17, 2011, America's absurd stab at systematising sock puppetry, The U.S. has a chance to move on from a history of clandestine foreign policy – instead it acts like a clumsy spammer, The Guardian, http://goo.gl/omR7P.

63   Fielding, Nick, and Ian Cobain, 17 March 2011, Revealed:
      U.S. spy operation that manipulates social media, Military's
      'sock puppet' software creates fake online identities to spread
      pro-American propaganda, The Guardian,
      http://goo.gl/CyrMB.
64   Right Web, Tracking militarists' efforts to influence U.S.
      foreign policy, American Israel Public Affairs Committee,
      http://goo.gl/0GHkb.
65   Findley, Paul, 2006, Representative Paul Findley Dares to
      Speak out—Again, Patriotic American National Productions.
44   Farr, Warner D., LTC, U.S. Army, The Counter proliferation
      papers, Future Warfare Series N. 2, USAF Counter
      Proliferation Center, Air War College, Air University,
      Maxwell Air Force Base, Alabama, http://goo.gl/4PpLy.
66   McArthur, Shirl, November 2011, A Conservative Estimate of
      Total U.S. Aid to Israel more than $123 billion,
      http://goo.gl/gsjmF.
67   Human Development Report, UNDSP, 2011, Sustainability
      and Equity: A Better Future for All, http://goo.gl/oH1an.
68a   U.S. inflation calculator, http://goo.gl/ufmuL
68   Stauffer, Thomas, 2003, The Costs to American Taxpayers of
      the Israeli-Palestinian Conflict: $3 Trillion, Washington
      Report on Middle East Affairs, pages 20-30,
      http://goo.gl/7IpXW.
69   Iraq Resolution Markup, January 24, 2007, C-SPAN,
      http://goo.gl/DCvTO.
70   The Huffington Post, November 29, 12, Countries that voted
      against Palestine at UN include Unite States, Israel, and
      Canada, http://goo.gl/XdCbH.
71   Collins, Dan, August 2, 2009, Israel to U.S.: Don't Delay Iraq
      Attack, http://goo.gl/bzjur.
72   Moore, Molly, December 6, 2003, Israel linked to Iraq
      intelligence failure, general says, The Age,
      http://goo.gl/xR2jG.
73   Findley, Paul, 1989, They Dare to Speak Out, People and
      Institutions Confront Israel's Lobby.
74   Zunes, Stephen, June 3, 2011, Netanyahu's Speech and
      Congressional Democrats' embrace of Extremism, Truthout,
      http://goo.gl/OajBe.
75   Israel Lobby, 2008, Volgendre Keer VPRO.NL.

76   Keinon, Herb, August 8, 2011, 81 Congressmen to visit Israel in coming weeks, http://goo.gl/XyuCR.

77   Mearsheimer, John, and Stephen Walt, February 12, 2009, Is it Love or the Lobby? Explaining America's Special Relationship with Israel, Security Studies, University of Chicago, http://goo.gl/4dIf0.

78   The News Hour, Mark Shields, David Brooks, with Judy Woodruff, January 4, 2013, The likely nomination of Chuck Hagel for Secretary of Defense. PBS, http://goo.gl/Jhcc8.

79a   The Republic Report, March 14, 2012, Analysis: When a Congressman Becomes a Lobbyist, He Gets a 1,452% Raise (on average), http://goo.gl/xoJud.

79   Lobbying Database, Center for Responsive Politics, http://goo.gl/eqQ3.

80   Weiss, Daniel J., Jackie Weidman, and Rebecca Leber, February 7, 2012, Big Oil's Banner Year, Higher Prices, Record Profits, Less Oil, Center for American Progress, http://goo.gl/rYo5Y.

81   Center for Responsive Politics, Energy and Natural Resources Sector lobbying cost in 2012, http://goo.gl/ouxlF.

82   Center for Responsive Politics, Defense Aerospace expenditure on Lobbying in 2012, http://goo.gl/JzT7w.

83   Dvorak, Kimberly, June 6, 2012, War profiteering and campaigns perpetuate the War on Terror, The Examiner. http://goo.gl/1uTy8.

84   60-Minutes, November 6, 2011, Interview with Jack Abramoff: The Lobbyist's playbook, http://goo.gl/psWCA.

85   American Legislative Exchange Council, History, http://www.alec.org/about-alec/history/.

86   Granite State Progress, 2012, ALEC Exposed, Retrieved March 28, 2012, http://goo.gl/3QM6o.

87   McIntire, Mike, April 21, 2012, Conservative Nonprofit Acts as a Stealth Business Lobbyist, *The New York Times*. Retrieved May 15, 2012, http://goo.gl/5EP31.

88   People for the American Way, ALEC: The Voice of Corporate Special Interests in State Legislatures, http://goo.gl/Lbr5X, 2011. Retrieved March 28, 2012.

89   Wikipedia, Tillman Act of 1907, http://goo.gl/SjCoL.

90   Wikipedia, Federal Corrupt Practices Act, http://goo.gl/dN4wK.

91   Wikipedia, Taft-Hartley Act, http://goo.gl/uuY0.

92   Wikipedia, Federal Election Campaign Act,
        http://goo.gl/6V6Mz.

93   Buckley v. Valeo, (No. 75-436), January 30, 1967, Legal
        Information Institute, http://goo.gl/M2B07.

94   First National Bank of Boston v. Bellotti – 435 U.S. 765
        (1978). No. 67-1172. Decided April 26, 1978.
        http://goo.gl/SrSk6.

95   Austin v. Mich. Chamber of Commerce – 494 U.S. 652
        (1990), Justia US Supreme Court Center,
        http://goo.gl/vAzXG.

96   Citizens United v. Federal Election Commission - 08-205
        (2010), Justia US Supreme Court Center, http://goo.gl/xe0yD.

97   The White House, Office of the Press Secretary, January 21,
        2010, Statement from the President on Today's Supreme
        Court Decision, http://goo.gl/aqZg.

98   Seligman, J, May 6, 2010, Is the corporation a person?
        Reflections on Citizens United v. Federal Election
        Commission, http://goo.gl/M4YaU.

99   Heard, Alexander, 1968, Political financing, In: Sills, David I.
        (ed.) *International Encyclopedia of the Social Sciences*, vol.
        12. New York, NY: Free Press - Macmillan, 1968, pp. 235–
        241.

100   Paltiel, Khayyam Z., 1981, Campaign finance - contrasting
        practices and reforms, In: Butler, David et al. (eds.),
        Democracy at the polls - a comparative study of competitive
        national elections. Washington, DC: AEI, 1981, pp. 138-172.

101   Paltiel, Khayyam Z., 1987, Political finance, In: Bogdanor,
        Vernon (ed.), *The Blackwell Encyclopedia of Political
        Institutions*. Oxford, UK, Blackwell, 1987, pp. 454–456.

102   Nassmacher, Karl-Heinz, 2011, Party finance, in: George T.
        Kurian, et al. (eds.) The encyclopedia of political science. Vol.
        4, Washington, DC: CQ Press, 2011, pp. 1187-1189.

103   Wikipedia, Political Finance, Campaign finance in the United
        States, http://goo.gl/WGPKC.

104   Legal Information Institute, Cornell University Law School,
        14th Amendment, http://goo.gl/q3Dsy.

105   The Library of Congress, Virtual Programs and Services, 14th
        Amendment to the U.S. Constitution, http://goo.gl/Vy3P4.

106   Wikipedia, The New Deal, http://goo.gl/caqRL.

107   Picchi, Aimee, March 28, 2013, More Americans than ever
       using food stamps, MSN, http://goo.gl/NQa6Q.
108   Meyers, William, November 13, 2000, The Santa Clara Blues:
       Corporate Personhood versus Democracy,
       http://goo.gl/HjX9c, Retrieved on September 2, 2012.
109   Bakan, Joel, 2004, The Corporation: The pathological pursuit
       of profit and power.
110   Nicole Winfield, August 18, 2011, In trip to Spain, Pope
       demands greater ethics in economic policy, The Washington
       Post, http://goo.gl/aYbL4.
111   Reclaim Democracy, Our Hidden History of corporations in
       the United States, http://goo.gl/FKTEt.
112   Wikipedia, Corporate Capitalism, http://goo.gl/uOQce.
113   Frutman, Lee D., The History of the corporation,
       Citizenworks.org, http://goo.gl/xZQmm. Retrieved September
       2, 2012.
114   Pistor, Katharina, Yoram Keinan, Jan Kleinheisterkamp, and
       Mark D. West, The Evolution of Corporate Law, A Cross-
       Country Comparison, The University of Pennsylvania Journal
       of international Economic Law, Vol.23, Issue 4, pp.791-871,
       http://goo.gl/ICKvt.
115   Justia, US Supreme Court Center, Santa Clara County V.
       Southern Pacific R. Co. – 118 U.S. 394 (1886),
       http://goo.gl/g0fQO.
116   Archer, Jules, The Plot To Seize the White House.
117   Justia, US Supreme Court Center, See v. City of Seattle – 387
       U.S. 541 (1967), http://goo.gl/Ejw6w.
118   Justia.com, US Supreme Court Center, Marshall v. Barlow's,
       Inc. – 436 U.S. 307 (1978), http://goo.gl/Tf6bT.
119   Justia.com, US Supreme Court Center, Buckley V. Valeo –
       424 U.S. 1 (1976), http://goo.gl/ieFTW.
120   Wikipedia, Buckley v. Valeo, http://goo.gl/dEfY & Legal
       Information Institute, Cornell University Law School,
       http://goo.gl/M2B07, and Wikipedia, http://goo.gl/fo2H &
       Justia US Supreme Court Center, Buckley v. Valeo – 424 U.S.
       (1976).
121   Justia.com, US Supreme Court Center, First National Bank of
       Boston v. Vellotti – 435 U.S. 765 (1978), http://goo.gl/SrSk6.
122   Federal Election Commission, Bipartisan Campaign Reform
       Act of 2002, http://goo.gl/nlXBd.

123 Legal Information Institute, Cornell University Law School, http://goo.gl/rMbDo, & Wikipedia, Citizens United v. The Federal Election Commission, http://goo.gl/igTu.

124 Justia.com, US Supreme Court Center, Citizens United v. Federal Election Commission – 08-205 (2010), http://goo.gl/xe0yD.

125 Marinez, Elizabeth, and Arnoldo Garcia, What is Neoliberalism?, July 27, 1996, CorpWatch, http://goo.gl/Kg6Ep.

126 Toplin, Robert Brent, 2008, Radical Conservatism, The Right's Political Religion, Wiley. http://goo.gl/cLZ3T.

127 Office of the United States Trade Representative, November 25, 2009, History of the WTO: Part one, http://goo.gl/xrrae.

128 Makwana, Rajesh, November 23, 2006, Neoliberalism and Economic Globalization, Share The World's Resources, http://goo.gl/LTW0w.

129 Sherman anti-Trust Act, 1890, Our Documents, A National Initiative on American History, Civics, and Service, http://goo.gl/KYNxQ.

130 Tax Justice Network, http://goo.gl/5YNul). Retrieved on September 2, 2012.

131 Wikipedia, World Trade Organization, http://goo.gl/THSBn, Retrieved on September 2, 2012.

132 Davis, Ronald L.F., Slavery in America: Historical overview, California State University, Northridge, http://goo.gl/bWteR.

133 Curtis, Edward E., 2009, Muslims in America: A Short History, Oxford Press, http://x2t.com/202591.

134 Grantham, Jeremy, April 2011, Time to wake up: Days of abundant resources and failing prices are over forever, GMO, The Revina Project, http://goo.gl/n2REC.

135 Martinez, Elizabeth and Arnoldo Garcia, 26 February 2000, What is Neo-liberalism?, http://goo.gl/JgSWl.

136 Levy, Jonah D, 2006, The State After Statism: New State Activities in the Age of Liberalization. Cambridge, MA: Harvard University Press. pp. 469.

137 Brenner, N., N. Theodore (2002-06), Cities and the Geographies of Actually Existing Neolibarlism, Antipode 34 (3): 349-379.

138 Kurlantzick, Joshua, June 28, 2012, The Rise of Innovative State Capitalism, The Economist, http://goo.gl/qLE5W.

139   Wooldridge, Adrian, The visible hand, 21 January 2012, The Economist, http://goo.gl/OlwIF.

140   World Economic Forum, http://goo.gl/vR1tC.

141   The Economic Times, January 26, 2012, World Economic Forum Davos 2012: Davos elite confronts crisis of Western capitalism, http://goo.gl/dbGUk.

142   The Economist, Politics This week, February 4, 2012, http://goo.gl/W14Ec.

143   Wikipedia, China National Petroleum Corporation, http://goo.gl/SGfYf. Retrieved September 2, 2012.

144   Grossman, Zoltan, From Wounded Knee to Libya, A Century of U.S. Military Intervention, http://goo.gl/0igc7, Retrieved September 19, 2012.

145   Archer, Jules, The Plot to Seize the Whitehouse, Jules, http://goo.gl/AUuy2.

146   White House, Budget of the U.S. Government Fiscal Year 2011, http://goo.gl/H0aJQ.

147   Interview with Donald Rumsfeld on January 1, Rumsfeld confirmation, January 11, 2001, http://goo.gl/BImT2.

148   Sirgany, Aleen, February 11, 2009, The War on Waste, CBS News, http://goo.gl/cOqT.

149   Bumiller, Elisabeth, April 17, 2012, Panetta Reassessing His Travel Options, The New York Times, http://goo.gl/Ni7eA.

150   Lindorff, Dave, a *founder of "This Can't Be Happening"* http://thiscantbehappening.net/, and a contributor to Hopeless: Barack Obama and the Politics of Illusion, published by AK Press, http://goo.gl/yLf6B. In an interview by U.S. radio host, Dennis Bernstein.

151   Wikipedia, 2012 United States Federal budget, http://goo.gl/zoqAR.

152   Wikipedia, June 20, 2012, Military budget of the United States, http://goo.gl/a9iM.

153   Stockholm International Peace Research Institute (SIPRI), April 11, 2011, World military spending reached $1.6 trillion in 2010. http://goo.gl/Qv1ZN.

154   Press Release, December 21, 2010, US Government's 2010 Financial Report Shows Significant Financial Management and Fiscal Challenges, US Government Accountability Office, Retrieved 6 January 2012, http://goo.gl/GhwtC.

155   Weiss, Daniel J., Jackie Weidman, Rebecca Leber, February 7,

2012, Big Oil's Banner Year, Higher Prices, Record Profits, Less Oil, Center for American Progress, http://goo.gl/rYo5Y.

156   Wikipedia, List of countries by military expenditures , http://goo.gl/FQEmA, Retrieved on September 2, 2012.

157   Wikipedia, List of countries by population, http://goo.gl/mbbz, Retrieved on September 2, 2012.

158   Wikipedia, McCarthyism, http://goo.gl/OZUT. Retrieved on September 2, 2012.

159   U.S. History, McCarthyism, http://goo.gl/BWh0S.

160   American Heritage Dictionary, http://goo.gl/TpFn6.

161   Anziska, Seth, September 16, 2012, A Preventable Massacre, The New York Times, http://goo.gl/ONsZU.

162   Okhovat, Sarah, December 2011, The United Nations Security Council: Its Veto Power and Its Reform, The University of Sydney, http://goo.gl/2c9ar.

163   Nelson, Steven, September 9, 2011, Former Senator Works to get new 9/11 investigation approved by voters, The Daily Caller, http://goo.gl/A7O4w.

164   National Post Staff, The National Post, Aug 17, 2011, 9/11 skeptics to meet in Toronto on anniversary, http://goo.gl/Tyvf1.

165   Perdana Global Peace Foundation, International Conference on "9/11 Revisited – Seeking the Truth," November 19, 2012, http://goo.gl/fdcTD.

166   Beck, Glenn, November, 15, 2006, CNN's Beck to first-ever Muslim Congressman, "what I feel like saying is, 'Sir, prove to me that you are not working with our enemies,'" Media Matters for America, http://goo.gl/uiD5V.

167   Telhami, Shibley, January 6, 2008, Cartoon villains, The New York Times, http://goo.gl/wxd3Q.

168   CIA report released by the Senate's Intelligence Committee, September 9, 2006, BBC, Saddam 'had no link to al-Qaeda', http://goo.gl/uI934.

169   Zakaria, Fareed, October 14, 2001, The Politics of Rage: Why Do They Hate Us?, Newsweek Magazine, http://goo.gl/XTe5c.

170   Cartalucci, February 13, 2012, Egypt: US-funded Agitators on Trial: US "Democracy Promotion" = Foreign-funded Sedition, The Global Research, Center for Research on Globalization, http://goo.gl/6p5D1.

171   Cartalucci, February 13, 2012, Egypt: US-funded Agitators on

Trial: US "Democracy Promotion" = Foreign-funded Sedition, The Global Research, Center for Research on Globalization, http://goo.gl/6p5D1.

172   Reaves, Jessica, February 12, 2003, Living with Terrorism: A how-to Guide, Time Magazine, http://goo.gl/kBzSb.

173   Tierney, John, March 17, 2003, Ridge gets the joke, but he hasn't lost his focus, The New York Times, http://goo.gl/wK5wr.

174   Syria: US-NATO Backed Al Qaeda Terrorists Armed with WMDs. Chemical Weapons against the Syrian People, Global Research, http://goo.gl/EqAlJ.

175   Barrett, Kevin, April 13, 2013, Al-CIAda aims to wreck Muslims, West in clash of civilizations, PressTV, http://goo.gl/ALFgF.

176   Thompson, Mark, June 29, 2011, The $5 trillion War on Terror, The Time, http://goo.gl/Gf2g4.

177   Kenny, Charles, November 18, 2012, Airport Security is Killing Us, Bloomberg BusinessWeek, http://goo.gl/OepJh.

178   Tully, Andrew, July 7, 2009, International Poll Finds U.S. Still Viewed As World's Bully, Radio Free Europe, Radio Liberty, http://goo.gl/wI0K0.

179   Pew Global, June 13, 2012, Global Opinion of Obama Slips, International Policies Faulted, http://goo.gl/DOkoo.

180   Haas, Michael, America's War Crimes Quagmire, from Bush to Obama, April 5, 2012, Publishing house for Scholars, www.USwarcrimes.com.

181   Ridley, Yvonne, 12 May 2012, Bush Convicted of War Crimes in Absentia, Foreign Policy Journal, http://goo.gl/VHzLI.

182   Agence France-Presse, 22 November 2011, George W. Bush and Tony Blair found guilty of war crimes in Malaysia, The National Post, http://goo.gl/tyUJW.

183   Agence France-Presse, 28 May 2012, Tony Blair interrupted by protestor at media inquiry.

184   Burns, John F., and Alan Cowell, May 28, 2012, Antiwar Protester Disrupts Inquiry as Blair Testifies, The New York Times, http://goo.gl/Tv5MF.

185   60 Minutes, April 29, 2012, Hard Measures, http://goo.gl/CZOEX.

186   Kurlantzick, Joshua, January 23, 2012, Freedom's Fizzle,

Bloomberg Businessweek.

187   The Guardian, 31 August 2011, Extraordinary rendition: a
       backstory, http://goo.gl/3EQBi.

188   Cobain, Ian, and Ben Quinn, August 31, 2011, How U.S. firms
       profited from torture flights, Court documents illustrate how
       US contracted out secret rendition transportation to a network
       of private companies, The Guardian, http://goo.gl/x5UHa.

189a The Rendition Project, http://www.therenditionproject.org.uk.

189   Wikipedia, Extraordinary Rendition, http://goo.gl/efah

190   Justice and Home Affairs, European Parliament, February 14,
       2007, CIA activities in Europe: European Parliament adopts
       final report deploring passivity from some Member States,
       http://goo.gl/Iefqe.

191   Jenks, Chris, and Eric Talbot Jensen, November 12, 2010, All
       Human Rights Are Equal, But Some Are More Equal Than
       Others, The Extraordinary Rendition Of A Terror Suspect In
       Italy, the NATO SOFA, and Human Rights, Harvard National
       Security Journal, Vol. 1, p. 171- 202, http://goo.gl/h2pbd.

192   CBC News, October 19, 2007, U.S. legislators apologize to
       Maher Arar, http://goo.gl/2SPcv.

193   Benen, Steve, December 1, 2011, Detainee policy gone
       horribly awry, Washington Monthly, http://goo.gl/PI8At.

194   Dolan, Eric W., November 29, 2011, Sen. Paul: New
       indefinite detention rule puts every American at risk, The Raw
       Story, http://goo.gl/5TRHo.

195   Chesney, Robert, December 1, 2011, Does the NDAA
       Authorize Detention of U.S. Citizens?, http://goo.gl/gbEpE.

196   Kain, Erik, December 5, 2011, The National Defense
       Authorization Act is the Greatest Threat to Civil Liberties
       Americans Face, Forbes, http://goo.gl/Gw0uD.

197   Martin, Patrick, November 20, 2001, U.S. planned war in
       Afghanistan long before September 11, World Socialist Web
       Site, http://goo.gl/gG8.

198   The Daily Mail Reporter, November 3, 2011, The Daily Mail,
       One U.S. veteran attempts suicide every 80 minutes: Hidden
       tragedy of Afghanistan and Iraq wars, http://goo.gl/ElQeH.

199   Lee, Ann, 2012, What the U.S. Can Learn from China, An
       open-minded guide to treating our greatest competitors as our
       greatest teacher. http://goo.gl/W2J3f.

200   Gusovsky, Dina, An empire of US military bases, February

14, 2011, Russia Today, http://goo.gl/WMrP4.

201   Strenger, Carlo, March 4, 2013, Leading Palestinian intellectual: U.S. was never a fair broker of Israeli-Palestinian peace, Haaretz, http://goo.gl/Y3aTy.

202   Johnson, Chalmers, 2004, The Sorrows of Empire Militarism, Secrecy, and the End of the Republic, http://goo.gl/thdVq.

203   Frank, Barney, Jan/Feb 2012, How to save the global economy-cut defense spending, Foreign Policy Special Report, http://goo.gl/MBkAG.

204   Kirkpatrick, David, and Steven Erlanger, September 22, 2012, Egypt's New Leader Spells Out Terms for U.S.–Arab Ties, The New York Times, http://goo.gl/rsQ9z.

205   Weisbrot, Mark, April 27, 2011, 2016: When China overtakes the US, The Guardian, http://goo.gl/hKokg.

206   Subramanian, Arvind, Eclipse, living in the shadow of China economic dominance, Watch an interview of the author at: http://goo.gl/wV3zs.

207   The U.S. Department of State, Milestones: 1937-1945, The Bretton Woods Conference, 1944, http://goo.gl/zYXpS.

208   Wong, Edward, and Natasha Singer, December 26, 2011, Currency Agreement for Japan and China, The New York Times, http://goo.gl/I6T9E.

209   Goh, Brenda, July 25, 2011, China, Iran eye barter plan to bypass U.S. Sanctions—Financial Times, Reuters, http://goo.gl/1T4pg.

210   Fisk, Robert, October 06, 2009, The Demise of the dollar, The Independent, http://goo.gl/t4sSI.

211   Fox Nation, November24, 2010, Russia Quit Dollar, Fox Nation, http://goo.gl/DJaHZ.

212   Rooney, Ben, February 10, 2011, IMF calls for dollar alternative, CNN Money, http://goo.gl/aSG2H.

213   Tuteja, Ashok, March 29, 2012, BRICS nations to promote trade in local currencies, The Tribune News Service, http://goo.gl/77GWs.

214   Zhang, Amei, 1996, Economic Growth and Human Development in China, United Nations Development Program, http://goo.gl/8EMRT.

215   The World Bank, World Development Indicators 2012, http://goo.gl/lLX1y.

216   Index Mundi, GDP-Real growth rate, http://goo.gl/JZ6WZ.

217   Gideon Rachman, January/February 2011, Think Again: American Decline, This time it's for real, Gideon Rachman chief foreign-affairs commentator for the Financial Times and author of Zero-Sum Future: American Power in an Age of Anxiety, http://goo.gl/9MXSb, Foreign Policy.

218   Inoue, Yuko, and Julie Gordon, August 12, 2011, Japanese manufacturers concerned about China's restrictive export quotas on essential rare earths may have found a way to resolve their supply concerns—relocate production to China, http://goo.gl/ytnXq.

219   Navarro, Peter, Greg Autry, Death by China: Controlling the Dragon – A Global Call to Action, 2011, http://goo.gl/hX54i.

220   The Economist, How China runs the world economy, July 28, 2005, http://goo.gl/K9Q47.

221   Tsui, Enid, Simon Rabinovitch, January 4, 2012, China pushes minimum wage rises, Financial Times, http://goo.gl/zkQEu.

222   Rabinovitch, Simon, China labour costs soar as wages rise 22%, Financial Times, http://goo.gl/AowHl.

223   Bradsher, Keith, 30 March 2012, The New York Times.

224   Xiaoshu, Quan, Yu Fei, Li Huizi, and Ji Shaoting, august 23, 2012, China unveils ambitious space projects, Space Daily, http://goo.gl/5gGw0.

225   The Province, February 29, 2011, Chinese investors targeting international city real estate, http://goo.gl/PwGm0.

226   Francis, Diane, April 13, 2012, To tame Toronto's housing bubble, ban foreign buying, The National Post, http://goo.gl/C01pd.

227   Johnson, Simon, 2012, White House Burning: the Founding Fathers, Our National Debt, and why it matters to you, Greenpeace, 11 April 2012, Banned pesticides found in teas produced by popular Chinese tea brands, http://goo.gl/RVgPV.

228   Kelleher, Dennis M. (President and CEO, Better Markets, Inc.), July 10, 2012, Testimony on "The Impact of Dodd-Frank on Customers, Credit, and Job Creators, " The Committee on Financial Services, Subcommittee on Capital Markets and Government Sponsored Enterprises, http://goo.gl/C1NZY.

229   Transgenerational.org, The demographics of aging, retrieved September 1, 2012, http://goo.gl/OwUGU.

230   Greenberg, Stanley B., July 30, 2011, Why Voters Tune Out

Democrats, The New York Times, Sunday Review, http://goo.gl/nA1sv.

231   Economic research, Federal Reserve Bank of St. Louis, July 2012, Personal Saving Rate, http://goo.gl/mVS8E.

232   Investopedia, Quantitative Easing, http://goo.gl/ZKr3y.

233   Wikipedia, Global currency reserves, http://goo.gl/s6DtK, Retrieved September 1, 2012.

234   People's Daily online, January 19, 2012, China signs currency swap deal with UAE, http://goo.gl/sjDo3.

235   Recknagel, Charlets, November 01, 2000, Iraq: Baghdad Moves to Euro, Radio Free Europe, Radio Liberty, http://goo.gl/nJEZw.

236a Law Library, American Law and Legal Information, Glass-Steagall Act, http://goo.gl/W5Kms.

236   The Free Dictionary by Farlex, http://goo.gl/EAiky.

237a Wikipedia, Savings and loan crisis, http://goo.gl/hPhiR.

237   Sekar, Anisha, The Glass-Steagall Act Explained, Nerdwallet, http://goo.gl/50ztL.

238a Feeney, Lauren, January 27, 2012, Byron Dorgan's Prophetic Words, Moyers & Company, http://goo.gl/cI2ae.

238   Dingell, John, CSPAN, House Session on November 4, 1999, http://goo.gl/6lvjJ.

239a Wikipedia, Gramm-Leach-Bliley Act, http://goo.gl/9JAOe.

239   Greenspan, Alan, Remarks on October 12, 2005, *Economic flexibility,* Before the National Italian American Foundation, Washington, D.C., http://goo.gl/ieQGH.

240   Hilsenrath, Jon, Luca Di Leo, Michael S. Derby, January 13, 2012, Little Alarm Shown at Fed At Dawn of Housing Bust, The Wall Street Journal, Retrieved January 13, 2012, http://goo.gl/ITrSS.

241   Associated Press, January 16, 2013, JPMorgan CEO gets pay cut by half after $6 billion loss, http://goo.gl/fgeJd.

242   Fitzgerald, Patrick, and Mike Spector, May 21, 2012, Corzine pay plan topped $8 million, The Wall Street Journal, http://goo.gl/XeE8s.

243   WSJ, May 21, 2012, CEOS Who delivered the most and the least bang for the buck, The Wall Street Journal, http://goo.gl/A2LGS.

244   Waldron, Travis, May 22, 2012, Former MF Global CEO Jon Corzine Gets $8 Million Pay Package After Firm Went

Bankrupt, Think Progress, http://goo.gl/BlPo3.

245 Wikipedia, Economy of the United States, http://goo.gl/KztCp.

246 Treasury Direct, U.S. Historical Debt Outstanding – Annual 2000 – 2010, http://goo.gl/Hu8e, Retrieved September 1, 2012.

247 U.S. Treasury Direct-Monthly Statement of the Public Debt, March 2012, http://goo.gl/H7oD8.

248 Bureau of economic Analysis-GDP News Release-March 29, 2012, http://goo.gl/XgEF.

249 National Bureau of Economic Research (NBER), http://goo.gl/4LQb.

250 McCaffery, Edward J., Public Debt Acts, Major Acts of Congress, Enotes.com, http://goo.gl/JyZMS, Retrieved September 1, 2012.

251 Free Government Reports, January 1, 2010, A Brief History of the U.S. Federal Debt Limit, http://Freegovreports.com.

252 Bill Summary & Status – 111th Congress (2009–2010) – H.J.RES.45 – CRS Summary – THOMAS (Library of Congress). Thomas.loc.gov., February 4, 2010, http://goo.gl/ltO6M.

253 Buffett, Warren, 2002, Letter to shareholders of Berkshire Hathaway Inc., http://goo.gl/vyLNk.

254 Choan, Peter, June 9, 2010, Big Risk; $1.2 quadrillion derivatives market dwarfs world GDP, Daily Finance, http://goo.gl/qKZbe.

255 Hilsenrath, Jon, Luca Di Leo, Michael S. Derby, January 13, 2012, Little Alarm Shown at Fed At Dawn of Housing Bust, The Wall Street Journal, http://goo.gl/lJvf6, Retrieved January 24, 2012.

256 Joyner, James, January 13, 2010, Derivatives Market 20 Times Size of American Economy, http://goo.gl/GUzw9.

257 Wikipedia, 2007–2012 global financial crisis, the free encyclopedia, http://goo.gl/UwKN1, Retrieved September 1, 2012.

258 Fitzpatrick, Dan, and Liz Rappaport, May 10, 2012, J.P. Morgan Chase takes $2 billion in losses on 'poorly executed' derivatives bets, Wall Street Journal, http://goo.gl/OJFrt.

259 60 Minutes, Wall Street: The Speed Traders, 10 October, 2010, http://goo.gl/TQF7.

260   Durden, Tyler, September 29, 2010, Senator Ted Kaufman's Final Remarks on market structure and integrity, http://goo.gl/4N2PX.
261   Wikipedia, Credit default Swap, http://goo.gl/W2Enl.
262   Guina, Ryan, The 2008-2009 Financial crisis – causes and effects, Cash money life, http://goo.gl/V8zpJ.
263   McFadden, Luis, Congressman McFadden on the Federal Reserve Corporation, Remarks in Congress, 1934, http://goo.gl/AtrAe.
264   Sanders, Bernie, June 12, 2012, Fed Conflicts detailed by GAO, http://goo.gl/5zcDx.
265   Eichler, Alexander, An Darby, Wife of New York Fed President, Gets $190,000 A year from JPMorgan Chase, July 12, 2012, The Huffington Post, http://goo.gl/LxsYf.
266   Sanders, Bernie, June 12, 2012, Jamie Dimon is not alone, http://goo.gl/gC4mq.
267   Sanders, Bernie, June 12, 2012, Fed Board Member Conflicts Detailed by GAO: Banks and Businesses Took $4 Trillion in Bailouts, http://goo.gl/Cq17K.
268   Andrews, Edmund L., October 23, 2008, Greenspan Concedes Error on Regulation, The New York Times, http://goo.gl/TxOPn.
269   Brown, Ellen, October 2008, Who Owns The Federal Reserve? The Fed is privately owned. Its shareholders are private banks, Global Research, http://goo.gl/vmn8.
270   Wikipedia, List of recessions in the United States, http://goo.gl/TlE9C.
271a Wikipedia, Too big to fail, http://goo.gl/ah5Ky.
271   Stern, Gary H., and Ron J. Feldman, February 2004, Too Big To Fail: The Hazards of Bank Bailouts.
272   Kavoussi, Bonnie, October 23, 2012, Alan Greenspan: We've got to get rid of too big to fail banks, http://goo.gl/YoxDj.
273   Greeley, Brendan, July 5, 2012, the Price of Too Big to Fail, Business Week, http://goo.gl/y680e.
274   Kowalski, Alex, October 6, 2010, Stiglitz Says Fed Rate Policy May Cause Asset Bubbles, Bloomberg.com, http://goo.gl/5ZNfB.
275   Philips, Matthew, May 10, 2012, Where has all the trading gone?, Bloomberg Businessweek, http://goo.gl/pcbyH.
276   Clarke, Dave, May 11, 2012, J.P. Morgan's Dimon loses clout

as reform critic, Reuters, http://goo.gl/RrA3Q.
277 Bank of North Dakota, http://goo.gl/2oxIO.
278 Public Banking Institute, Public Banking Model for a State, http://goo.gl/hi8WF.
279 OECD, 2011, An overview of growing income inequalities in OECD countries, http://goo.gl/2UiT8.
280 The U.S. Census Bureau report, September 2011, Income, Poverty, and Health Insurance Coverage in the United States: 2010, http://goo.gl/BplbK.
281 Stiglitz, Joseph, Of the 1%, by the 1%, for the 1%, Vanity Fair, May 2011, http://goo.gl/Bgi9t.
282 Alterman, Eric, October 6, 2011, Think Again: The Era of the '1 Percent', Center for American Progress, http://goo.gl/sZ4vK, May 2011, Think Again: The Era of the 'One Percent', Vanity Fair, http://goo.gl/4cfLf , and Huff Post media, Canada, October 6, 2011, http://goo.gl/UUMUB197.
283 Moyers, Bill, February 10, 2012, Bruce Bartlett on Where the Right went wrong, http://goo.gl/Ll3ri.
284 Piketty, Thomas, and Emmanuel Saez, 2007, How Progressive is the U.S. Federal tax System? A Historical and International Perspective, Journal of Economic Perspectives-Volume 21, Number 1-winter 2007, Pages 3-24.
285 Damon, Andre, March 26, 2011, US corporate profits hit record high, new home sales at record low, World Socialist Web Site, http://goo.gl/IU2No.
286 Tavernise, Sabrina, September 13, 2011, Soaring Poverty casts spotlight on ;Lost Decade', The New York Times, http://goo.gl/xaEOm.
287 Economic Policy Institute, The State of Working America, Inequality between the top 1 percent between 1913 and 2008, http://goo.gl/9D2Af, Retrieved September 7, 2012.
288 Freeland, Chrystia, march 8, 2012, A U.S. recovery, but only for the 1 percent, The New York Times, http://goo.gl/KzJRj.
289 Atkinson, Anthony B., Thomas Piketty, and Emmanuel Saez, 2011, Top income in the long run of history, Journal of Economic Literature, 2011, 49:1, 3-71, http://goo.gl/XFWFR.
290 Lowenstein, Roger, February 26, 2012, Is Any CEO worth $189,000 per hour?, Bloomberg Businessweek,
291 AFL-CIO America's Unions, Executive Paywatch, http://goo.gl/1zAWp.

292   Bivens, Josh, November 9, 2011, CEOs distance themselves from the average worker, The Economic Policy Institute, http://goo.gl/0uRCu.

293   Duhigg, Charles and Keith Bradsher, 21 January 2012, How the U.S. lost out on iPhone work, http://goo.gl/R4Lym.

294   Ryle, Gerard, Marina Walker Guevara, Michael Hudson, Nicky Hager, Duncan Campbell, and Stefan Candea, April 3, 2013, Secret Files Expose Offshores' Global Impact, The International Consortium of Investigative Journalists, http://goo.gl/3fqgh.

295   Tax Justice Network, http://goo.gl/IDcT9.

296   Henry, James S., July 2012, The Price of Offshore Revisited, Tax Justice Network, http://goo.gl/viuvi.

297   Too Much, Institute for Policy Studies, http://www.toomuchonline.org.

298   Shaxson, Nicholas, John Christensen, and Nick Mathiason, 19th July 2012, Inequality: You don't know the half of it –Tax Justice Network, http://goo.gl/Uiiig.
      Nicholas Shaxson is author of *Treasure Islands: Tax Havens and the Men who Stole the World,* Random House, 2011. John Christensen is former Economic Adviser to the UK tax haven of Jersey and is director of the Tax Justice Network. Nick Mathiason is a business correspondent at the Bureau of Investigative Journalism.

299   Boyce, James and Leonce Ndikumana, 2001, Is Africa a Net Debtor. New Estimates of Capital Flight From Several Severely-Indebted Sub-Saharan African Countries, 1970-98, Journal of Development Studies, Vol. 38, No. 2, pp. 27-56

300   Brent, Paul, June 2010, Good Business or Cheating the taxman?, Rogerson Law Corporation, http://goo.gl/8pwAE.

301   G20, Declaration on Strengthening the Financial System – London Summit – Leaders' Statement, April 2, 2009, http://goo.gl/PxJO9.

302   The Economist, February 16, 2013, Tax Transparency, Automatic Response, The way to make exchange of tax information work, http://goo.gl/UpSxV.

303   Vellacott, Chris, and Sinead Cruise, July 26, 2012, Tax Haven clampdown yields cash but secrecy still thrives, Reuters, http://goo.gl/IKJqA.

304   Financial Secrecy Index, http://goo.gl/VPN7k.

Bloomberg News, August 16, 2010, China Overtake Japan as World's Second-Biggest Economy, http://goo.gl/5wYL.

305 Moyer, Bill, February 10, 2012, Bruce Bartlett on Where the Right went wrong, http://goo.gl/Ll3ri.

306 Blodget, Henry, 12 July 2011, The Truth About Taxes: Here's How High Today's Rates Really Are, Business Insider, http://goo.gl/zE7fV.

307 Federal Tax Receipts as a percentage of GDP, http://goo.gl/4hMTe.

308 US Government Revenue, http://goo.gl/55uLz.

309 Peterson, Pete, 1999, Grey Dawn.

310 Gross, Bill, Skunked, http://goo.gl/wAc5L.

311 Buffett, Warren, August 15, 2011, Stop Coddling the Super-Rich, the new York Times, http://goo.gl/eSQ9Q.

312a Federal Individual Rate history nominal adjusted 2013- (1862-2013), http://goo.gl/oW1iX.

312 Leonard, Andrew, April 11, 2012, The Buffett rule, explained, The Salon, http://goo.gl/QFFe4.

313 Societe Generale, Cross Asset research, 2010.

314 Robin Hood Tax Organization, http://goo.gl/RoIa9.

315 Barber, Brad M., Yi-Tsung Lee, Yu-Jane Liu, and Terrance Odean, Do Individual Day Traders Make Money? Evidence from Taiwan, http://goo.gl/zBMLb.

316 BBC News, 29 January 2012, Sarkozy announces French financial transaction tax, http://goo.gl/lPYvg.

317 Clark, Gordon, Sorry, I must have misheard. I thought you said '$1 billion', 14 May 2012, the Province.

318 Parussini, Gabriele, February 29, 2012, French Front-Runner Pledges 75% tax bracket, The Wall Street Journal, http://goo.gl/3mKhx.

319 Easton, Nina, July 17, 2012, Millionaire taxes hurt the masses, from Newark to Paris, Fortune, http://goo.gl/7H9gz.

320 Dieter, Heribert, 2003, Reshaping globalisation: a new order for international financial markets, Institute for Global Dialogue. pp. 7, http://goo.gl/leBTB.

321 Jacobson, Darien B., Brian G. Raub, and Barry W. Johnson, The Estate Tax: Ninety Years and counting, IRS, http://goo.gl/8SY4u.

322 Hodge, Scott A, April 01, 2012, The countdown is over. We're #1, The Tax Foundation, http://goo.gl/tkCZF.

323a   Neate, Rupert, November 4, 2012, Apple paid less than 2% on overseas profits in 2011, The Guardian, http://goo.gl/Sh1Kn.

323   Pozen, Robert, February 22, 2012, How to tax US companies' foreign profits, The Financial Times, http://goo.gl/TWQdF.

324   Murphy, Richard, 2012, Country-by-country reporting, Accounting for globalization locally, prepared for the Tax Justice Network, May 2012, Tax Research.org.uk. www.taxjustice.net. Country-by-country reporting at http://goo.gl/TIZzG.

325   British Houses of Parliament at http://goo.gl/IDcT9.

How to contact the author

Readers of this book are encouraged to contact the author with questions, comments, or ideas for future editions.

To get in touch with Dr. El-Rayes about his availability for speeches, interviews, seminars, contact him by email at:
hamdy.elrayes@gmail.com

or by phone at: 604-630-6865

You may also visit http://www.TheNewEraClubs.org to learn about the New Era Community Club in your neighborhood or to start a new one.

www.ingramcontent.com/pod-product-compliance
Lightning Source LLC
Chambersburg PA
CBHW062213270326
41930CB00009B/1727